HEART DROPS OF DHARMAKAYA

Tonpa Tritsug Gyalwa

HEART DROPS OF DHARMAKAYA

Dzogchen Practice of the Bön Tradition

Lopon Tenzin Namdak on the *Kun Tu Bzang Po'i Snying Tig* of Shardza Tashi Gyaltsen

The full title of the text translated herein is:
The Teachings of the Progressive Great Perfection called the Heart Drops of Dharmakaya ('od gsal rdzogs pa chen po'i lam gyi rim pa khrid yig kun tu bzang po'i snying tig shes bya ba bzhugs)

Translation and commentary by
Lopon Tenzin Namdak

Introduction by Per Kvaerne
Edited by Richard Dixey

The purpose and practice of mind is the subject of this text and by this you can remove all the negativities and obscurations of mind. Also you can remove all disturbance and stop desire with the mind. Ultimately you will achieve the final Dharmakaya. This text is not restricted and is for the benefit of all beings.

Snow Lion
Boulder

Snow Lion
An imprint of Shambhala Publications, Inc.
4720 Walnut Street
Boulder, Colorado 80301
www.shambhala.com

14 13 12 11 10 9 8 7

Second Edition
Printed in the United States of America

♾ This edition is printed on acid-free paper that meets the American National Standards Institute Z39.48 Standard.
♻ This book is printed on 30% postconsumer recycled paper. For more information please visit www.shambhala.com.
Snow Lion is distributed worldwide by Penguin Random House, Inc., and its subsidiaries.

Designed and typeset by Gigantic Computing

The Library of Congress catalogues the previous edition of this book as follows:

Bkra-śis-rgyal-mtshan, Śar-rdza, 1859–1933.
'od gsal rdzogs-pa chen po'i lam-gyi rim-pa khrid-yig kun-tu bzang-po'i snying-tig shes-bya-ba bzugs. English
Heart drops of dharmakaya: teaching on the Kun-zang Nying-tig / by Shardza Tashi Gyaltsen; translation and commentary by Lopon Tenzin Namdak; introduction Per Kvaerne; edited by Richard Dixey.—1st ed.
p. cm.
Includes bibliographical references.
ISBN 978-1-55939-012-5 (first edition)
ISBN 978-1-55939-172-6 (second edition)
1. Rdzogs-chen (Bönpo). I. Namdak, Tenzin, 1926– . II. Dixey, Richard.
III. Title.
BQ7982.3.B53713 1993
299'.54—dc20
93-12487
CIP

Contents

Preface

The publication of this text is a first for two reasons. It is the first time a text from the Bönpo tradition has been published in its entirety, demonstrating the vitality and importance of this tradition which has survived intact from very ancient times. Secondly it is the first time a complete text concerning Dzogchen has been made available to a general Western audience, and gains from the fact that it was actually written in modern times, almost certainly after 1930. Written by Shardza Tashi Gyaltsen (1859-1935), a famous Bönpo master who gave teachings to students of other schools of Tibetan Buddhism as well as to many students from the Bönpo community, it belongs within an unbroken lineage that remains active right up to the present day.

Reappraisal of the Bönpo and their role in the development of Tibetan culture has been a feature of Western scholarship of the last twenty years, and we hope that this volume will help in this task. Toward this end we have included with the text a short history of Yungdrung (Eternal) Bön from their own perspective, as well as biographies of Shardza Tashi Gyaltsen and Lopon Tenzin Namdak, the Bönpo master responsible for this translation.

It is important to note here that the Lopon recognises three distinct types of Bön—the old Bön, which is entirely shamanistic; the new or reformed Bön, which arose in response to competition from other Buddhist schools; and the Yungdrung or Eternal Bön, which is the tradition presented here. Yungdrung Bön shares many similarities with the other traditions of Tibetan Buddhism, but traces its origin to a much earlier teacher than Shakyamuni Buddha, namely Tonpa (Buddha) Shenrab, who taught in a country to the west of Tibet. The tradition then spread to the western regions of the Tibetan plateau, most notably to the kingdom of Zhang Zhung in the Kailash region, and was already ancient when King Songtsen Gampo (*srong brstan sgam po*) conquered the kingdom in the seventh century.

When dealing with an ancient history that tells a story significantly different from the Buddhist histories of Tibet, one struggles to find pointers that can help either validate or at least locate some of the events within a western conception of cultural progression. In particular, the idea that the culture of Yungdrung Bön originated in the region of Persia, and that many of the teachings originated from the west of the Tibetan plateau instead of from the Indian subcontinent, and did so in a period that predated the time of the historical Buddha, seems almost incredible to those used to the received history of the conversion of Tibet in the time of the kings of the seventh century.

Indeed, due to the periodic upheavals that have occurred in the region and the fragility of the paper on which the texts were written, any attempt independently to assess this history is made immeasurably more difficult by the rarity of ancient texts that can be dated in their original form. Furthermore, in the case of the Bönpo, the early lineage was entirely transmitted orally so it would appear that no direct records remain to give an insight into the early history.

There are two exceptions to this conclusion, however. The first concerns important elements of ancient Tibetan culture, including both architecture as well as religious concepts, that have been noted by scholars as bearing comparison with ancient Persian culture.[1] Since these elements date from the period when the Bön religion was preeminent in Tibet, they lend credence to the idea that Persian influences were important in ancient times.

The line of evidence is more direct as regards the style and origin of the Bönpo chorten monuments. Here, as in many other elements of Bönpo culture, it has been claimed that the Bönpo copied the Buddhist stupa style in an attempt to compete with Buddhist culture even though there are important differences between them. Most notable are the Bönpo texts indicating temple enclosures within the structure of chorten, which in consequence are often drawn with a box-like lower storey beneath the recognisable stupa structure above. Another important difference is the use of a trident with a central flaming sword as the symbol on top of the structure, instead of the sun and crescent moon used in the Buddhist style.

Recently two studies have been published concerning the images depicted in ancient rock carvings in the Karakoram and in Ladakh to the west of Tibet.[2] These carvings are of particular interest as they can be dated

1 See Giuseppe Tucci, *The Religions of Tibet* (London: Routledge and Kegan Paul, 1980) concerning the origins of the "Tibetan Book of the Dead"; H. Richardson and D. Snellgrove, *A Cultural History of Tibet* (Boston: Shambhala, 1986) concerning architecture; and Giacomella Orofino, *Sacred Tibetan Teachings on Death and Liberation* (Bridport: Prism Press, 1990) concerning the similarities between Tibetan and Zoroastrian dualism.

2 Concerning the Karakoram carvings, see Karl Jettmar, *Between the Ghandara and the Silk Road: The Rock Carvings of the Karakoram Highway* (Mainz: Verlag Phillipp Von Zabern, 1987), illustration no.14, or *Antiquities of Northern Pakistan*, edited by Karl Jettmar (Mainz: Verlag Phillipp von Zabern, 1989), Vol. I, plates 5-6. Regarding the Ladakhi carvings, see Giacomella Orofino in *East and West* 1991.

by other means and so provide direct chronological evidence about the early period of Tibetan culture. It is therefore of some importance that one such carving from the Karakoram dated as first century C.E. clearly shows the characteristic style of a Bönpo stupa with the opening in the base and the trident symbol, as well as the swastika symbol of Yungdrung Bön. Such evidence must make one wonder about the confident assertions that such a style was copied from the Indian Buddhist culture that did not arrive in Tibet until six centuries later! The Ladakhi carvings add to this picture, for although they were made by soldiers at the time of the expansion of Tibetan influence that coincided with the arrival of Buddhism from India, they all use the Bönpo stupa style along with inscriptions in the archaic language of Western Tibet, Zhang Zhung, that was supplanted by Tibetan. Again, the generally accepted idea that written language arrived in Tibet with Buddhism from India seems less credible in light of these findings.

The Translation of the Text

The text presented here is in the style of personal instruction from Shardza to his students. Such texts are called *mengagde* (*man ngag sde*) in the tradition of Dzogchen, and this text is a condensate of a two-volume work by Shardza in the same style.

The translation was carried out in the month of August 1991 by Lopon Tenzin Namdak in the course of teaching the text to a small group of Western students in his monastery in the Kathmandu Valley in Nepal. As the rain fell around us, Lopon spent some two hours every morning translating and teaching from the text, which was typed on a portable word processor as he taught it. It was also tape-recorded, which enabled us to check that the typed text was accurate, and that no unwarranted omissions occurred from the Tibetan original. The typing and the correcting of the English was done by me, whilst the checking of the typescript against both the tape and the original text was carried out by Monica Gentile, who is completing her thesis on aspects of Tibetan culture at the Sanskrit University at Benares, India. The final version was then read back to the Lopon, who checked it for a second time against the Tibetan original. Apart from the omission of some quotations in early sections, this process was applied to all sections of Shardza's original, and the appendices that accompany it. Thanks here are also due to Cheh Goh, who helped translate the biography of Shardza Tashi Gyaltsen, and Tadeusz Skorupski, who translated the short history of Bön that forms Appendix 2.

As well as being an acknowledged master of Dzogchen, Lopon Tenzin Namdak is a remarkable teacher with an encyclopedic knowledge of Bönpo culture and a lifetime's experience of teaching it to trainee monks, both in Tibet and India. Not only could he translate the text as he read it to us, but he was happy to answer any points of clarification or problems of interpretation as they arose during our sessions, and his answers form almost another *mengagde* text alongside the original. These comments are to be found in the copious footnotes that accompany the text, and should be read as a commentary to it, at the same time. Reading it now in London there are many other questions I would like to have asked him, but hope that many questions will be answered by presenting the text in this way.

Following the suggestion of Per Kvaerne, who very kindly offered to write an introduction to the text as well as check my English for inconsistencies, this text is better described as an exegetical commentary than as a strict translation. As it is a commentary of what is, after all, a personal instruction by a great master of Dzogchen, this need not cause too much of a problem, and we hope it preserves some of the flavour of the text as it was taught. For those new to Dzogchen, however, a comprehensive resumé of background reading is given by Professor Kvaerne in the bibliographic essay that follows the text.

The final point concerns the vexed question of how to present Tibetan terms in English, and we decided to use spellings that enable a rough enunciation of the Tibetan original, followed by the more precise Wylie transliteration in brackets afterward, so that the ease of reading the text would not be interrupted.

As mentioned in the first line of this preface, this is indeed a rare event, and we hope that this wonderfully clear and concise text will be both comprehensible and useful to whoever reads it. It describes a tradition that is utterly extraordinary in the truest sense of that over-used word, yet is still active and available. May it serve to benefit beings.

Richard Dixey
London
October 1991

Introduction

It is still not widely known that Buddhism is not the only religion in Tibet. Buddhism, introduced in the seventh century C.E. under the patronage of powerful Tibetan kings, became the dominant religious faith in the eleventh century, and has remained so until today. Nevertheless, alongside Buddhism a second religion has survived down through the centuries. This religion, for which there is no other term than its Tibetan designation *bon*, claims to be the very same religion that had long been established in Tibet when Buddhism entered the scene; Bön, so its adherents claim, has a proud and ancient history long antedating the origins of Buddhism in India. This claim has generally been dismissed by Western scholars who have stressed the innumerable points of similarity—in fact, often identity—between Bön and Buddhism, and thus concluded that Bön is, essentially, nothing more than a highly heterodox form of Buddhism.

There is, however, a growing feeling among some scholars that the claim of Bön to be a separate religious tradition with an identity of its own has to be taken seriously. Nor should it be forgotten that Tibetan Buddhists, too, have on the whole regarded Bön as an entirely distinct, non-Buddhist religion. This does not mean that the Bönpo version of history necessarily has to be accepted at face value, at least as far as the period preceding the seventh century is concerned. It does mean, however, that if, instead of focusing on monastic life and metaphysical doctrine (where the merging with Buddhism often appears to be complete), one looks at the sources of religious authority and legitimation, the distinctiveness of Bön, as understood by most Tibetans, becomes immediately apparent. The Bönpos—as opposed to Buddhists—do not derive religious legitimation from the Buddha Shakyamuni, but from an Enlightened Being, Tonpa Shenrab (*ston pa gshen rab*, "the teacher Shenrab"). Long before Shakyamuni, Tonpa Shenrab lived as a prince (and later as king) of Olmo Lungring, a land situated, so the Bönpos assert, to the west of Tibet. Olmo Lungring is often identified with Tazig, generally held by Tibetans to be the Iranian or Persian world. Furthermore, the doctrine which Tonpa Shenrab preached, i.e. Bön, is believed to have come to Tibet not from India as Buddhism did, but rather from a land the historical existence of which (though little else) is fully attested, viz. Zhang Zhung, located in what today is, in a broad sense, western and northern Tibet.

The Bön religion is alive and indeed to some extent even flourishing today—not only in Tibet itself, where, especially in the east (Kham) and northeast (Amdo) entire districts still firmly adhere to Bön, but also in Nepal (Dolpo and Lubra) and in the Tibetan exile communities in India. Both in Tibet and in exile there are several erudite and spiritually highly accomplished Bönpo lamas, one of the most venerated of whom is Lopon (*slob dpon*, "Head Teacher") Tenzin Namdak. For an increasing number of Tibetan and Western disciples and friends, his learning and warm, compassionate presence have been a profoundly moving experience.

The present text should be seen as the fruit of an encounter between a highly qualified Tibetan Bönpo lama, willing and indeed eager to share his vast store of knowledge, and a Western pupil equally eager to learn and communicate to others what has been learnt. As a document resulting from such an interaction the text will repay study. It gives an indication, a kind of rough hint, of the spiritual treasures to be found in the Bön religion. At the same time, it is essential to realize what this text is not. It is not a real translation. The careful work of interpretation and collation, based on a close and competent study of a large number of texts in the original Tibetan remains to be done, and it is this alone which may, at some future time, make accurate and adequate translations possible. The reader is well advised to have no illusions about this. Even less should the text be taken to be a "do-it-yourself" manual for those who aspire actually to practice the spiritual discipline, to attain the "Great Perfection" described therein. For such practice the personal, regular guidance of a qualified, experienced lama is absolutely indispensable. Those wishing to experiment on their own may be assured that whatever mental experiences they may have will be either delusive, or—the danger is a real one—destructive.

The Great Perfection (Dzogpa Chenpo, Dzogchen, *rdzogs pa chen po*) is regarded by Bönpos as the highest, the ultimate religious practice. It has been preserved in several distinct traditions. Also, the Nyingmapa school of Buddhism has a Dzogchen tradition, which it claims goes back to the great siddha Padmasambhava (eighth century C.E.) and his disciples. A comparative study of the Bönpo and the Nyingmapa varieties of Dzogchen remains to be undertaken. Nevertheless, in recent years a fairly lively interest in Dzogchen has been evident both among a number of scholars and among the more numerous Western adepts. The bibliographic essay appended to the text is not complete but should be useful to those who want to find further information and perhaps return to the present text with a better understanding of its subject matter.

Per Kvaerne
University of Oslo

Shardza Tashi Gyaltsen

Biography of Shardza Tashi Gyaltsen

In general, there are three sections to a master's biography: the external (which is also the general biography), the internal and the esoteric biography. Here, only the general biography is described, but in it there are some parts which concern the specific internal and esoteric aspects as well.

There are eight sub-divisions of the external biography:

1. His birth
2. How he began learning the religious path
3. How he began thinking and practising according to the path of Yungdrung Bön
4. How he received teachings, initiations and vows
5. How he practised in solitude
6. How he worked for the doctrines of Tonpa Shenrab and for the benefit of all beings
7. The teachings and works he left behind
8. How he manifested his great knowledge as a rainbow body

HIS BIRTH

When Shardza Tashi Gyaltsen (*shar rdza bkra shis rgyal mtshan*) was born, there were many auspicious signs. In the sky there were many rainbows and there was a shower of flowers. The country in which he was born is in the Kham region of East Tibet. It is a place in between two rivers, the Dza Chu (*rdza chu*) and the Ngul Chu (*dngul chu*), and is called "Da Gang", or "the range of Da Gang (*zla gang*)". This is a place where many saints have previously been born, or have stayed and visited. It is known, in short, as Dzakog (*rdza khog*).

The name of the village in which Shardza was born is Da (*brda*), in the foothills of that place. His father belonged to the clan of Hor (*hor*), and was called Tashi Ga (*bkra shis dga'*) and his mother was called Boleg (*bo legs*). He was born on the eighth day of the third month of the earth-sheep year (1859).

From his childhood, he did not give his parents much trouble and was easy to raise. Even from his infancy he always had good manners and behaved with calm and composure. He also showed the auspicious signs of teaching other children, building stupas and chanting, and in this way pretended to be the teacher. Sometimes he also saw forms of divinities in space.

When he was nine years old, a great siddha called Tenzin Wangyal (*bstan 'dzin dbang rgyal*) whose secret name was Drenpa Dudul (*dran pa bdud 'dul*), told his parents, "Your son must become a monk." But the parents refused because Shardza was their only son. Soon after, Shardza developed some mental sickness, and for many days neither ate nor slept. So the parents took him to Tenzin Wangyal, who again said, "This child is connected to the religious way of life. You should send him on the religious path, otherwise he will not be useful for you." This time, the parents understood and decided to let the child become a monk. When they returned home, the child's mental sickness gradually lifted, and he was finally released from it.

HOW HE BEGAN LEARNING THE RELIGIOUS PATH

Tenzin Wangyal recognised that the boy had a very long-lasting connection with him over many past lives. So he was very kind to this boy from the beginning and the boy was always very devoted to him. When the child was born, he had blessed him with long life. After the boy became older, he took the refuge vow from Tenzin Wangyal, who prayed that the boy would become beneficial to all sentient beings. Thus he gave the boy the name Tashi Gyaltsen. He also made a special prayer to the red Sipa Gyalmo (*srid pa rgyal mo*) to bless the boy.

When the boy was twelve, he went to his uncle Yungdrung Gyaltsen (*gyung drung rgyal msthan*) to learn how to read and write. Soon after, the boy received many initiations, teachings and transmissions from the special master Tenzin Wangyal.

Tenzin Wangyal knew that the boy would be important for Tonpa Shenrab's teachings and for the benefit of all sentient beings, so he advised the boy to take the Vinaya vows, the Tantric vows and the Dzogchen vows. He also told the boy to practise and meditate diligently, learning Sutra, Tantra and Dzogchen.

One day, Tenzin Wangyal put a huge volume of books on the boy's head and prayed for a long time and said, "You will be the owner of this doctrine." From that moment, Shardza had a great change of feeling, and this was the beginning of his receiving auspicious signs. This was the beginning of the mental initiation and blessing that Shardza was to receive from Tenzin Wangyal. The boy now became very sharp and intelligent, had great devotion, stopped all desires for the worldly life, and naturally increased his compassion and devotion to both the doctrines and his masters, particularly to Tenzin Wangyal, who transferred his mental blessing to him.

One springtime there was a drought, and the local people asked Tenzin Wangyal to call for rain. Tenzin Wangyal took the boy with him as assistant. He gave the boy a sword and asked him to "push down the wind." Shardza held onto the sword, and after some time the master returned suddenly, took the sword forcefully away from the boy, and showed the face of anger. He used the sword to hit the boy, who fell unconscious. After a while, the boy woke up, and at that moment he received the heart transmission from his master and realised the natural state clearly, on the same level as his master. From then on whatever he studied, it was as easy for him as if he had known it before, and he meditated with the recognition of this natural state day and night. He was never again in any doubt, and was never in fear of not having the knowledge of the natural state.

He also started learning grammar and poetry. From then on he began keeping notes for his books called the *Five Treasures*, a collection of thirteen volumes of his writings. Besides, his meditation was very stable and developed without his having to practise as hard as other people. He also had special knowledge of the nine ways of Bön. Yet, he behaved in the same way as an ordinary young boy.

HOW HE RECEIVED TEACHINGS, INITIATIONS AND VOWS

When he was young, he kept the vow of refuge and other simple vows very strictly. Everyone praised his manner of keeping the vows. When he was older, the abbot of Yungdrung Ling (*gyung drung gling*), whose name was Kelzang Nyima Togi Gyaltsen (*skal bzang nyi ma tog gi rgyal mtshan*), came to Kham. He was invited to Dza Tengchen Gonpa (*rdza steng chen dgon pa*), the boy's monastery. There, many people took their vows from this abbot, and each received a name at the same time. When it came to Shardza, he received the name Tenpa Drudrag (*bstan pa 'brug grags*) from the abbot, who repeated the name three times. All those who were taking the vows burst out laughing loudly. The abbot said that it was a very auspicious sign, and that the boy would become a great man.

The reincarnation of Tazhig (*stag zhig*), whose name is Shengyal Tenzin (*gshen rgyal bstan 'dzin*), came to the Dzakog (*rdza khog*) country upon the invitation of Shardza's monastery. He was the holder of the vinaya vows of the Menri (*sman ri*) lineage. In front of the abbot, the lopon (*slob dpon*) or teacher, a witness, and an interpreter,[1] all four of whom were high monks, Shardza took the highest and final vinaya vows. He kept his original name, Tenpa Drudrag, and additionally received the name Drime Nyingpo (*dri med snying po*). From that time onward, he never took any alcohol, never ate meat nor wore the skin of animals, and he conducted himself completely according to the vinaya rules. Altogether he observed two hundred and fifty vows.

The second vow is the vow of bodhicitta, which he took from Samten Yeshe (*bsam gtan ye shes*). At the same time, he received the name Gyalse Zhenpen Norbu (*rgyal sras gzhan phan nor bu*). He practised the two kinds of bodhicitta: one that is according to the absolute truth, and the other according to the relative truth. When he took the vows, he offered hundreds and thousands of butter lamps, flowers, incense and torma (ritual cakes). From then on, he always kept the vows precisely and paid attention to all details.

In the tradition, different texts mention different vows as part of the bodhicitta vow. Some mention twenty vows, some mention an extended form of 360 vows, some mention a medium form of 108 vows and some twenty-eight vows. These vows can be described as the four kinds of bodhicitta vows, all of which Shardza practised. In addition he also practised the ten perfections.

---

1 The presence of an interpreter is to ensure that the vow explained to the person taking the vow is clearly understood. The recipient thus cannot claim at a later date that the meaning of the vow was not explained clearly.

The Tantric Vows

Shardza took the tantric vows from his root master, Tenzin Wangyal. He took the initiation of the yidam called Walse Ngampa (*dbal gsas rngam pa*). At the time of the initiation, he was introduced to the nature of mind, the four initiations of the yidam and the initiation of Dzogchen called Gyaltab Chilug (*rgyal thabs spyi lugs*).

From another master called Rigdzin Tsewang Dragpa (*rig 'dzin tshe dbang grags pa*) who was also known as Dechen Lingpa (*bde chen gling pa*), he received the initiation of the peaceful and the wrathful form of the same yidam, Walse Ngampa. Also he received the Dzogchen initiation of Rigpai Tselwang (*rig pa'i rtsal dbang*), as well as the preliminary and essential teachings of Atri (*a khrid*), besides many other tantric initiations.

In the tantric vow, there are five root vows and twenty-five branch vows for the Kyerim (*bskyed rim*), and five root vows and one hundred branch vows for the Dzogrim (*rdzogs rim*). In Dzogchen, there are thirty vows. Shardza kept all these vows carefully and clearly. In the Bönpo tradition, all the vows mentioned above are those that can be taken by a person who can take all three types of vows, which he did.

Altogether Shardza had twenty-four teachers, from whom he learned different subjects. Usually in those days people were satisfied after learning from one or two masters. But Shardza was special. He continued to seek and learn all the time. To the following masters he offered all his wealth and from them he received all the teachings of different subjects, initiations and transmissions:

1. Dzatrul Tenzin Wangyal (*dza sprul bstan 'dzin dbang rgyal*)
2. Dechen Lingpa (*bde chen gling pa*)
3. Dudul Lingpa (*bdud 'dul gling pa*)
4. Samten Yeshe (*bsam gtan ye shes*)
5. Shengyal Tenzin (*gshen rgyal bstan 'dzin*)

6. Tsewang Gyurme (*tshe dbang 'gyur med*)
7. Rinchen Namgyal (*rin chen rnam rgyal*)
8. Kelzang Nyima (*bskal bzang nyi ma*)
9. Meton Nyima Gyaltsen (*me ston nyi ma rgyal mtshan*)
10. Paton Nyima Bumsel (*spa ston nyi ma 'bum gsal*)
11. Yungdrung Wangyal (*gyung gdrung dbang rgyal*)
12. Tsultrim Namdak (*tshul khrims rnam dag*)
13. Sonam Gyaltsen (*bso nams rgyal mtshan*)
14. Tsultrim Pelzang (*tshul khrims dpal bzang*)
15. Sonam Pelzang (*bso nams dpal bzang*)
16. Nyima Özer (*nyi ma 'od zer*)
17. Togden Gede (*rtogs ldan dga' bde*)
18. Yeshe Tenzin (*ye shes bstan 'dzin*)
19. Lama Tengyal (*bla ma bstan rgyal*)
20. Yezhin Wangyal (*yed bzhin dbang rgyal*)
21. Sangngag Lingpa (*gsang sngags gling pa*)
22. Chime Tsugpu (*'chi med gtsug phud*)
23. Nyima Zangpo (*nyi ma bzang po*)
24. Dawa Dragpa (*zla ba grags pa*)

HOW HE PRACTISED IN SOLITUDE

When Shardza was about thirty-four years old, one day he felt great disgust for living in this worldly life. So he decided to go stay in solitude completely. The place he went to stay was Yungdrung Lhunpo (*gyung drung lhun po*), which bordered Shardza, his country. When he went there, many auspicious signs appeared, so he decided that it was a suitable place. There he built a small hut, just big enough for him to sit inside. At this place, he completely stopped all external and worldly activities and connections, and internally his mind stopped thinking of plans and desires, including relatives, friends and wealth. Living in solitude, he only had simple food and one set of clothes. In this way he practised with a rested body, speech and mind.

He started, as was done normally, by doing the preliminary practice of the teaching. He also did the refuge, bodhicitta and the esoteric practices. At that time, people generally learned and practised the Bönpo teaching only for food and wealth. Those people considered it sufficient just to do some rituals and prayers to please those who demanded it. However, Shardza saw all the essential points of the Bönpo teachings and practised accordingly, without paying any attention to such worldly thoughts.

In his own country, the tradition of the teaching was mixed up with the new Bön. He was able to see clearly the historical and pure part of the old Bön teachings, and completely left out the new Bön teaching, keeping strictly to the old (Yungdrung) tradition.

In Bönpo there are five high clans or families of people, which are the Dru (*bru*), Zhu (*zhu*), Pa (*spa*), Me (*rme*) and Shen (*gshen*) clans. Each one has its own lineage tradition and strict rules, even though they are all Bönpos. He respected all these traditions, but he followed the Dru tradition, because this is the lineage holder of Menri.

From the beginning he practised the relative bodhicitta and the absolute bodhicitta. He practised with great hardship in solitude. He also practised the Kyerim and Dzogrim of various yidams in the tantric teachings. He divided the twenty-four hours of a day into four sessions, and practised most of the yidams, particularly peaceful Kunzang (*kun bzang*), Drenpa Namkha (*dran pa nam mkha'*) and Tsewang (*tshe dbang*), or Black Kila. He practised everything, including tummo, Dzogrim and mantra. Even though he mainly practised the recitation of mantra, he especially did the practice of Trekchö (*khreg chod*) and Tögel (*thod rgal*) all the time.

HOW HE WORKED FOR THE DOCTRINES OF TONPA SHENRAB AND FOR THE BENEFIT OF ALL BEINGS

He worked for the preliminary teachings and the history of Sutra, Tantra and Dzogchen. Hence, he compiled them into two volumes. His commentaries on the nine ways of Bön and on Trekchö and Tögel of Dzogchen in particular were compiled into two volumes. He held the lineage of *Zhang Zhung Nyengyu (zhang zhung snyan brgyud)* teachings. He also wrote many ritual texts for prayers and gana puja, as well as chöd teachings, sutra and tantra teachings with various subjects in the sutra and their commentaries. All his work is like the lamp for the old Bön tradition. Later in our time, when people eagerly want to know something about Bön, his works are like a key to the whole tradition.

He had many disciples following his teaching. Among them, the best disciple was called Terchen Sangngag Lingpa (*gter chen gsang sngags gling pa*). His successor was his nephew Lodrö Gyatso (*blo gros rgya mtsho*). Besides these disciples, he also had many others to whom he gave special transmissions.

He was always teaching and giving transmissions. He never showed tiredness when people went to him for teachings. Aside from that, he still strictly kept his own sessions of practice.

THE TEACHINGS AND WORKS HE LEFT BEHIND

He helped his monastery, Dza Tengchen Gonpa (*rdza steng chen dgon pa*), to rebuild. For the exterior he reconstructed the temple, and for the interior, he restored the images. Three images are two stories high—about eighteen feet tall. There are many other smaller ones which are one storey (about nine feet) tall. On the outside of these images he made many decorations of precious things, and inside he hid relics and books of important teachings and mantras.

Below his hut for solitary retreat one of his students, Sangngag Lingpa, proposed to him that he build a meditation centre. The place where the centre was built was called Gethang (*dge thang*). There he built a temple with images inside. Gradually people offered him properties, and he used these places to build many temples. Inside these temples he built several hundred images of various sizes. He also carved many blocks for printing books, particularly his collected works, which amount to thirteen volumes. Altogether 330 volumes of books were carved in blocks. Five huge prayer wheels and several large stupas were also made. All of these things together with the properties offered to him were, in turn, offered to his master from time to time. He also made offerings to all the temples and monasteries in his country, regardless of whether they were Buddhist or Bönpo. Whenever there were practitioners who were in need, he also helped them with their living.

He always offered flowers, incense, butter lamps, water and mandala on a regular basis. Every tenth day of the month, he made offerings of gana puja. Even though he was teaching a lot, he remained in his solitary retreat hut. Gradually, however, his students began to teach extensively in many teaching centres in the east of Tibet. Later, he made his nephew the successor to the meditation centre in Gethang and this nephew took over the teaching responsibility when Shardza was getting old. In all his teaching centres, the vinaya vow was strictly observed, while the meditation practice was Dzogchen.

HOW HE MANIFESTED HIS GREAT KNOWLEDGE AS A RAINBOW BODY

When he was seventy-five, in the water-bird year, Shardza changed his manner of teaching. In addition to the more serious topics, he gave more general kinds of teaching to his students, giving them advice. Usually he only had one meal a day, but then he began to accept all offerings regardlessly. He also liked to play with children more, and began behaving very freely, without any consideration of how his worldly manner should be. Some of the students began to see him (manifesting) as the form of various divinities. Some of his helpers also saw him walking away with his feet above the ground. Some saw him leave his bowl floating in mid air. At night they could not see his body throw any shadow in the light of the lamps. This was noticed very clearly.

He also said to his disciples,

> I, the old man Shardzapa, don't know when I am to pass away. I have been teaching specifically for the past eight years and I have taught many important teachings and I hope that you are not going to waste them. I advise you not to waste any of these teachings you have received but continue to practise until you are stable in your natural state. I think you are all very lucky, because it is very rare to receive these teachings. Since you have received them, you must try to realise yourself. They are very precious, can you understand?

When he was seventy-six, in the wood-dog year, one of his disciples, Kelzang Yungdrung (*bskal bzang gyung drung*), was praying and practising in order to bless some medicine. Shardza told this disciple to finish his prayers before the fourth month, because after that they would not meet again. Then on the second day of the fourth month Shardza was presented with the blessed medicine with the prayer complete. He said, "Now I have to go to the empty places." So he went to the place called Rabzhi Teng (*rab zhi steng*) to stay. He put up a small tent there. Several of his students followed him and he told them, "The base of all knowledge is faith, devotion and vow. So you must realise this and carefully practise." In addition, he also gave them much advice. Very often his gazes were straight into space.

On the thirteenth day of the fourth month, he made a gana puja offering of Tsewang Bö Yulma (*tshe dbang bod yul ma*), and he sang many teachings in the form of songs. He then ordered his disciples to sew the tent completely closed, and not to open it for many days. Then he went into the tent and said "good luck" to his students, as well as prayers. Then he sat inside in the posture with five characteristics.

On the next day, his students saw many rainbows above his tent. Some were big, some were small, some were round, others were straight, horizontal or vertical, all with many colours. Particularly at night white lights like long white scarves shone forth brilliantly, which everyone saw. On the fourth day, there was an earthquake, and there were loud and strange sounds. Also showers of flowers rained down. Between the stitches of the tent many lights with different colours—some with five colours, some with only a single colour—came out like steam. His student called Tsultrim Wangchug (*tshul khrims dbang phyug*) said, "If we leave the body for much longer, everything will disappear and there will be nothing left from the corpse. We should have something as relics for our devotion." So he opened the tent, and prostrated. The body of Shardza was completely wrapped up with light, and the size had shrunk to that of a one-year-old boy. It was suspended above the mattress at a height equal to the distance between the outstretched finger tip and the elbow of an arm. He went into the tent, and saw the fingernails had come out of the fingers and were scattered on the mattress. When he touched the body, the heart was still warm. He wrapped up the body with a cloth and kept it for forty-nine days. He then did a puja of the 1000 names of the Buddhas, as well as many gana puja and other offerings. After, when visitors saw the body and touched it, everyone had many special feelings rising in themselves. All the people saw lights, rainbows and rains of flowers every day. All the local people visited the body and strong devotion arose in all of them and they had great belief in him.

Some of the non-devotees were saying that, "The lama was not so special when he was alive, but is more special dead. So he is better dead than alive."

His successor, Lodrö Gyatso (*blo gros rgya mtsho*), and his younger brother, Tsultrim Tenzin (*tshul khrims bstan 'dzin*), saw to it that all his properties were given as offerings and donations to all monasteries, both Buddhist and Bönpo, particularly to his own monastery, Dza Tengchen Gonpa. They also asked the monasteries to do prayers for many weeks, and gave them properties so that every year they would recite prayers on the anniversary of the manifestation of his rainbow body—the thirteenth day of the fourth month. They also made a large memorial stupa, with gilded copper, and his body was put inside in the niche of the ball of the stupa. Even much later people still could see the reflection of lights and rainbows and sparks coming from it.

Extracted and translated by Lopon Tenzin Namdak from the biographical account by Sula Kelzang Tenpai Gyaltsen (su la bskal bzang bstan pa'i rgyal mtshan) (1897-1959)

Heart Drops of Dharmakaya

Introduction

In this text there are three subdivisions according to whether the student is clever, medium or not bright. By following these practices, the first will achieve Buddhahood in one lifetime, the second in the intermediate state and the third after several lives of using the Dzogchen methods. [1]

1 These subdivisions occur in every section of the text and do not refer to the four major books into which it has been divided.

Gyalyum Sherab Jamma

Book One
Preliminary Practices

[Tibetan text 3a, line 2]

First there is a preliminary practice which is described in two sections. The purpose of the first practice is to distinguish between samsara and nirvana; the purpose of the second is to stop desire for body, speech and mind.

THE FIRST PRELIMINARY PRACTICE CYCLE: TO DISTINGUISH SAMSARA FROM NIRVANA

The first practice is further subdivided into external and internal practices.

External Practice

Go to a quiet place without any people and stay there. First make offerings to the mountain gods or whoever is powerful and spiritual in the area so that they are not disturbed. Tell them where you are practicing so that you do not disturb them.

Then, thinking that you must stop desire for samsara, ask what is the purpose of so much attachment? You need to ask why you have this desire. Imagine that you are naked and born in hell, screaming and suffering as if you are actually there. Then imagine that you are born in the realm of the hungry ghosts (*pretas*) with endless hunger and want. Imagine you are born in the animal realm, doing as animals do. Then think that you are born as a human with servants—imagine that life; then as a titan (*asura*) fighting with another—what is the purpose of that? Finally imagine that you are born as a god (*deva*) and spending life in leisure without thinking of the next life—what is the purpose of this? Imagine that you are circulating from one realm to the next. Do whatever comes to your mind—in vision or imagination.

Then imagine what it is like to be a *yidam* (tutelary deity); or that you are in Shambhala and are teaching the bodhisattvas; or in the tantric realms with the siddhas as disciples; or in Sukhavati or Olmo Lungring teaching Dzogpachenpo. Pretend that you are actually doing this. Finally dissolve all visions into the natural state. What is left? Then dissolve even your thought itself into the natural state so there is nothing left. Then you will realise that everything is made by your thought—everything comes from there. You have to realise how things are created.

You must practice this seriously for at best three months, or at least one month.[2]

---

2 Lopon comments that it is necessary to practise in this way as a preliminary to the main practice—so the mention of time requirements is quite serious and deliberate. Think that it is very important to make such a period of preparation, and not just for a little while. Therefore prepare as much as you can.

Apart from eating and sleeping, this practice should be carried on for the entire day. If you go to an empty valley or cave, what else is there to do? This is serious practice, not like the common ngondro. This is for the person who is absolutely fed up with worldly life. Otherwise it is difficult to give up all the other things.

Regarding this we asked Lopon whether it was absolutely necessary to go to a solitary place for this practice, and he said that it was not. If we can't, we should at least

The result is seeing that everything is created by your thought. Once you finally realise this you can check back to find its origin. All things are created by your thought and mind—and if you look back to the source of your thought and mind you find that it disappears. It dissolves and goes back to its nature. That is the limit; every individual thing is dependent on the mind. All worldly life, all the beings in the six realms are in the same situation. The purpose of this practice is to stop all desire for the worldly life—to see that it is all created by our mind. The world is like a common mind. All human beings share the same vision, the same karma. Likewise for the beings in the other realms—they all share a karmic vision of the world.[3]

---

keep to regular sessions and do it seriously in order to have results. He said that in the Western lifestyle we have many free periods in which we can practice, so sometimes it may be even better than being a monk, because a monk has so many different duties and rituals to perform.

Lopon further comments that with regard to the content, the six realms visualisation is one means, but there is also the realisation of samsara as such. This is done exclusively. If you try to practise alongside all the worldly activities then it is very difficult not to be distracted. And if you don't do the ngondro seriously then the other practices will only look like leisure.

3 Lopon comments that although humans look at water and see water, beings of other realms look at the same thing and perceive it differently. When animals see it they only see it as something to drink, but not water. The hell beings see it as fire or ice; the pretas as some sort of dirty thing. What we see is always conditioned by our previous actions. We only see our own karma; that we can check from the clear example that if two or three people go together to see something they all see and feel different things. This gives an idea.

Take the individual mind, for example. One person might think that he is good although others think he is bad;

Internal Practice

The second part of the first preliminary practice is to stop desire through internal visualisation and recitation. It should be done for at least seven weeks. The actual practice is not described in this text. Briefly, there is a mantra and sending lights to the six realms to purify all defilements. It is more connected to the tantric system.[4]

THE SECOND PRELIMINARY PRACTICE CYCLE: TO STOP DESIRE FOR BODY, SPEECH AND MIND[5]

The Practice for the Body

Here one practices with the body. One stands up and places the soles of the feet together with the knees out and the hands joined above the head. The neck is bent to the chest. That is the body posture. One visualises oneself as a three-pointed dorje, flaming and blue.[6]

---

a mother may see a man as her son, but his wife sees him as a husband. All this is created by individual minds—people see others through their preconceptions. Everything is created. This realisation makes it possible for us to develop in positive or negative ways. But we are covered with our ignorance, for always we are grasping. If things exist as our grasping mind sees them, as objects that are real and fixed, then nothing can change in this world. But nothing is fixed. That is how we are deluded. It is to break this deluded perception that is the purpose of this practice.

4 Lopon comments that Shardza composed his own collections here which are described in the main text. They are taken from the *Zhang Zhung Nyengyu (zhang zhung snyan brgyud)* which has been published in Delhi. These internal practices are best done alongside the external practice in the same session.

5 Lopon comments that the three types of practice are best carried out in the same session, one type after another.

Inhale the breath and hold it. Hold that posture until you cannot hold it any longer. At that point fall down backwards, exhaling with *HAH* strongly. Do this many times.

This practice serves three purposes: first, it purifies the body; second, the demons see the flaming vajra and leave you alone; and third, it stops desire for the body.

The Practice for the Speech

The second type of practice is for the speech. There are four subdivisions: Gyedapa (*rgyas gdab pa*; 'sealed'), Tsel Jongpa (*rtsal sbyong pa*; 'practice'), Nyen Tselpa (*mnyen btsal pa*; the training'), and Lamdu Zhug (*lam du gzhug*; 'to put in the way').

(1) The Seal (Gyedapa). There are three subdivisions.

(a) External Gyedapa. HUM is a seal for the impure mind. *HUM* is used since it symbolises the Buddha mind. The practice is to sit cross-legged and gaze into space. Visualise your mind at the heart as a blue *HUM*, then sound *HUM* slowly many times. At the same time visualise the blue *HUM* emitting rays of little *HUM*s which come out through the right nostril filling up the universe with *HUM*. Whatever the *HUM* touches turns into another blue *HUM*, everything both internally and externally. Your mind is completely absorbed into *HUM*—nothing else is happening. Always sound the *HUM*, soft and long.

(b) Internal Gyedapa. Now sound *HUM* in a fast rhythm, and imagine that all the *HUM*s dissolve one into another and come back to the heart through the left nostril. When they come to the inside of the body all the flesh and blood turns into *HUM* so that the body is filled with *HUM*. Hold this vision for a long time.

6 The three points of the dorje are made by the elbows and the hands.

(c) The Purpose (dgos pa) of Gyedapa. Thus you realise that no object, not even your body, is self-sustaining. Nothing, not even your body, has independent material existence—everything can be easily changed. When you have practiced long enough signs come, such as an unexpected vision of *HUM* externally, or that you suddenly feel that your body is filled with *HUM*. That is a sign that you have practiced *gyedapa* enough.

(2) The Practice of Visions as Reflections (Tsel Jongpa). Whatever vision comes to mind is *tsel* (reflection), so this practice is to destroy whatever comes and dissolve it into mind. The practice is similar to before. Sitting with the five-point body posture,[7] visualise a dark blue *HUM* inside the heart. Now you should sound the *HUM* very strongly, very sharply, and visualize the *HUM* as a very strong fire with swords, throwing off sparks like lightning. This *HUM* comes out through the right nostril in the form of many *HUM*s and whatever they touch they destroy. Finally they go through everything and destroy in all directions. Everything is destroyed by this strong *HUM*. Then again it comes back through the left nostril and destroys all the material of your body. It also helps to send away all sickness and disturbance. It can even help in the formation of the *jalu* (*'ja' lus*; the body of light) by stopping all desire for the body.

The signs that this has been practiced enough are to have the sudden vision that the universe is just an illusion and that your body is thin like a net, insubstantial. That is the sign.

(3) The Training (Nyen Tselpa). The purpose here is to tame your mind and bring it under control. You practice by placing a stick in front of you and sounding *HUM* continuously like a beat. Then many *HUM*s come out from the heart like beads, leave the body through the

---

7 This is to sit with the legs crossed, back straight, neck slightly bent, eyes looking to the chest, and mouth slightly open.

nostrils, and go to the base of the stick. They climb the stick like ants, wrapping around it. When the first one comes to the top of the stick it stops, facing you; the rest are wrapped around in a spiral. When thoughts disturb you, all the *HUM*s come back to the first *HUM* at the heart. You have to spend some time doing this, and it brings the thoughts under control so you can meditate for as long as you want to.

(4) To Put in the Way (Lamdu Zhug). This means to put the body, speech and mind into the right way—to put them into the natural clear light. The practice is to think of a blue *HUM* the size of the distance from your elbow to your finger tips. This represents your body, speech and mind—everything. When you sound *HUM* it moves to the right and left and then it moves off, travelling over the countryside, until finally it goes to countries that you have never seen. All the while say, "*HUM, HUM*" continuously. Then stop it by saying "*PHAT!*" strongly and suddenly. The vision disappears and you rest as you are—you remain in your nature. This *HUM* can go to the heavens or to Shambhala; suddenly you stop it by sounding *PHAT*. By sounding *PHAT* you will stop thoughts and remain in the natural state. By carrying out this practice you will begin to have experiences (*nyams*) of bliss, emptiness and clarity.

The sign that you have carried out this practice enough is that you will be able to remain in the natural state without any doubt or effort.

The Practice for the Mind (Sem Jongpa; sems sbyong pa)

These are direct methods of introduction to the natural state. The methods described above are all material ways to bring you to the natural state. Below are given nine methods to bring you directly to this state.[8]

---

8 Lopon comments that this part of the preliminary practice is done in sessions—first a section for body, then for speech and finally one for the mind, all in one session. As

The first three methods come under the title *Where does it come from, where does it stay and where does it go?*

Holding the five-point body posture, look back to the origin of thought and enquire whether the natural state is material, visible or invisible. You have to check back. You cannot find where this object is or who is searching for it. When you try you lose everything. Like the sky—that is the empty mind—you start to realise the empty mind.

Checking the Normal Worldly Vision. When you realise this point you can try to destroy it but you will find nothing. Whatever you do, it is not possible to do anything with this empty nature. Even when all thoughts are stopped there is still a very bright and clear presence that is empty. That is called Clear Natural Mind.[9]

If things were independent and self-sustaining then you could find out by checking all your visions as described above to discover their nature. But when you practice in this method, although vision comes as nor-

---

before this is an intense process; sometimes go out, but most of the time practice.

9 Lopon comments that we see all things as independent objects; we cannot see that all are reflections of the natural state. What we are seeing are all delusions that do not in fact exist independently. They are like the visions that come in dreams. However, if these visions were all independent and self-sustaining we would be able to determine this through a process of enquiry.

Take this table, for example. If we ask whether the table can be found in the top, the sides, the legs or the bottom, we cannot find it. If something was independent and self-sustaining (i.e. had inherent existence), it would remain after such enquiry.

This is a very widely used method of analysis in Buddhism; see Jeffrey Hopkins' *Meditation on Emptiness* (London: Wisdom Books, 1983). Checking the object in this way is a simple procedure and not so difficult; the problem is in the reconstruction of perception.

mal, your understanding is different. You see that all visions are illusion. You have realised the nature of nonstop illusion.

Looking to Where the Reflections Come, the fifth method: The visions come to the mind, but where do they appear and who understands them? Who tastes sadness and happiness? If you look back to the mind's situation you will see that everything is made by the mind. But if you look to the mind you will see that the mind too seems to have no independent existence.[10] However, if the mind is not there, then who called the names and made the causes of existence? Therefore the mind must exist, and everything else exists in dependence on mind. Nothing exists independently of mind.[11]

---

10 Lopon comments that philosophy can be useful to introduce the Dzogchen view. Although you cannot explain the nature of mind, you can point to the place where it can be found—like a child pointing to the moon. Usually Dzogchenpas do not discuss the view from a logical or analytical standpoint, because they are not trained to do so. This is not the case in the Bön tradition, however, where a school of philosophy unique to Dzogchen has developed. In any case, the least a Dzogchenpa can do is explain what he or she is doing and thinking.

11 Lopon comments that this use of ***mind*** is not in the sense of 'consciousness'; it is the mind as the 'nature of mind'. It is not like the Cittamatra (Mind Only) view.

This reference to Cittamatra concerns the store consciousness or ***kunzhi (kun gzhi);*** in this view it is where all the karmic traces are kept, and if you purify it you achieve Buddhahood. Although this term is used in Dzogchen, there it means the natural state, the base, and there is no concept of purification. The base is primordially pure—*kadag (ka dag)*—pure from the beginning. So the practice is not purification but recognition of that state.

Take the external world, for example. In Cittamatra it is explained like the two halves of a hard-boiled egg that is cut down the middle, so that the object side and the subject side

Nothing exists beyond the natural state. Earth is not independent of the natural state; stone is not independent of the natural state; visions are not independent visions. Everything is a vision of the natural state.

The natural state is like a single point; the natural state is like where birds fly—behind there is no trace. If you understand this point you will realise that the natural state is the creator of all things—the king of creators.

---

of an individual existence match. But Dzogchen says that everything is encompassed by the natural state, which has the power to make and take reflections. What is reflected in the mind does not independently exist; both internal and external are spontaneous reflections in the natural state.

To do this is a natural quality of the primordial state, but it does not mean that these reflections are solid, independent and inherently existent. They arise from the natural state and go back to it; it is our ignorance that grasps them as independent. So Cittamatra philosophy is often confused with Dzogchen. In Cittamatra it is said that both the objective and the subjective worlds arise from karmic causes. In Dzogchen however the world spontaneously exists; it is conditioned by karma but its source is the natural state.

Madhyamika philosophy does not accept the concept of kunzhi at all, however; it only accepts the six types of consciousness (senses and mind) rather than the eight of Cittamatra and Dzogchen. In those systems after the six senses the seventh is *nyonye (nyon yed;* emotions) and the eighth is *kunzhi*. An analogy is sometimes used: the mind is the husband and nyonye is the wife; kunzhi is the storehouse and the senses collect the goods that come into the storehouse from the outside.

So Dzogchen holds many aspects in common with Cittamatra, and the object side and the subject side are inseparable in both systems. Crucially, however, in Dzogchen the natural state is pure from the beginning and is always present. There is nothing to purify and nothing to reach.

Realisation Without Speaking or Thought, the sixth method: One might say that if the natural state exists then somewhere it must appear, but nothing appears so therefore the natural state does not exist. It is always without a trace, in past, present or future. But even though the natural state does not appear it is always there. This awareness is of a sort that you can never catch by thought, and you cannot name it or show it by letters. If you try to show it by sounds or signs you never go exactly to the nature of this awareness. Whatever you do to study or check in this way, you will be like a dumb man who tastes sugar—he can taste but he cannot explain to others how the flavour tastes. In the same way this nature cannot be thought and cannot be captured by words. When you understand this then you realise the natural state without speaking or thought.[12]

The Natural State Does Not Exist Because It Is Not Material, the seventh method: The natural state does not exist either, because there is no method to remove it. It cannot both exist and not exist; neither is the natural state beyond existence and non-existence. There is no place for it to rest; therefore the nature of mind is completely beyond

---

12 Lopon comments that Tsongkhapa's criticism of Dzogchen was based on the notion that all Dzogchenpas do is ask about the nature of mind and find that mind has no colour or size or material. According to him that is the Dzogchen view. But this criticism is mistaken for this is the view of the Vipassana schools. As was mentioned in note 11, Dzogchen stresses the difference between the mind and the nature of mind. My nature of mind and your nature of mind are different. There are as many natures of mind as there are sentient beings. When someone takes a rainbow body everyone else is left the same. Just as each sentient being has a different body, so they also have different minds. But the quality of all their minds is the same; the mind is completely individual but its qualities are common to all. One can only study one's own nature even though the qualities you discover may be the same for all beings.

limits. If you understand this you understand the 'Great Limitless Mind that is beyond the Four Limits.'[13] Thus you have nothing to grasp at. If you grasp at things you must bind them by one of the four limits.

The Realisation That Is Beyond Thought and Without Name, the eighth method: In the first place the natural state is completely beyond thought and the objects of thought. It is in no way an object of thought. You cannot show it by example. Whatever you do you can do nothing with this. However when you check back to the source of thoughts you cannot find anything—you just come back to the nature of mind itself. It is not separate from object and subject, nor from names, nor can any thoughts seize its nature. When you understand this without thinking you realise the mind without name that is beyond thoughts.

The Realisation of the Spontaneous Mind Without Doing, the ninth method: Even if you do not search or study anything the natural state is always with you from the limitless beginning. There is nothing to lose and nothing to find. If you search in yourself can you find it? Therefore you should not speak about searching for the nature of mind. From the beginning it was always with you and never separate from you. No other beings can see the nature of your mind. It is always self-originated. When you realise this you have realised the 'Naked Basic Dharmakaya'.

13 Lopon comments that these are existence, non-existence, both or neither.

THE DZOGCHEN VIEW

Checking Where the Natural State Comes From, Where It Stays and Where It Goes

In this section you first check *Where does the natural state come from and who is coming?* The method to check this is, when a thought comes without planning, to ask the question whether it comes from existence or non-existence. Look into where it comes from. If you think it comes from existence and the external realms, say from the earth, mountains or houses, or from the internal realms inside the body or brains, then check each possibility individually. Check them and go back to these items. If you do this where can you find the source?

Secondly, you might think it is coming from the empty sky—but if so then where is the source in the sky? This source must be one of the elements, but if you look at air, fire, earth or water you cannot find your thoughts there. If you check in this way you still cannot find where they come from. The natural state is like a wind that comes suddenly from nowhere.

So just look to the natural state, whether it is something material, whether it has colour, what it looks like. Can you find out anything about it? Nothing can be found. Then suddenly you have lost both subject and object;[14] that is called the 'Endless View'. It is the basic Dharmakaya for the base, the path Dharmakaya for the path and for the fruit the Final Dharmakaya. When you understand this nature you understand the nature of the Dharmakaya.

Where Does It Stay and Who Stays There? We must check these things. If you think that the natural state exists, then where is it right now? If you take all the material

14 That means that you realize it without grasping. It is a method for introduction—a preliminary practice, not the final Dzogchen view.

things and check them, things go back to the atoms and finally disappear like the sky. You cannot find the place where they reside. And if you cannot find the place where they stay, who stays there? What remains is a very bright clearness that will stay with you.

If you try to recognise who is staying in both realms you cannot find anything—neither in the object side nor in the subject side. Without thinking or speaking, it is the presence of brightness and clarity. The presence is very clear. According to the path it is called the 'Self-Brightness of Practising', and according to the fruit it is called the 'Unstoppable Sambhogakaya'.

Where Does It Go and Who Goes There? After a little while you will have to think back to ask where the thoughts go. If you look externally, you cannot find their destination. Everything just disappears. Even if you were to find something, you would have to ask, Who is going? When you try to find out, everything disappears. It is self-disappearing; it is self-purified. You did not do anything but delusion was purified. You do not try to purify nor do you do anything with the pure perceptions. Everything spontaneously appears and is self-liberating into emptiness. According to the path this is called 'Without Trace of Acting', and according to the fruit the 'Unseparable Nirmanakaya'. You must look hard to where the thoughts are going. Just as a wind disappears, they disappear into space. They are self-liberated and go into self-liberation. When you have this experience you see the 'Ungrasping Nirmanakaya'.

Usually we think that it is my mind that is always thinking. But when you ask where it comes from, where it goes and where it stays you cannot find any place. That is called the 'Collapse of the House of the Mind'. When you realise this you reach the 'Great Nature and Selflessness without End', *Tadrel Chenpo (mtha' 'brel chen po).*

When you come to this nature there is no need to check or to do anything—there is no action and there is nothing to do. This is the unification of brightness and emptiness and is the great nature of Dzogpachenpo.

When you realise this it is called the 'Coming to Direct Cognition of the Natural State'.

So ends the preliminary practice.[15]

15 Lopon comments that you must not go on beyond this point unless the realisation it describes has been reached— without checking, object, or any grasping. This is bright clarity and emptiness united. You must not even grasp for the unification itself. Only when this has been reached can the practises that follow bear fruit. There must be a clear presence with no grasping; that is the fruit of the preliminary practice.

དྲན་པ་ནམ་མཁའ།།

Drenpa Namkha

Book Two
The Practice Of Trekchö

[Tibetan text 20b, line 5]

ESSENTIAL TEACHINGS FOR THE PRACTICE

First of all we should get into the right state for the essential ripening of the mind. For this purpose it is necessary to receive the initiation. However, if you come through this preliminary practice you will receive initiation with the practice itself.[1]

Leading to the essential teachings there are two subdivisions. The first division explains the context of the teachings and the second teaches in detail the practice.

---

1 Lopon comments that when you receive initiation it is to show you the natural state. Afterward you can check whether you received anything by seeing whether you then perfectly understand the natural state. However, if you do the preliminary practices you will see the natural state. So that is the initiation in itself.

THE CONTEXT

This section begins with a quote from the *Namkha Truldzö (nam mkha' 'phrul mdzod)*. It says that in Dzogchen there are three types of wrong teachings. The first are wrong teachings that are incorporated into Dzogchen, the second are misinterpretations of the teaching and the third category are the wrong teachings that are automatically stopped.[2]

For example, the way the mistaken teachings have been incorporated into Dzogchen is by putting the views of the eight lower vehicles into the teachings.[3] But according to the Dzogchen view you do not need to see that the eight views are negative—they are spontaneously dissolved into it.[4]

Quote from the *Yetri Tasel (ye khri mtha' sel)*: "In the ultimate Dzogchen view, you do not need to remove anything. You do not need to grasp, for Dzogchen does not follow the traces of the path and fruit of the stages. All grasping to external or internal view is liberated by itself. It is beyond the subject, object, obtaining the fruit or removing of defects. This view is the object of the best knowledge of the practitioner."

The second mistaken view is to always wish and hope for very bright clearness or emptiness—strongly grasp-

---

2 This text is like the last category; if it is taught correctly, misunderstandings are automatically stopped and examples of this are given in the text that follows.

3 It is said that they have to be removed. The Dzogchen view is beyond these ways; it is the best and has to be practised. But this view is itself mistaken because in thinking that the other ways are negative and Dzogchen is the best view you are keeping two sides—the negative side and the positive side; but Dzogchen has no sides. If you are still grasping for the two sides you have not achieved the Dzogchen view.

4 If you remain in the liberated state you do not need to keep or reject anything.

ing for many things, holding and wishing. It is bounded by wishing. That is also not good Dzogchen practice. If one is asked what is one's view, one answers, "Without negative or positive—things should be left as they are. Then all bindings and obscurations are liberated by themselves."

This view is beyond the decision of practicing and meditating. Without doing anything—without any attempt to change your nature—just let it go on continuously. Then all the negative side and all the positive side is dissolved into its nature. There is no wrong view. For example, if a flood comes from the mountains, it washes all the shrubs and bushes and trees down to the valley. It is in this manner.

Now in this Dzogchen text we have three systems of teaching the pupils. One of these is called 'the system of teaching', the second the 'system of direct introduction' and the third the 'traveller who crosses mountains and having mistaken his way is then helped to find the right path'.

If you ask which system is being taught here, it is the first system. What is the second system? It is to introduce Trekchö and Tögel directly. The third system means to give gradual teachings.[5] This teaching is of the first type because all teachings are contained in this one.

The students that do not have the highest capacity must be taught gradually in self-awareness so as to remove slowly the obscurations of thoughts and thus move from samsara. This method I have already taught in the text *Dzogpachenpo Kusum Rangshar (rdzogs pa chen po sku gsum rang shar)*.[6]

The teaching here is for the practitioners of best capacity. So how is it taught? The manner of its teaching

5 Especially bardo and phowa teachings, which are given in Book 4 of this text.

6 In this work Shardza collected many quotations from different sources on Trekchö, Tögel and Dark Retreat, etc.

is suddenly to introduce everything in a moment like a lightning strike. The basis (of it) is naturally liberated from the beginning. To this base you add nothing but are introduced directly to it so that you understand it fully.[7]

Details of the Practice

The practitioner of best capacity does not need to meditate or contemplate, but needs to make a decision. By this firm decision he or she is liberated. This is the method of the Trekchö system.

By the teachings of Tögel one reaches the fulfilment of the visions of the three kayas and so achieves the rainbow body at the end of the lifetime.

THE TEACHINGS OF TREKCHÖ

There are two subdivisions according to two capacities of pupils.

For the lower division there is a quote from the medium book of the *Zhang Zhung Nyengyu*,[8] the *Dringpo Sorzhag ('bring po sor bzhag)*: "The visions are all introduced[9] into the mind, the mind is introduced to the emptiness and the emptiness is introduced to the clear light. The clear light is introduced to the unification and the unification is introduced to the great bliss."

The reason for this is that when you introduce the visions to the mind this causes the cessation of the sense that appearances are self-sustaining. When you introduce the mind to emptiness, that causes the cessation

---

7 Buddhahood is then self-achieved. During this life you achieve the base and so you feel very safe and secure. You live with the confidence of a tulku, for whom samsara has no fears.

8 The book of collected experiences of practitioners called colloquially the *Nyamgyu (nyams rgyud)*.

9 "Introduced" means "shown directly."

of the ignorant thoughts that grasp after truth. When you directly show the clear light to emptiness, that causes the cessation of the misunderstanding of your nature. And when you show the unification to the clear light that is the unification of awareness and nature. When you directly show the great bliss to the unification you realise the naked nature of emptiness and awareness without being born, stopping or resting in any place.[10]

Now for this first system of teaching, 'the direct showing', one needs the personal advice of the teacher in this manner. The vision itself is not mind, and the mind is neither form nor vision. If you ask what the mind is you must understand that all the visions come from karmic traces.[11] Because the mind has kept various karmic traces, they can be awakened, and so by the cause of the traces of previous action the visions appear. Even though these visions appear they have no inherent existence.[12]

---

10 Lopon comments that if you grasp after the emptiness, it is not right, if you grasp after awareness that is not right and even if you grasp after unification it is not right. The real Dzogchen nature is unification, but unification is a state of being, not an object of knowledge.

11 Like the Cittamatra (Mind Only) system.

12 The Lopon comments that this is a reference to the Cittamatra view of the vision of the elements. Even though things seem to happen when we are awake, as if they were permanent and real alterations to the world, they are still karmic traces; nothing has happened in the absolute sense.

All vision is like a dream. In a dream, a vision is just a vision to the mind, even though whatever appears looks like real material to the dreamer. It is just the same when we are awake. All appearances come from the karmic traces—they all come to the mind. Apart from the mind nothing exists at all. The difference between dreaming and awakening is just in time—that is all.

THE DIRECT INTRODUCTION ACCORDING TO SEMDE *(SEMS SDE)*

The basic nature of the natural state (bodhicitta) is the base of all reflections. It is like an ocean; all kinds of reflections can appear in it.[13] Thus the ocean equally reflects all images—the sun, the moon and the stars. That you must know.

From the point of view of bodhicitta (the natural state), you cannot explain the difference between the base, the energy or the reflections. That is because its nature is emptiness (i.e. the natural state) and to emptiness there is no distinction between them. For example, in the ocean itself, the clearness of the water (energy) and the reflections in it are not different from the water—they appear but they are not beyond the water. If you look from the point of view of the reflections (i.e. individual things) there is no contradiction either. From that perspective you can see that the ocean and its clarity and reflections are distinct from one another. However, according to the natural state none of the reflections has a real base. There is no inherent existence in them.

A quote from *Lugyudang Drawai Dampa (lus rgyud dang 'dra ba'i gdams pa)*: "In this connection there is no speaking about emptiness and vision. Both emptiness and vision have no base."

Therefore the Semde system is only for leading the followers of lowest capacity into Dzogchen, and it is also called the Great Seal (Mahamudra).[14]

---

13 The energy to reflect (*tsal*) is a property of the ocean, so the reflections (*rol pa*) and the energy are unified in its nature (*gzhi*). Sometimes only two terms are used: *gzhi*, the base, and *tsal*, reflections, these two referring respectively to the capacity to take reflections (subject side) and the reflections themselves (object side).

The text *Chagtri (phyag khrid)* by Trugel Yungdrung (*bru rgyal gyung drung*) and his followers was accepted as the highest teaching but this is not the case. It cannot

---

14 You cannot say the natural state is empty or has reflections or whatever. Like water which is also wet it is both things at once—neither term captures this reality, which is beyond words. You can't say it is empty because it is not graspable—if you say that it is empty you try to enter the state whilst grasping the concept of emptiness. The real fact is beyond all concepts. This is a reference to the Mahamudra system. Semde is the aspect of Dzogchen that most stresses emptiness and so the author here says that it is similar to Mahamudra. Mahamudra emphasises and grasps emptiness, but here nature is left as it is, without trying to act upon it, without meditating, visualising or contemplating.

Lopon comments that Semde (*sems sde*), Longde (*klong sde*) and Mengagde (*man ngag sde*) are all aspects of Dzogchen because they recognise as the final truth the unification of awareness and emptiness. Semde emphasises more the emptiness side, and Longde the awareness. But both are unified which is the essence of the Dzogchen view (the union of emptiness and awareness). Mahamudra is the union of emptiness and bliss, and as Tsongkhapa explained very clearly the emptiness referred to is that of the Madhyamika view; this is not the view of emptiness referred to in Dzogchen.

Many schools have terms and propositions which are very similar to those of Dzogchen, and this has led to some confusion when this label has been applied to other systems. For example, Sakya Pandita was very explicit in condemning Dzogchen as not being a Buddhist view at all. All the Dzogchen texts make special mention of the need to separate out all the other views in order to make clear the meaning of the terms in the context of Dzogchen alone.

At the very beginning you must know the other views, but they are to be discarded as this is the highest and best vehicle. Many Dzogchen teachers at present are teaching that Mahamudra and Madhyamika and Dzogchen views are not different. But this is not found in the literature at all.

be compared with the highest teaching any more than the earth can be compared with the sky.[15]

THE DIRECT INTRODUCTION ACCORDING TO MENGAGDE

For the best practitioners there is a second direct introduction. They can be liberated just after being shown directly. This instruction is given in two subdivisions: the first is the direct introduction, and the second concerns the decision to enter into the great non-action.

THE DIRECT INTRODUCTION

Now concerning the direct introduction there are three methods of teaching. The first is to comment on the importance, the second is to tie up and the third is to bind.

The First Method: The Comment on the Importance

Here there are two methods: to show directly the root awareness and to show the view, practice, action and fruit.

To Show Directly the Root Awareness. There are three descriptions of awareness (*rig pa*). The first is encompassing awareness, the second is awareness of thinking and the third is primordial awareness. The first means the awareness of the Buddha who encompasses all beings. The second is that of some of the schools of meditation like Vipassana (insight) where awareness is practised in meditation. There if you do not practise it you do not see the awareness, and sometimes it is clear and sometimes not. The third is according to this view—it is

---

15 Lopon comments that Trugel Yungdrung was the author of the *A Khrid in Fifteen Sessions*, which was composed in the eleventh century. Shardza is criticising this text because it is mainly Semde.

the real awareness of Dzogpachenpo. It is always there whether you are practicing meditation or not, or whether you realise it or not. Whether you know it or not does not matter. What follows below is to show you this awareness directly.[16]

The View, Practice, Action and Fruit. First of all sit down in the seven-point posture.[17] Then the master calls to the student and says, "Oh good child, is there any watcher or thing that is watched? And to where? Or not? You cannot find any object to be watched or a watcher who watches it. At that moment everything goes as the sky. Do not change or do anything. That nature is inexpressible. At that moment there are no names or concepts of clarity, emptiness or unification.

"You cannot show this by example; you cannot check it or recognise it by thoughts. You are unable to remove it, yet it never goes away. There is no root—it is empty. While you are in this state clarity is there without ceasing, nonstop and purified. The clarity is the self-created clarity and there is no antidote. It will always be in bliss. Always naked, it cannot be deluded. You can't say what

---

16 Lopon comments that this third type of awareness is with you whether you know it or not. But normal sentient beings are not aware of this part of their nature. This can best be explained by a little story. There was once an old lady who had a lump of gold lying on the floor of her thatched cottage. One day a prince came and saw the gold, and he asked the lady, "Why are you so poor?" The old lady answered that she was just a poor peasant. The prince pointed out that a treasure was there, since the old woman had not recognized the riches that were hers. Only when the prince (the teacher) came did the old lady (sentient being) see the riches (the natural state). Of course, the gold was unaffected whether the old lady saw it or not.

17 The seven-point posture is to sit with crossed legs, hands in equipoise, spine straight, neck bent, eyes open, mouth open, tongue on palate.

you have seen, but it is always bright. Its nature is without ceasing. It is the inexpressible nature and unremovable wisdom. There is no subject, for the visions are just there; without thoughts clarity is there.

"Without distinguishing subject and object, wisdom is there. This is the wisdom without object or subject, without substance. It is the Great Secret Path of the Great Perfection—the heart blood of the dakinis—and is the gift of Drenpa Namkha (*dran pa nam mkha'*). It is also the essential teaching of Rigpa Rangshar (*rig pa rang shar*).[18]

"Have you understood? You realised it? Wonderful! "

The Second Method: To Tie Up

[This is given in four sections: the view, the practice, the activities and the fruit.]

The View of Tying Up. This means that all the views are tied up in emptiness because all the visions and mind are kept without change or trying to change them; everything comes as it is. Without doing anything and with no delusions you can see clearly. The vision comes suddenly like the flash made when lightning strikes. It is called 'the vision that comes as suddenly as lightning comes down'.

A quotation from the text *Namkha Trulgyi Dzöchen (nam mkha' 'phrul gyi mdzod chen)*: "Just now these visions and minds are all seen without any covering, very brightly and clearly. They come without planning; therefore they are sudden. They are self-originated; therefore they are called lightning. All the visions are without stopping and without inventing. They come

---

18 Drenpa Namkha was a mahasiddha who was the father of Guru Padmasambhava according to Bön history. He was a great reformer and wrote many commentaries. Rigpa Rangshar is the secret name of Shardza Tashi Gyaltsen; he is also known by the name of Drime Nyingpo (*dri med snying po*).

spontaneously, and everything is self-originated. This is why they are said to be like lightning."

This is the first of the four ways to tie up (with views).

The Practice and Activities for Tying Up. All the practice is aimed at seeing directly with full awareness. This is because when the thoughts suddenly arise, just at that moment they are self-liberated (if you are aware of them). That is called 'directly hit'.[19]

Quoting from the text as before: "Thoughts arise suddenly. There is no certainty as to where they are coming from; therefore it is directly hit. Whatever appears is only self-originated. Thus, ignorance has no place to hide and it is called directly hit."

It is clearly seen how awareness and normal vision are connected and this is called directly hit. When awareness and vision are left as they are—without any change—that is called directly hit. Once you have understood these methods there is nothing beyond them, nothing to meditate on. That is called directly hit.

Now all the activities are tied up with the self-originated wisdom that comes naturally. Whenever you perform any of the four activities,[20] without trying to plan or change anything but simply leaving everything as it is, that is called the 'Spontaneously Originated Wisdom'.

From the same text another quote: "Nothing is being stopped and everything appears naturally; it comes automatically. Nothing is being done particularly. This is why it is said that everything is coming automatically. If you act normally there is nothing wrong. Whatever you do, everything is the reflection of emptiness, and therefore it is the 'Automatically Originated Appearance'.

---

19 Lopon comments that while you are in awareness, when thoughts arise, then they are self-liberated. If you are not in awareness, then the thoughts can lead you.

20 The four activities are eating, sleeping, sitting and defecating—so at all times you should keep the natural state!

There is nothing to remove, collect or desire—therefore it is automatically originated. Everything comes into the emptiness and there is nothing to agree or disagree with—therefore everything is automatically originated. All the time your body, speech and mind are left as they are—there are no antidotes. That is the looseness without binding and tightness. It is a happy mind."

The Fruit of Tying Up. All the fruits are tied to the three bodies that are self-originated because whatever appears and whatever comes it is as though it does not matter, good or bad. This is because thought is self-originated from the natural state—and that is called the fruit 'self-originated from the three bodies'.

Quoting from the same text: "The self-originated Dharmakaya is like the sky. The Sambhogakaya is self-originated like the four elements of earth, water, fire and winds. The Nirmanakaya is self-originated as the six realms of beings. Wisdoms are all self-originated as the five poisons of the emotions. All things self-originate naturally from awareness and all are connected with awareness. Therefore there is nothing left to remove or to tie up with practicing."

Now one might ask, If everything is self-originated and goes back to the natural state, then what is this samsara that we are living in? Do you think this is the final truth and that there are not defilements? What you said is contradictory!

The Dzogchen view replies that there is nothing contradictory in this statement, because to the Dzogchen practitioner everything is self-originated. In this natural state there is no antidote to apply, for there are no negatives—there is nothing to be removed.

This is proven by the following quote from the *Melong Gudu Öselgyi Gyu (me long dgu 'dus 'od gsal gyi rgyud)*: "The view is like lightning that comes from the sky—no one can stop it. The practice of meditation is like the sun shining in the sky—all the darkness naturally disappears. When a flood comes from the mountain it washes all the rocks and trees and shrubs down to the valley—

that is like the activity. When you have found the wishing jewel your wishes are perfectly fulfilled—that is the fruit."

The Third Method: The Binding

This is again described in four sections—view, meditation, activities and fruit. All of these are bound into normal vision which has no base. It is just left as it is—that is the binding.

Concluding Summary

The conclusion is that everything is awareness and emptiness. That is the single point; everything is in this. There is nothing to do with body, speech and mind. This view ties up all the ends. All samsara and nirvana are liberated without doing anything. This is the natural unification which is unborn and unending without doing anything—you just leave it as it is. That is to tie up with the five points.[21]

---

21 The five points are (1) to stop; (2) to put into one single point; (3) to tie up without doing anything; (4) to liberate all samsara and nirvana; and (5) that everything is unified ceaselessly into the 'Unified Natural State'.

THE DECISION TO ENTER INTO THE GREAT NON-ACTION

Decisions without action has three subdivisions. The first is in general to remove all faults; the second is to explain what the decision without action means; and third is to decide to practice without practising.

As a general introduction, someone may challenge the view by asking, If as you say everything is self-liberated whether you understand or not, and samsara and nirvana are self-liberated for all time past and future, then surely you do not need to do anything. It seems that you hold the wrong view that there is nothing to do.

In reply one says that if one decides to enter the great acting without action, then there are twelve methods of acting. If one does more than these one is doing too much and one will circulate in samsara even more deeply.[22]

A quote from the *Trödrel Namkhadang Nyempai Gyu (spros bral nam mkha' dang mnyam pa'i rgyud)* amplifies this point: "If you are doing too much you cannot stay in the real truth. If you take on many activities that means you are following the path of evil. Therefore remain loosely and without delusion in the 'self-liberating path without action'."

But then some may say, Surely is this not still the mistaken view that you don't need to do anything because everything is self-liberated?

One replies, Yes, this is the case, but it is neither mistaken nor contradictory. I do not need to do a thing more. Now all visions are helpful and without fault. Truly, once you are in the natural state every action is like practising the accumulation of merits.

---

22 These twelve are described in the sections that follow, as the four achievements, the three capacities of understanding and the five points of the decision without action.

The Decision Without Action

The second subdivision explains in detail the nature without action; it has three parts. First of all there are the four achievements, then there are the three capacities of understanding, and finally there is the decision without action, which has five points.[23]

The Four Achievements. These are:

1. To be able to do the opposite of what one thinks is the right action.[24]
2. When one has achieved this capacity of acting without any concept of good or bad, it does not matter if one is criticised or not; everything is equal.
3. The person who has achieved this capacity is never involved in actions or thoughts.[25]

---

23 Lopon comments that these are descriptions of the practitioner who has the capacity to achieve Buddhahood.

24 If you do not fully understand the natural state, then all practices, such as reciting mantras, etc., are seen as effort. But when you fully understand that state then none of these actions are important any longer. Thus you are able to do things in the opposite way. A similar point was made by Longchenpa (*klong chen rab 'byams pa*): "When you don't understand the natural state you must try to accumulate merits and practise bodhicitta and confession, etc."

But the opposition spoken of here is not opposition in the sense of adopting the views of the heretic schools or even that of an opponent. It means that once one is continuously in the natural state one is not deluded—so whether one recites, or practises visualisation or whatever it does not matter. It is like being in space. Whether you paint black or white on space it leaves no trace.

When you first begin to hear these teachings this can be misleading, as it is valid only for the person who can remain undisturbed and not distracted in the natural state. Such freedom is the result.

4. If one who has achieved this capacity is criticised, that person does not modify his or her view. One is not deluded by others.

These are the four achievements of the person who has achieved the natural state.

The Three Capacities of Understanding. These are:

1. Of course the practitioners who have achieved this capacity will have clairvoyance. But they do not care for these signs even if the Dharmakaya appears very brightly in front of them. They have fully understood that everything is part of their nature, so they are neither happy nor sad to see this. That is the first sign that no one can remove the practitioner from his or her nature.
2. Of course even if sickness and miseries come, the practitioners do not care. If the King of Hell comes and puts molten metal in their mouths, if the demons come to take them away, they know that these appearances are not separate from their own nature. So no one can make the practitioner afraid. That is the sign that he or she will not fall down.

---

25 Lopon comments that if you don't do anything it does not matter from the point of view of emptiness; of course, it is different from the point of view of the practitioner. These differences are not different at source so there are not two truths; the practitioner is not, after all, the source. There is only one source, but to one who is grasping there is a limited point of view.

Many teachings seem very similar to Dzogchen, but all teachings are bounded by thought. If you go back to their origin there are always precepts that say this is the right way and that is the wrong way. Once you have this background you are bounded by thoughts. But Dzogchen has no background; this is difficult to explain as everything Dzogchen says is for the practitioner with capacity. This difference of view is very important to understand.

3. Of course practitioners can spontaneously give many teachings without study, as the teachings will be known spontaneously by the power of their understanding. Thus they will have a good reputation and so achieve power and knowledge to conquer their critics. They do not care—even if they see the Sambhogakaya or see Tonpa Shenrab teaching under his umbrella—they never change from their nature. They know that everything is not different from their nature. So they do not follow good or bad. That is the sign of the capacity of the practice—the practitioners will never be stopped, nor will they go back from their nature.

Practitioners have no hope to achieve nirvana nor are they frightened to fall down to samsara.[26] They do not wish to do good things. Those practitioners who have this capacity do not doubt any longer. But if a practitioner is still doubtful as to whether he or she is acting in the right way or not, or whether he or she has got the right sign or not, then that person has not yet achieved this capacity. He or she will continue to circulate in samsara.

---

26 Lopon comments that when other Buddhist schools hear these teachings they have been very upset in the past and have said that Dzogchen is not Buddhism at all. But Dzogchen is not like the view of Indian or Western materialist philosophy in which the actions in the life have no ultimate consequence because body and mind have the same nature—the view that they are born together so it doesn't matter whether you perform good or bad actions because finally they both go to ashes and no trace is left. The natural state is not material at all—after all, as is continuously stated in the text, where can you find it?

The Decision Without Action. Now comes the third part, the decision without action, which has five subdivisions. They are:

1. Activity can not bring Buddhahood because all activities are material and therefore impermanent. Nature and final truth are like the sky; no activity can bring emptiness. Therefore just decide to enter the 'Great Nature Without Action'.

   A quote from the *Trödrel Namkhadang Nyempai Gyu*: "If anyone enters the 'Nature Without Action', whether that being is a god or a human or in any one of the six realms, the nature of mind will always be purified spontaneously into natural truth. And whoever wants to get into this nature should not make any kind of action—only remain in the final truth."

2. There are no obscurations or negativity in the natural state. From the beginning everything is liberated into the realms of 'Great Bliss of Self-Clarity'. Therefore there is no need to apply antidotes.

   A quote from *Kunzang Dewai Lung (kun bzang bde ba'i lung)*: "From the highest mandalas of Buddhas down to the ground, including all the external and internally existent things, nothing is beyond the Great Bliss. Therefore everything is not far from Buddhahood."

3. Whatever appears or comes, everything is the reflection of wisdom; everything is like an ornament of the natural state and is self-liberated. All the visions appear as wisdom. Therefore one must decide to enter 'the Path of the Equal Taste'.

A quote from the *Desheg Gongpa Dupai Gyu (bde gshegs dgongs pa 'dus pa'i rgyud)*[27]: "Whatever your thoughts are doing, rising or moving, the natural state and awareness has never been damaged by them. Everything spontaneously exists. That is the great fruit of the 'Self-Pure Liberation'. It is also the 'Pure Clarity Wisdom'. All the various visions are like reflections of the natural state."

4. All the existences that belong to samsara and nirvana are reflections that come from the natural state. All of them will be liberated into the natural state. Just at the moment when they are reflected they are ready to be liberated—there is no need to try to liberate them. Therefore decide to enter the 'Self-Liberation'.

A quote from the tenth chapter of the text above: "This is the automatic cutting off of the mistakes or obscurations. From the beginning it is beyond the views of nihilism and eternalism. Here nothing is said about them for all are naturally liberated into the 'Pure, Great, Naturally Liberated'."

5. From the standpoint of the natural state, whether you understand this natural self-awareness or not does not affect it. It is completely beyond the ends of samsara and nirvana.[28] If you do not realise the natural state, the natural state never goes bad; therefore its nature is completely be-

27 This text has unfortunately been lost in the massive destruction following the Chinese invasion of Tibet.

28 Lopon comments that this means it has no end at all and is beyond concept; the Dzogchen Nature has no end and no beginning. From an individual point of view nirvana might be seen as having a beginning, however, for the practitioner must become a Buddha. But in this teaching all things are Buddha—equal.

> yond samsara. It is liberated beyond the end of samsara. If you try to search or to look, you have only understood a little part. In this nature there is no side to be taken; therefore this is 'Liberated from the Ends of All the Eight Paths.' Whatever you do, everything is naturally self-liberated. There is nothing to look for and nothing to find. And there is no certain action. Therefore now you can live without worry, for you have realised the open space of your mind.

Deciding to Practice Without Practicing

When you have fully understood the natural state then all doubts are stopped.

A qualm: Surely if everyone who exists acts without action then whatever practices are done in the lower eight paths must be without purpose?

The Dzogchen reply is that everything that is practiced in those paths is made up by thoughts, and their practitioners never achieve the stage of acting without action, without thoughts.

Dzogchen never pursues them, but all their achievements, like Sambhogakaya or Dharmakaya or purification of knowledge are naturally present in Dzogchen Buddhahood. The reason for this is that all existing things are like illusions coming from the natural state. Therefore there is not any misview, as everything is liberated into the natural state.[29]

---

29 Lopon comments, "Why do they criticise this view? It is because all these schools, even the tantric schools, depend on visualisation, body posture, breathing, etc."

Quote from the same text: "The ways of the eight practices are outshone like the stars are outshone by the rising sun. Dzogchen does not need a plan to achieve Buddhahood; everything comes from remaining in the natural state—to spontaneously exist."[30]

Therefore to the nature of the Dzogchen view there is nothing to do with acting. Day and night remain in the natural state—without any action, even planning or thinking, no expecting, no reciting, no visualising—even during sleep. So the practitioner practises days, months and years without distraction in the natural state. All the four actions are carried out without distraction.

The practitioner is contemplation. Everything is the 'Unstoppable Action'. Whatever the practitioner experiences, whatever comes is an experience for the practice—happiness, bliss or whatever. He or she does not even care if the thoughts are racing—there is no hope or path—so thoughts are left as they are. That is the method of practice. Sometimes there are raging emotions, like anger or sorrow or whatever, and the practitioner does not care. They are just left as they are. This is the teaching.

Whether the practitioner collects merits or sins does not matter, things are left just as they are. Not far away from the natural state, the practitioner leaves behind no trace.[31] There is no base of keeping past actions.

---

30 Lopon comments that in a horse race the horse has no time to look at the ground and pick flowers or grass; in the same way when you practise the natural state all thoughts and activities are naturally liberated into the natural state without plans or actions.

31 Lopon comments that while the practitioner is not distracted but is continuously in the natural state it is as if he or she is in space—whatever is done, no traces are left behind. As we said, whether you paint black or white on space nothing remains. The base that keeps the traces is lost; it is empty.

Of course this only applies to a practitioner who has

That is the practice of the Dzogchenpa. There is no trying to practice antidotes or removing negativities—that is the fruit. And not to seek antidotes—that is the commitment. Everything is to be left as it is. [32] There

---

achieved continuous contemplation. For other people who still grasp their karmic traces this does not apply. When the Lopon first came to Swayambhu in Nepal in 1944 he met some Tibetans with whom he travelled for some days. One man was a former monk who had a wife and children and was carrying a huge load of luggage on his back. When he was a monk he had met Dega Rinpoche, a famous Dzogchenpa, in the mountains and consequentially he gave up his robes because he felt he was too tied up with the vinaya vows. But Lopon pointed out that he was equally tied up with his children. The man replied that in Dzogchen it is said that it does not matter what you do—so he was free to do anything and that was OK. But this is a complete misunderstanding of Dzogchen. The teachings only apply when you are totally absorbed in the natural state. It depends on your practice and only you can judge.

So it is a paradox that beginners must take actions even though the ultimate Dzogchen view has no action. The beginner must take a very strong action—a decision—otherwise there will be doubt and hesitancy. All the preparatory methods help us realise the natural state. But once it is seen and understood then the situation is different. The experienced Dzogchenpa would not need to do preparatory practices at all.

32 Lopon comments that this means not hesitating or meditating, and this is why many Buddhist masters criticised Dzogchen. For example, Tsongkhapa asserted that the natural state in Dzogchen is just like being unconscious. Far from that, this awareness is very bright and clear. But the Indian commentators on the Prajnaparamita, such as Nagarjuna, did not understand this awareness that is present after thoughts have stopped. They do recognise something similar, the undeluded direct cognition of sunyata (void). This cognition is inseparable from its object and undeluded; but it is not the same.

is no measure of being understood or not understood—that is the sign of the practitioner's knowledge.

Another criticism might be put in this way: You say that the Dzogchen view is not limited; yet here you say no action is your view. Is this not a contradiction?

The answer to this lies in non-action. From the Dzogchen view this term means no action, but from the practitioner's point of view this is not a choice—one just does what comes next in the natural state. But to explain it a term must be used. Whether it is to look or not to look, to act or not to act, everything is self-liberated; therefore there is no missed view or right view—I do not care.[33]

It may seem the same because here the object is sunyata and the subject is direct cognition; but the difference is that this cognition is the fruit of practice by thought. First you practise and then you have the experience. You develop it until the thoughts gradually diminish and the object becomes more and more clear. Finally the object is perceived directly; so it is a result of thought.

Even if there is a gulf in the progression to the final stage of direct cognition, the connection between thought and direct cognition cannot be denied. If there was no link between the two then nothing could bridge it. But from the Dzogchen point of view the nature is already connected; it is not linked with thoughts because it is already there. It has always been there. It is not invented. Whatever is in you, that you can realize.

Purification is needed for Dzogchen, however; that is the reason for the preliminary practises. It is a great error to try to apply these teachings without this period of preparation. You must always understand the perspective of any comment—be it about the natural state or the individual. Otherwise you fall into nihilism.

33 Lopon comments that in the philosophical background to Dzogchen there are various mistaken views which are described in the *Namkha Truldzö (nam mkha' 'phrul mdzod)*, a major text on the philosophy of Dzogchen taught at Dolanji:

"The view that you must meditate, or that you must not meditate; that there is no source of existence or that samsara has no end; the view that Dzogchen must be learnt in order to know it or that Dzogchen has no connection with mind; the view that it has nothing to do with anything else or that the Dzogchen view is not certain—anything goes; that everything is nothing so you can do whatever you like, or that the view says that everything is faultless. These are the ignorant views.

"Better views but still mistaken are *kadag (ka dag)*—that the view is pure from the beginning; *lundrub (lhun grub)*, which means that everything spontaneously exists; that the view is not certain so it can be this or that; or that the real natural state is nature and reflections. These are all partially complete views.

"Some of the masters of Dzogchen introduce the view directly with a crystal or mirror; some say you must go to a quiet place to meditate; some say you must have hardship and others that you must be a beggar. Some of the masters say that you must give up all your property and go and live in a cemetery or in the mountains; some again say, "Go now and live as a madman!" Some say, "Don't desire anything, go and live as a small child." Others say you must live the opposite of what they teach; some say, "You should avoid objects that cause anger and desire and don't expect to have a good reputation!" Others say whether people say good or bad things about you, you should not care. These are the sayings of the Dzogchen masters.

"But according to this system we don't accept any teachings of theirs; we don't think that their teachings are either good or bad—we don't care. Why? Because we are completely outside of the judgement of their points. There is no point in arguing or judging; we don't care. Like the elephant—if he is thirsty no one can stop him from going to the water! All these different views have been bounded by thought and so are grasping."

This process has the purpose of bringing out doubts to clarify them—like washing stains from a cloth so that one sees the material clearly.

Book Three
The Practice of Tögel

[Tibetan text 27a, line 6]

The Tögel section has two parts: first there is the explanation of why Tögel is higher than Trekchö, then there is the teaching of the Tögel path.

First, in the text *Yetri (ye khri)* there are ten points to distinguish Trekchö from Tögel; here is a summary in seven points.[1]

The first is in 'the ways of purifying grasping'. In Trekchö all the mountains, rocks and countries have to be thought of as illusions, otherwise this teaching cannot liberate directly on its own. Tögel, however, de-

---

1 Lopon comments that the distinctions are being made between the two techniques in order to clarify them in relation to one another, and not to suggest that either can work on its own. Without the fundamental practice of the Trekchö view, the Tögel will have no meaning, although it will work. Without Trekchö the foundation is not safe for Tögel. Many people are keen to do dark retreat straight away, but without Trekchö there is no base for the visions to come.

If you hope to see strange things you can, but it will have no meaning. This is explained below.

Tugkyi Trowo Tsocho Kagying

pends on the five lights by which all the objects of existence are completely liberated into light.

Quote from the *Yetri*: "It is originally purified; there is no grasping. That nature is called the 'Great Buddhahood'."

The second point is in 'the matter of the self-vision of the body'. In Trekchö the body cannot become the light body—it can only be made to disappear to the level of the atoms.[2] There are many systems to make the physical body disappear, such as the temporary illusory body. Even in the practice of shamata the physical body can disappear. But they are not true or final. Tögel, however, completely transforms the physical body into pure light.

If you don't achieve the rainbow body then you do not achieve the final body. Likewise, if you do not achieve the Great Rainbow Body you have not achieved the final Buddhahood. In Tögel all your physical body and the objects that you share go into the rainbow body.[3]

---

2 Lopon comments that this refers to the body becoming so subtle that you cannot see it with the naked eye, as if it transforms into very fine particles. There are many other results of practice in the other traditions. In Mahamudra, for example, the body disappears and the illusory body is realized. It is not that the physical becomes the illusory body; the physical body dies as in the normal case but the mind realizes the illusory body.

3 Lopon comments that just as the karmic causes make the world of experience, each individual person has his or her share of this common vision. For example, a person, say a man called John, is part of the common vision, but his mother will see him as her son, and his wife will see him as her husband. That is their personal share. So along with the physical body, whatever is a person's share goes into the body of light in the final transformation; the body of light is all that is left after all karmic vision is purified. The entire body goes into light, but not the material things and property—they remain part of the common karmic vision.

འཕྲིན་ལས་འབྲུག་གསས་ཆེམ་པ་ཞེག།

Purba Drugse Chempa

If one becomes a rainbow body one's light body has no defects; it is completely purified and karmic causes have completely stopped. Previously one practiced bodhicitta; now one has received the result, so until samsara is finished one will help sentient beings.[4]

When a man dies, he leaves behind possessions, furniture and houses, but the vision that 'this is mine' or 'that is mine' dies with him. No one will think 'this is mine' of one of his former possessions unless it has been given to her or she buys it.

So karmic links are everything but there are two aspects, the public side and the personal side. This is not like the Hinayana view, however, in which it is believed that after the Buddha showed the Parinirvana there were no traces left, for he had completely gone—non-existent. That is the final body of the Dharmakaya, permanent because it is nonmanifest. The rainbow body is the manifest body of Buddhahood, the Sambhogakaya form, in which all the body, speech and mind are completely purified of all karmic traces.

As a Sambhogakaya form, this body is impermanent, although someone who has achieved the jalu (*'ja' lus*) realises all three kayas of the Buddhas. The Dharmakaya can be seen only by the Buddhas; the Sambhogakaya can be seen by the high Bodhisattvas; and the Nirmanakaya form can be seen by ordinary beings, but only if they have the karmic causes to do so. All manifest bodies are impermanent; even the Dharmakaya has two forms—the wisdom Dharmakaya (the awareness side), which is impermanent, and the nature Dharmakaya (the empty side), which is permanent.

4 The unmanifest Dharmakaya cannot help beings, but its manifest aspect—the Sambhogakaya form—does so due to the everlasting bodhicitta. Such is the union of clarity and emptiness.

When you have purified all the defilements your mind is called the Dharmakaya and your body is called the Sambhogakaya. At the same time you have emanated teachings to all beings; that is called Nirmanakaya. Generally we say

Quote from the *Yetri*: "The visions of the five aggregates (*skandhas*) are not removed but are purified into self-vision."[5]

The third point, 'the matter of purifying consciousness': In Trekchö you only see emptiness, but do not see the pure light visions, so the deluded vision cannot be removed or purified. You have to think that it is *kadag* or pure from the beginning, but it does not appear that way. It is therefore always linked with ignorance, and the visions are not completely pure. For this reason one can be easily distracted, and it is difficult to achieve liberation. In the Tögel, however, you use methods for understanding illusion directly, so it makes the achieving of self-liberation rapid. After self-liberation, deluded vision does not occur and therefore does not cause distraction. The visions of Tögel lead very directly to understanding.

Quote from the *Yetri*: "There are eight objects of the eight consciousnesses (five senses with emotion, mind and *kunzhi*). They are the self-vision dakinis and they spontaneously exist without any searching. Therefore this is called the 'Great Vision Owner of Wisdom'."

Fourth, 'the method to help others from the viewpoint that nothing exists inherently': The natural state spontaneously exists as sounds, rays and lights, and

---

that Dharmakaya is permanent but the kayas are impermanent; but here the Dharmakaya has two divisions. We say that the Buddha's knowledge is purified but that it is impermanent; what is permanent is the nature of emptiness. The Buddha's mind is not permanent.

5 Lopon comments that in the Trekchö it is not easy to make pure visions, but in Tögel one experiences the source of visions and their nature and how they are liberated. Therefore it is easier to purify all common objects and subjects. Trekchö is like reading a description of the view instead of seeing the view itself.

those all appear. By the method of Tögel you see this and so everything becomes rapidly purified. In Trekchö, however, there is no direct method to see this. Trekchö is also gradual—it takes a long time. However, Tögel is very direct and by itself can purify so that you can help other beings very quickly.

Quote from the same text: "All the visions come from themselves and are seen by themselves. Everything is the reflection from itself. There are no objects inherently. Everything is the 'Great Vision'; therefore there is no way to help others."

Question: If you realise that everything is your own vision then how can you help other beings? What is the answer?

The answer is that you can help them because they are self-vision.[6] Beings are also self-vision. Inherently helping them is not possible.

Fifth, 'the matter of not searching for fruit': All of these matters are without any searching for fruit. During the Trekchö time all the visions are inherent vision even though you understand that they have no inherent existence.[7] Tögel allows the development of special vision that mixes with the normal vision so that it easily turns into the vision of reality. It is a quick and practical path to develop the self-liberated vision. Nor do you need to

---

6 It is sometimes said that you only perceive your own karma. Lopon comments that if you stop to help beings, that would imply that other beings are inherently real. But if you believe this you cannot help others in actuality. Helping beings is part of your own self-vision, within the Natural State of Spontaneous Self-Arising.

7 Lopon comments that visions still appear as inherently existent in Trekchö even though you understand fully that they are all reflections that come from the Natural State. So in Trekchö the visions do not change—they are the ordinary visions we all experience. You understand and they are self-liberated but the visions do not change.

pray any more. By this method you quickly achieve Buddhahood.[8]

Quote from the *Yetri*: "It is itself a great fruit, so there is nothing to search for. If you do not search for this fruit everything spontaneously exists; therefore it is excellent."

Sixth, 'the matter of directly seeing the self-visions': In Tögel you directly see the self-vision. During the Trekchö the six sense organs are not purified, and therefore they have to search for the purified visions. In the Tögel the doors of clear light are opened by the wisdom wind. From there the four lamps will appear and by them are purified all the views of delusion. According to this method you understand that all visions are self-liberated visions while at the same time you are developing the Trekchö view.[9]

Quote from the *Yetri*: "The point is to understand the means of self-vision so that there is nothing separable and it comes together."

Seventh, 'the matter of the bhumis (stages)'[10]: In Trekchö everything is connected with the natural state but the vision and body are unable to rise to the final level (because the method is lacking). In Tögel there are no antidotes to remove obscurations—it naturally

---

8 Lopon comments that even though you understand that vision is self-created in Trekchö, your visions are still mixed with deluded vision; therefore you should practise Tögel and mix the Tögel visions with the normal ones. The visions in Trekchö are still waiting to be purified, so to reach Buddhahood by this method will take a long time. It is far quicker with Tögel; Trekchö is gradual.

9 Lopon comments that this view is of vision and unification. You cannot separate pure vision and unification—they develop at the same time.

10 Lopon comments that literally *bhumi* means 'earth', but here levels of mind is meant. The ten bhumis represent the increasing capacity of developing knowledge.

sends you to the final stage. Tögel therefore achieves the 'Great Bhumi of Swastika'.[11]

Quote from the *Yetri*: "This unchangeable bhumi has no methods to remove all activities, so it is the greater way."

---

11 The Swastika is the ancient symbol of Yungdrung (Eternal) Bön. Lopon comments that the bhumis referred to here are levels according to the Bönpo Prajnaparamita. If you look at them panoramically they all seem to reflect one another. Each has its own beginning, object to be purified and knowledge to be achieved. At each stage there are different views and each bhumi has its own deities. When you achieve the bhumi you will see the divinity and they will teach you how to develop further. When you achieve the first bhumi you see the loving Goddess of Dana (giving), the Sambhogakaya of the goddess of generosity. She will teach the antidote and how to remove the obscurations. The second is moral behaviour or *shila*; higher levels form in like manner.

The Bönpo philosophy has a background completely independent of the Indian and is much earlier. Later it found its way to India and the Indians accepted some of its concepts. An interesting example of this is the cosmological system of Vasubandhu. His system has nothing in common with other Buddhist cosmological systems. And the Buddhists used to say that this system was his own special system. In fact it is almost identical to the Bönpo system. The root text of the Bönpo text is called the *Dzöpu (mdzod phug)* and is written in the Zhang Zhung language with a Tibetan translation beneath it. It is still in use.

HOW TO PRACTISE THE TÖGEL

From the *Rigpa Khujug (rig pa khu byug)*[12] there comes the following quote concerning the practice of Tögel. This is followed by a commentary.

> There is a proverb about the forty-two methods of Tögel: 'When the king of awareness travels magically to beings he rides on a red bird with a long beak that comes from the white-stepped red rock, and riding on this bird he goes to the different places. At that time four kings are all serving him and lift him from down below. The four queens of the seasons are supporting him from the sides. Four magic winds are moving him along, and four great rivers are extending his virtues and magic. Four fires give equal heat; they dwell in the golden earth and eight clear mirrors decorate the body. Three secret letters are set into mind; five bright lamps shine from the crown of the head; all the stars and planets are shining brightly on his breast. Four servants are all serving him. He works for beings without lacking any methods, and all benefits come from this mount.'

In this allegory are combined all the methods of the Tögel practices. They were taught by the Dharmakaya to the Dakinis who kept them secret in this proverb. The early siddhas and scholars did not comment but thought to leave it to Shardza Tashi Gyaltsen for his share (of comments).

---

12 Lopon translates this as 'the Awareness of the Cuckoo' though this is a different text from the famous Tun Huang manuscript of the same name.

THE COMMENTARY

The long-beaked bird means the source of vision (the five rays of coloured lights, the very beginning). In the centre of the heart the awareness rests, and from the heart a channel the size of a straw joins the awareness to the lungs. Through this channel the winds are coming and going, and to them the visions attach. That produces thoughts. When the winds touch the source of the visions, that is called mind. The wind is like a blind horse and this mind is a like a lame man with eyes who rides him. When the wind stops all the visions dissolve into awareness and all thoughts disappear and dissolve into their nature.

This nature has three qualities—emptiness, awareness and unification (or inseparability). That is the base from which the reflections come. If you use the methods of Tögel, those reflections which the base contains spontaneously appear through the channel of the light which is joined to the eyes. Each eye has two channels joined to it.[13]

This purifies the impure visions and you see the visions of wisdom. There are forty-two methods of Tögel and here they will be taught sequentially.

---

13 Lopon comments that one channel is the normal eye consciousness and the other is the one discussed here, so the doorway is the same although the Tögel visions are generated internally. In Tibetan medicine this inner path is named the *yangje karpo (yang rje dkar po).* It travels between the eyeball and the lungs via the occiptal foramen over the outside of the brain, and through it come the Tögel visions. Normally it is not used until it is opened by the methods of Tögel; in Trekchö you still use the normal channels of the eye.

The four kings that lift from beneath

The four kings are the four methods—the first method concerns the body, speech and mind; the second concerns the eye organ that stands at the doorway; the third is the object of vision and the fourth is to slow down the awareness and winds. For example, Tonpa Shenrab goes to the four great kings to invite them respectfully and he controls the three realms of existence. In the same way there are four methods to use and the awareness controls all the visions.

The First Method of Body, Speech and Mind

The Methods of Body

The first method has three subdivisions. The body is kept in a posture to control the channels and winds. Controlling the posture helps the practitioner to see the clear light directly; this is why posture is important.

Quote from the *Wonderful Beads of Gold (gser gyi phreng ba mdzes):* "The Dharmakaya posture is like a lion sitting, the Sambhogakaya posture is like an elephant sitting and the Nirmanakaya posture is like a rishi sitting."

The Dharmakaya Posture. The posture of the lion sitting is to place the balls of the feet on the ground, lift the bottom and hold the back straight, and close the lower door (anus). The head is held back slightly and the two hands are placed on the ground between the legs. The position is like a squat. Some teachings say the whole foot should be placed on the ground but in our tradition only the front of it is put down. The purpose of this is to remove the wind that produces disturbing thoughts and to open the central channel so that visions start. Also it helps to stabilise the natural state.

The Sambhogakaya Posture. In the posture of the elephant lying down, you squat with the balls of your feet on the ground so that the knees are lifted up off the ground and touch the chest, and the chin is supported by the hands with the elbows on the ground. This calms the disturbing winds, stops thoughts of desire or anger and brings strong health. This posture helps to bring complete visions externally and to stabilise the natural state.

The Nirmanakaya Posture. The rishi position has the soles of the feet placed on the ground with the arms wrapped round the knees, which touch the chest. The neck is slightly bent back. Alternatively you can sit without crossed legs, supporting the neck with the hands, with the head bent back. The purpose of this posture is to bring you warmth and gradually to stop the thoughts. It also allows you to develop external visions, while internally you develop great experiences.

The postures are not to be held too strictly or held so tightly as to be uncomfortable, nor are they to be held too loosely. Too tight a position will be painful and disturb the meditation; too loose a position will give no assistance.

Then there is the posture like a duck moving sideways, useful for beginners to start to have visions. To do this, the practitioner lies on the right side with the right elbow placed on the ground supporting the chin. The left hand is placed on the thigh. The two legs lie on the ground one on top of the other with the knees slightly bent. This inserts the wind into the central channel so that extraordinary visions develop.

Finally, there is the antelope position which is not explained.[14]

14 Lopon comments that it is a very difficult position with the legs bent and the hands on the back of the neck looking up. These techniques are used to keep concentration and specifically to develop visions. In the Bön system all the four classes of tantra have their own postures as well.

The Methods of Speech

Quote from the *Taktse Dronma (rtags tshad sgron ma)* from the *Zhang Zhung Nyengyu*: "If you do not stop talking you cannot see the unspeakable nature and the one single point nature will not appear directly."

Shardza comments that you must talk less, and in the end stop talking and remain in your nature.

The Methods of Mind

The mind means the essence of the awareness according to the gaze of the eye. To stare into space makes the movement of the winds calmer and calmer. When the winds become calm the unification will be deeper and deeper.

Quote from the *Taktse Dronma*: "If you don't apply the gazes strictly, the awareness will not appear directly."

The Second Method of the Eye Organ that Stands at the Doorway

Now the second method is with the eyes. In ordinary vision the gaze does not help with the appearance of wisdom. So you must hold special gazes in accordance with the body postures.

Quote from the *Wonderful Beads of Gold*: "In the Dharmakaya body posture the eyes must gaze firmly upwards, for the Nirmanakaya posture the gaze must be downwards and for the Sambhogakaya posture it must be to the side, right or left."[15]

So the gazes can be of three types but the main thing is the appearance of the visions.

---

15 Lopon comments that as with the body positions, these gazes are not to be held too tightly, otherwise one becomes uncomfortable and this disturbs the meditation. The essential thing is to control the mind.

Quote from the same text: "With half-closed eyes and without being deluded,[16] look slightly below the sun at the distance of your fingers to your elbow. That is the method."

Practise this more and more until you can keep looking at the sun in this way continuously.

The Third Method of the Object of Vision

The third method is for space. In a high place without any disturbance, gaze into the clean and clear sky. Gaze through the eyes at the clear cloudless sky; there will appear the different clear light visions. Beginners should do this at sunrise or at sunset. In the morning face west, and in the afternoon face east and gaze into the clear sky.

Quote from the *Tingshok (mthing shog)*: "In the morning gaze into the west; in the afternoon gaze east...."

The Fourth Method to Slow Down the Winds and Awareness

The fourth method gives four stages of breathing—inhale, add a little, hold and exhale. Some teachers say this but they do not know the method of breathing here; in this case you should not change the breathing, but leave it as normal. Whether it is through the nose or mouth keep it the same as long as it is very gentle. If you keep this gentle breathing, then the thoughts and mind will be slowed down, and the mind will be easily seized as a prisoner, as the winds are not moving.

The mind is kept prisoner by the awareness. If you keep the wind gentle then the breath coming and going between the mouth and nose becomes calm, and when it becomes calm then the mind and wind meet at the channel at the heart. As there is no disturbance, no

---

16 "Without being deluded" means that the mind does not follow the vision.

thoughts are produced, and the mind is naturally absorbed into the naked nature.

Four magical winds are moving him along

There are four special channels. For example, the winds are all shaking and lifting the universe. In the same way, there are four great channels and all the visions of clarity are produced and developed (lifted) in them.

Quote from the *Tigle Drugpa (thig le drug pa)*: "In general four things combine to make the body. The channels or veins are like nets. In the body there are the four special channels of activity. The first is called 'the great golden channel' (*ka ti gser gyi rtsa chen*), the second 'the threads of white silk' (*dar dkar snal ma*), the third is 'the fine twisted thread' (*phra la 'khrul*) and the fourth 'the crystal tube' (*shel bug can*)."

The first channel connects the heart to the central channel at the level of the heart. Inside there is the essential clear light, and there all the reflections spontaneously exist with the peaceful divinities. From there it travels to the brain, where the wrathful divinities spontaneously reside. Also it has branches which each support the visions of tigle.[17]

Inside the second channel, the threads of white silk, it is fine and white. This channel starts at the heart level of the central channel and goes up the spine, leaving the central channel at the neck. From there it travels over the outside of the brain where it splits into two branches. One side is connected to the right eye channel where it supports what we see as external vision; the other runs to the crown of the head where it supports the appearance of the great thoughtless aware-

17 Lopon comments that with regard to tigle there are material tigle and natural tigle; the Tibetan for "natural tigle" means 'empty' (*thig*) and 'awareness' (*le*) and is translated into English as 'drop'.

ness. When the vision is perfected, it supports the nine tigle that are piled up one on top of the other inside the channel.

The third channel, the fine twisted thread, starts in the central channel at the level of the heart and then goes down to the base before rising again through the centre of the four wheels (navel, heart, throat and crown chakras) to pass over the outside of the brain to the left eye doorway. It supports all the visions of the natural clear lights that shine directly.

Finally the crystal tube travels from the heart to the eye; it supports the dissolving of all the visions into their nature.

Thoughts are generated when the unification at the heart level meets the winds from the channel from the lungs.

Four fires give equal heat

This refers to the four lamps—the lamp of water called *Gyangzhag (rgyang zhags chu'i sgron ma)*; the lamp of the empty tigle (*thig le stong pa'i sgron ma*); the lamp of pure emptiness (*dbyings rnam dag gi sgron ma*) and the lamp of self wisdom (*shes rab rang byung gi sgron ma*). These four lamps produce the visions of the mandalas and the forms of the divinities, and whatever vision comes they are clear. Whatever vision comes all of them are equally encompassed with wisdom and the ripening of the three kayas. Thus, as in the proverb, the great fire of existence makes all warm equally and produces fruits and leaves on the bushes. This is the important teaching for insight into the natural state.

Quote from the *Rigpa Tselwang (rig pa rtsal dbang)*[18]: "The four lamps are all inner essential teachings."

Commenting on the four lamps: First of all hold the body postures and eye positions as before. The first

---

18 This is from one chapter of the *Zhang Zhung Nyengyu*, the section for teaching and initiation.

lamp, the lamp of water, appears when the eye gazes into clear space and a dark blue clear colour appears.[19] From this extend the colours of the five lights and rays of different shapes like the patterns of colour that appear on the dark blue background of brocade silk. That is the beginning of the appearance of visions which exist spontaneously inside the heart.

Quote from the *Text of Molten Gold (gser gyi zhun ma)*: "In the external empty sky you will see the direct clear lights of the heart which are all blue, green, red, yellow, white and smoke-coloured."

The teaching refers to the sky—some commentators think that this refers to ordinary sky without clouds, but that is not correct because the ordinary sky has nothing to do with the practitioner.[20] The sky is just the base of the vision; the dark blue which appears to the practitioner spontaneously exists in his or her nature when this method of posture and gazes is used.

Quote from *Wonderful Beads of Gold*: "Into the external sky enters the lamp of internal space."

Here is an explanation about external sky and internal space differently put. Normally the sky is not the base of Tögel rainbow vision; it just turns into a rainbow when supported by the practitioners' visions. However, you must not conclude from this distinction that external space and internal space are two kinds of things.[21]

---

19 Lopon comments that this colour is what you see when you stare into the sky and notice the dark colour between the mountains and the sky. First of all you will see the dark blue colour, much darker than in other places; that means that the visions are beginning. It is like the moment when a film is starting and the screen goes dark.

20 Lopon comments that whether this vision—the first dark blue vision—comes or not depends on the quality of one's practice. It may appear in the sky but it has very much to do with the practitioner.

21 Lopon comments that when the practitioner practises it

The second and third lamps are the empty tigle and pure emptiness. They can be illustrated by a pond of water. If you throw a stone into a pond then ripples form around it. In the same way ripples come around the vision. At first they are without colour, but finally they appear in five colours. That comes from the purification of the coarse wind. If you gaze into the vision then you will see inside. The awareness becomes more clear and suddenly there are no objects or subjects—no grasping—and it nakedly appears. That is the lamp of self-wisdom.[22]

The fourth lamp is called 'the lamp of self-wisdom'. That is explained as naked without any grasping of objects—just left as it is.[23] If you have stabilised your

---

looks to him or her as if space is changing, but ordinary space is not the basis of these visions. They come from within.

22 Lopon comments that here there is no grasping or focussing—it is very bright and clear to you. This is the nature of the Trekchö view, the inseparable nature, nonduality. This is the Trekchö view of naked nature.

Without the Trekchö practices Tögel does not work at all; without Trekchö, Tögel will not be effective. So you should not practise Tögel alone—it should be practised alongside Trekchö. If you abandon the Trekchö view the visions of Tögel will be of no more significance than watching the television—better to go to the cinema! Visions may happen, but if there is no understanding of illusion the visions are of no value. Anybody can look into the sun and see visions and so forth, but it means nothing.

23 Lopon comments that this is again the Trekchö view. However, although in the Dzogchen view sounds, rays and lights spontaneously exist, if you practise only Trekchö then what spontaneously exists will not be able to appear to you. That is why Tögel makes the process of release from delusion so much quicker, since what spontaneously exists will appear to you. But its view is not different from the view of Trekchö.

lights, keeping in the natural state, then a very precise and clear knowledge will develop. This knowledge is much clearer than that which comes through studying. Indeed, whatever you say or teach comes without thinking or study—it comes automatically. Everything is perfect and precise. That is called the *tsel* (energy) of this nature.

Clarity appears like pearls and golden threads; the nature is wisdom and forms like this are the *tsel* of wisdom. Whatever visions you may have, these visions are all of the same nature and go back to the same truth. They are only distinguished by names.

They dwell in the golden earth and eight clear mirrors decorate the body

This means that the basic empty nature is the place where the visions come from and go to; both are in unification. The space is dark blue. From this dark blue space five colours all increase and appear. The real essence of awareness is inside the heart but the forms and colours appear like a mala of beads through the eyes.[24] When you are focussing on the sunlight you see threads, initially black or white. The two types of awareness are that of nature (the natural state) and the awareness of clarity (visions).[25] In the earth everything is golden; you cannot find stones there—all is gold. In the same way if everything is seen as reflections coming to or from the natural state then the visions are all seen truly like the empty nature, the unification.[26] Visions

---

24 Again the normal eye sees nothing; the vision comes from the unification.

25 Lopon comments that these two have the same nature, but when you are in the unification the awareness is called the awareness of nature, and when you practise Tögel and the visions come, that is called the awareness of clarity. Only the names are different.

26 There is nothing to take or remove; everything has the

are all whatever spontaneously exists with the unification. When these methods are practised the visions appear to the practitioner.

Four great rivers are extending his virtues and magic

The four great rivers are the four visions.

Quote from the *Trödrel Rigpai Tselwang (spros bral rig pa'i rtsal dbang)*, the initial text of the *Zhang Zhung Nyengyu*: "The first is the direct vision that comes from emptiness. Then there is vision that is developing, then vision that is complete and finally vision that dissolves back into emptiness."[27]

This is only a measure of how much you have practised; you cannot compare these with the bhumis. The path of accumulation is like walking, whereas this is like flying in the sky.

The First Vision—The Direct Vision That Comes From Emptiness. The four methods of practising (body, speech, mind and gaze) were mentioned previously. If you use these methods then from the heart chakra where the essence of the Buddha is (the natural state) the visions will come. When you begin to apply these four methods you will start to see rainbows and tigle, and from there visions will start. Initially there will be many tigle, sometimes piled up like beads and sometimes side by side, moving all the time; sometimes clear and sometimes not so clear. The reason for the visions is like the sun and its rays—the unification is the real nature, but that is unsayable. The visions are like rays that appear to the practitioner but not to the ordinary organs of sense perception. They are called the swastika tigle. They are

---

same nature.

27 Lopon comments that these four stages are not progressive like Prajnaparamita or tantric teachings with the four paths, which start with removal of obscurations, etc. Here, these visions are simply a reflection of how much you have practised; there is no sense of purifying or developing antidotes to obscuration.

like the mirror and your face—your face is reflected in the mirror, but you cannot distinguish between the mirror and your reflection—both of them are the same. In the same way, whenever you have visions you cannot split them from the unification. You must understand this.

If you don't understand this you will see the reflections as objects and understand yourself as the observing subject. The watcher and the watched are connected by thought, which is the mistake of grasping thought. By keeping to this method of practice all these visions are self-liberating. The sign of this is that they look like very fine beads (tigle) moving in many angular patterns. In the corner of the angles there are small and fine tigle.

These visions are connected with the winds which is why they are always moving. You must not follow these visions, however; neither give them too much attention nor care for them. That means that whatever tigle or visions come you have to be careful to see the visions without following them. You should remain in the natural state and not care what visions come.

Quote from the *Togbep (thog 'bebs)*: "There are two methods to use together—in the daytime and in daylight use the sun and the fire crystal (magnifying glass), and in the night use the moonlight and the water crystal (natural crystal). In the early morning or late evening use the light of butterlamps. Whatever light you use, do not gaze at it directly. The visions will become more bright and clear and stable. Your contemplation becomes more and more stable; that means that your winds and mind become calmer and calmer. Then experiences will develop. Suddenly you will know the different knowledge without study. One third of wisdom will be yours. During this period if you are disturbed by death you will be born in *Rangzhin Trulpa (rang bzhin sprul pa)*, the magically emanated realms of the intermediate state."

Quote from the *Tagdronma (rtags sgron ma)*: "That which is called the empty goes from the eyebrow level;

if you have passed away you will go to the magically emanated realms."

This is not only for visions of the natural state but also for the practice of contemplation. Therefore signs come of this type.

Quote from the *Tagdronbu (rtags sgrong bu)*: "Mixed with awareness and emptiness you will be born in the magically emanated realms."

The Second Vision—The Vision That Is Developing. In the first vision, as the vision comes, you still practise and then the unification of nature comes. In this first stage if you practise in this way the visions come but they are not even—sometimes bright and clear, sometimes dull; but they get more stable.

Now in this second stage the unification occurs. It is called 'to separate from the eyebrow'.

This symbolises the five wisdoms that appear as the five colours in rays that shoot straight upward from the eyebrow. They also go to the side, and sometimes can even appear as a triangle. They are much more developed than before and can seem even as large as a country. They are diaphanous like nets and have garlands of flowers, swastikas, jewels, palaces and mandalas. Many shapes can come. This is called the 'Space Visions Arriving in the Sky'. One can also see chorten, arrows and many other forms. That is the completion of nearly perfect visions. Between the visions there are bigger tigle. Their size is like shields which are round with five colours.[28]

That is called 'compounding the essence of awareness'.

---

28 Lopon comments that these visions can occur within tigle or outside them; tigle can also appear on their own.

All the stars and planets are shining brightly on his breast

This is explained by the comments on vision above. These visions all become stable according to the extent of practice. First they fly past like a hawk flying through the sky; at the second stage like deer running on the mountains; for the third stage like a *sharana* (a slow-moving mythological animal); at the fourth stage they are slow and gentle like the honey bees taking pollen from the flowers. Their stability depends on how much you have practised contemplation—the visions are as stable as your contemplation.

In the final stage the visions are as big as the universe and stable, and at the same time the contemplation is stable. When you start to have them, there are also techniques for changing the gazes according to how the visions appear.

Quote from the *Zhang Zhung Nyengyu*: "When the vision comes as a semicircle and white you should gaze upward and as hard as possible. When the colours are above and to the right and red you should look down. When the visions come in square shapes yellow in colour, the gaze is to the right. When they are round and green then look to the left. If the shapes are triangular and the colours are blue the eye should gaze straight ahead."

These are general instructions but the visions change so much that you should learn by experience.

If you don't develop the visions at all even though you practise, it is sometimes helpful to press on the eyes and hold the breath. Then suddenly open your eyes and exhale the breath, and the visions will appear temporarily. This may be necessary at the beginning.[29] After they

29 Lopon comments that this technique is only a temporary measure. If you don't develop these visions but only stay in the natural state then you will not develop quickly;

have gone just keep the natural state without any distraction. Sometimes if you are unable to control your thoughts then you should stop for a little while and calm the breath gently.

The gazes also help to calm the thoughts. Your contemplation is never deluded if you are in the natural state, so whether the visions develop or not, the mind should remain in contemplation in the natural state, always. The gazes can help to get into the natural state but the mind is the central key.[30]

It is important that your gazes are held looking into space and that you remain in awareness without distraction and with calm breath.[31]

---

conversely, if you don't practise the natural state you can have some visions but they are still not free. But then if the visions distract you from remaining in the natural state, that is again not right.

If you stay continuously in the natural state without visions then you do not understand the deluded vision, so you need both techniques. This is not like a game you play for interest; neither should you become attached to these visions and grasp after them. They are for practice. It is the same for dark retreat: you can have interesting experiences but they do not make much sense on their own.

30 Lopon comments that you should practise and discover what works for you—after all it is you that must enter the natural state.

31 Lopon comments that this is a basic instruction for all of the time. If you remain in the natural state then the visions come. Do not follow the visions, however; you should not be distracted by them.

There are three techniques in the *Zhang Zhung Nyengyu*—the gazes of the dark, of space and of light. The first is not described in this text, which only mentions the gazes of space and light. The practice of the dark is used to stabilise contemplation and for the initial development of visions.

At the beginning the visions start from inside the tigle, so only an upper half or a lower half appears, and not very clear. At this time you must still hold your gaze straight ahead in the natural state.[32]

This is generally true, but there are other qualifications. If you pass away when you are at the stage of the 'uniting of the four visions of wisdom', then in the same way in the intermediate state there are four visions of wisdom. At that time you will realise and be liberated. If you pass away when you see the triangle shapes in your vision then in the intermediate state you will be liberated. If the visions are round and like four-petalled flowers when you pass away, you will realize the clear vision in the first bardo of the intermediate state. In conclusion, if all the colours and the shapes are completed at the time you pass away, then when you are in the intermediate state you will realize what all the visions are before the bardo of birth (the sipai bardo; *srid pa'i bar do*) and you will be liberated.[33]

When the tigle are the size of shields and round then the visions have almost come to the ultimate. They do not get bigger than this. Each has five colours around the outside with mandalas of divinities with the consorts

---

32 Lopon comments that if you look for the other half of the image nothing will remain—they will all go. Better not to try to see anything. If you keep in the natural state then they will come naturally, for that is their source. But if you want to see more and try to focus on them, they will not remain; they are not objects of vision.

33 Lopon comments that this is a commentary on the *Zhang Zhung Nyengyu* text called *The Six Lamps*. If in this time you pass away you will be liberated in the intermediate state, because at the start of the bardo, visions begin as in this practice. If you realize that these visions are spontaneously arisen from the natural state then you will be liberated, since you will not grasp after them as real. This is explained in Book 4 of this text.

and different attendants inside. This is almost the final vision.

The Third Vision. Now comes complete vision. These visions all spontaneously exist within the natural state and you have used methods to develop them, so the visions appear to you. The visions do not come from outside. When the visions are all complete, then peaceful and wrathful divinities will appear—not as statues but directly from the natural state in Sambhogakaya or Nirmanakaya forms. Each will have the thirty-two special marks and eighty-one subsidiary signs. They appear because the practitioner has reached the complete vision. Just using the methods of Tögel and Trekchö and without any visualisation or mantra the divinities appear; therefore it is excellent.

Whatever the visions might be called, their nature is unification. They come to vision although they spontaneously exist. It is you that has come into the natural state, not them. You should not be limited by what visions come. Single or with consorts, dakinis, peaceful or wrathful—they appear because you have practised in unification and are stable and clear.

Therefore these visions come to you. There can be retinues and attendants and mandalas and so on, each with decorations and ornaments. They are naturally coming because everything spontaneously exists. You did not make any special thing; you only used the methods.

Quote from the *Togbep*: "The signs are the rays of clarity and the decorations of images."

Five bright lamps shine from the crown of the head

When the completed visions come the five wisdoms directly appear to the practitioner. At the same time all the visions mix with the external vision. Real vision mixes with external vision so that it is the same vision for you—the material things now mix with your vision. At the same time the visions are all liberating themselves. So the 'empty wisdom' has appeared to you—and whatever you see, wisdom appears. It does not matter whether you see friends or enemies—all are liberated in your vision. The visions are completely mixed without any conditions. All the normal visions in life are seen as the Buddha realms and the five Buddha families. You can see coming from your chest the five-coloured rays connecting you to these divinities. Also from your eyebrows rays come with tigle between them, becoming like the mandalas of the eighty-six wrathful deities, and inside the heart there are the forty-five peaceful deities that you can see.

The channels become completely purified and through them divinities and beings appear. At this time all the normal thoughts which are mixed with ignorance are completely purified and liberated. Awareness and wisdoms directly appear.

At that time you can focus on rocks and move them if you want to. Your mind can make imprints in rock; there is no attachment with the material body. Also the practitioner has the six kinds of clear voice and can see all the mountains as a paradise of the divinities. You can receive teachings from them and you have much knowledge that you receive without any learning.

The material body and channels being self-liberated, material things start to disappear. The mind and physical body are disconnected, so the physical body begins to disappear. You can see samsara and nirvana. You can see samsara and see that it is not your karmic cause, and you can see nirvana and that it is connected to you.

All the karmic causes and traces disappear like shooting stars disappearing into space. All the three kayas are completed in this time.

Three letters are set into his mind

All the visions and Nirmanakayas that have knowledge and purifications appear to the practitioner. This is a result of the practice of Dzogchen. No other schools can do this. To practice, see and use all the three kayas is unique to Dzogchen; therefore Dzogchen is the most esoteric path. In the practice of the eight ways, the realisation of the three kayas comes after the termination of the path (in the intermediate state). Here, they appear during this life so one can practise and have teachings directly from them.

Some of the masters say that these visions are all delusion. And some say this is the final truth. According to this text and my intention you cannot say this is either delusion or truth. What appears is what spontaneously exists—you cannot say that it is either true or false. To the practitioner the natural state appears spontaneously but the visions are neither external nor material. In the experience of the practitioner who has achieved this state all the visions are liberated into the natural state.

The Fourth Vision. The fourth vision is the completion of the natural visions. Here, depending on the methods which you have used, the visions of the natural state are fully developed. They are like the full moon. Just as when the moon is full it begins to wane, in the same way the visions also wane. They come down to the size of tigle again and the tigle dissolve into the natural state so that all that remains is the unification, nothing else. For this reason it is called 'finished'. Vision remains in the natural state as the final truth, just as the thirtieth day of the lunar month of the Tibetan calendar has no moon that you can see.[34]

The visions are bigger or smaller depending on the practitioner. The natural state is neither—it has always the same nature and is without size or colour.

There are two ways in which this completion comes about—gradual and sudden. In the gradual case the visions become full and then gradually diminish. Here the practitioner develops the four lamps sequentially and then the visions gradually disappear.

Although it is very rare, there are practitioners who are purified from practice in a previous life, and for them the visions suddenly start and equally suddenly stop.

---

34 Lopon comments that they start from the natural state and go back to the same source.

After the visions are complete all aspects of experience dissolve at the same time—not only the visions that you have, but also the normal vision, body and mind, sense organs and consciousness. Everything dissolves into your nature, because all aspects have been purified.[35]

---

35 Lopon comments that this is why after the taking of the body of light (*'ja' lus*) the nails and hair are left—you can cut them and it does not hurt, which indicates that they are outside the connection to the nature. Twenty nails and some pieces of hair are left.

One of Shardza's masters called Dawa Dragpa (*zla ba grags pa*) did achieve the complete resorption of his body in 1932. He asked his pupils to build a hut so he could take the rainbow body, and he asked them to keep its location secret especially from his very powerful brother who only lived one day away, because otherwise he would be disturbed. They built a hut, and they kept a small hole in it for a few days and then closed it completely. Just before he entered he took only a little milk and then nothing at all. It is said in the period just before he entered that sometimes he disappeared completely to the eyes of his students. Then he entered the hut, and around it they heard chanting and singing and saw rainbows of extraordinary shape, including square and linear ones. After one week they informed his brother, who was very upset that he had not been told. He travelled rapidly to the place and fought with the pupils and broke down the hut. This was nine days after Dawa Dragpa had entered it. When the brother looked inside it looked as though Dawa was there and he loudly exclaimed, "Everybody says you are dead but you are not dead!" So he shook the robes but there was nothing—only the empty clothes that Dawa was wearing, which fell to the ground. Searching for relics, he found some hair and nineteen nails, but could not find the twentieth. At that time Dawa's main student was not there either, and when he heard he made prostrations all the way to the place. He reached the hut where Dawa had disappeared and, searching for remnants of his master, found the missing

Why is it that all the external visions are dissolved? The reason for this lies in the process of awareness, which is generated at the heart by the arrival of winds from the channel that comes from the lungs. At the end of the visions this channel is completely disconnected and so the natural state becomes complete and pure.[36] Therefore all the visions are dissolved and this nature comes into the real final source.[37] If it does not reach

---

fingernail. This can be seen to this day in Dege.

When Shardza died in 1935 he left behind a body no larger than a plate; partial resorption of the body was also achieved by his nephew and his successor.

The most recent case was that of four students, one of whom was a personal friend of the Lopon, who went to practise with one of Shardza's main students in the 1950s. When the Cultural Revolution came they were brutalised along with all the monks; one died at this period and achieved the partial absorption of the elements of his body. The remaining pair lived on until after Mao died. One of them gave teachings to many people during the period of religious liberalisation that followed, and when he died in 1983 he also very nearly disappeared. Two of the monks who reside in Kathmandu were present at that time, as is described in Appendix I of this book.

Partial resorption of the body is simply the result of the stage of practice reached at the end of the life.

36 Lopon comments that just as the beginning of this process could be described as being like travelling down the English channel, at this stage the traveller has reached the open ocean and sees the shore no longer.

37 Lopon comments that this is not as if all external vision had disappeared and the practitioner were unable to see anyone or anything. The vision that dissolves is that connected to one's own personal traces; that is, the practitioner can see other beings and things that are part of the shared karmic traces but not his or her own. No thoughts can delude; were one to look into a mirror one would be invisible. Indeed, others can sometimes see the practitioner, sometimes not. It depends on the depth of absorption

the final nature then a small body is left behind because the visions have not all dissolved.

The Two Results

At that time the practitioner receives two kinds of things. First of all he or she receives the 'Free Birth' (this is explained below) and helps beings. The visions start to dissolve and when the practitioner looks at the fingers on the hands, he or she sees all the fingers wrapped up with lights. When the practitioner focuses on these lights and remains in meditation the body disappears and at the same time he or she sees the universe like the reflection of the moon in water. Also the practitioner can look at his or her own body and see that it too is like a reflection in a mirror. That time is called the 'Great Transfer'. The practitioner then becomes a member of the lineage of those who made the Great Transfer like the first twenty-four masters of the Dzogchen Lineage.[38] He or she then belongs to their community. And when he or she has a body like this, impure eyes see the practitioner as a normal person but he or she has a light body (hence the 'free birth'). In his or her body there is nothing material. The body can completely disappear or go through solid walls or fly in the air. An example is Tapihritsa who after he took a rainbow body was able to appear in any form at any time. In the *Zhang Zhung Nyengyu* it tells of him appearing to a rich man as a servant; this is because the man was the benefactor of

into the natural state.

38 This refers to the lineage of the *Zhang Zhung Nyengyu*; it was orally transmitted from master to pupil for twenty-four generations, with all lineage holders achieving the Great Transfer. The twenty-fifth master, Tapihritsa (*ta pi hri tsa*), asked his pupil Nangzher Löpo (*snang zher lod po*) in the eighth century to write it down, and many other rainbow bodies were recorded in the subsequent written lineage. It has remained unbroken to this day.

Nangzher Löpo, who was meditating nearby. After some time they realised that the servant was an emanated form, and Tapihritsa taught both the rich donor and Nangzher Löpo, finally appearing as the crystal-coloured form of the Dharmakaya.

Another example was Lungbon Lanyen (*lung bon lha gnyen*), who lived in the twelfth century in the Tsong province, who prayed for a long time to go to Tsewang Rigdzin (*tshe dbang rig 'dzin*). One day Tsewang Rigdzin appeared to him and then agreed to teach him. In fact more than one person received these teachings, which included the *Namkha Truldzö* Dzogchen that is quoted above.

The practitioner can meet an ordinary person and talk and then disappear and reappear at any time. He or she can also help all the six realms of beings at that time. If the connections are already there the practitioner can insert his or her mind into that of a pupil and change the pupil's mind. Gradually the pupils will practise and take their own rainbow bodies. That is the first result.[39]

The second result is called 'Gaining Free Entrance'. This means that if the practitioner has a bodily form which is not great or powerful in helping beings then when he or she sees his or her fingers wrapped with light there is no need to focus on them. The practitioner just remains in the unification. Soon thereafter the practitioner will completely disappear and all will disappear for him or her. Only the unification exists. This is called 'All the visions go back to the natural state'.[40]

---

39 Lopon comments that such appearances are rarer nowadays. Now people are not connected, that is to say that there must be a karmic cause on the part of the practitioner and a commitment from the master for such an appearance to happen.

40 Lopon comments that sometimes this is explained by analogy to an image that is placed inside an offering vessel. You cannot see the image from the outside of the vessel although inside it is there. In the same way, although the

Then the practitioner disappears and takes a rainbow body and, with the Buddhas, helps beings until samsara is finished. This is explained in the text *Treasure of Emptiness* written by Shardza, where it is described in detail.[41]

And the queens of the four seasons are all supporting him

That means the four supports are by his side. They are described in the following text.

Quote from the *Text of Molten Gold* (*gser gyi zhun ma*): "There are four supports. The first is the three unmoveable bases; the second is the three stabilities. The third is to fix as if with nails the three receipts, and the fourth is to show the signs of liberation and the four satisfactions."

The First Support Is the Three Unmoveable Bases. This is first to keep your body posture as stable as possible, so that your channels and winds all become calm. The second aspect is to not shift the gazes. This allows the visions to develop much more quickly. The third is to hold the mind without speaking in the natural state, which makes the unification more stable.

The Second Support Is the Three Stabilities. The first stability is that your body has no activity; the second is that if you stay quiet, without acting, then your winds all become calm and self-liberating. When the winds become calm the mind is not disturbed with thoughts. The third is that if the winds are not agitated with thoughts then the visions are all stable and they all quickly become developed and complete.

---

visions dissolve, something is there; the practitioner spontaneously exists in the unification. Although this analogy is often used it can be misleading—it must be remembered that the unification has neither inside nor outside.

41 Shardza was the prolific author of more than fourteen volumes of over three hundred pages each.

The Third Support Is to Fix as with Nails the Three Receipts. During this time the signs of how much you have practised come to the three doorways of body, speech and mind. How much you have achieved is also shown by dreams. The first signs come to the doorway of the body. It will feel like a tortoise put on a plate, unmoving in its shell. If you do this with the body then the channels and winds will be calm—that is the natural system. When the Great Perfection does not stop action [42] the lamps are fixed as with nails. So if you do this then all the bodily activities are liberated, and without acting the unification and awareness become more clear. This is the part of the body.

The second doorway is the speech; it is like drumming that does not cease. If you do not stop speaking then the mind goes into the channels and disturbs your keeping in the nature. If you stop talking no winds go through the channels and the unutterable nature is more clear and stable. You are more stable in unification and awareness.

The third doorway is the mind; it is like a bird caught in a tether trap. When all the thoughts and activities become naturally liberated then unification and awareness become clear and stable. And that makes all the visions unmixed and pure. Impure visions disappear and pure visions are stable and clear.

During the time that visions are developing the practitioner is like a very sick man who loses all shame regarding others. The practitioner who receives this sign does not care any more whether he or she is washed or not—one disregards one's appearance. So the practitioner cares for nothing. The reason is that the winds are inserted into the central channel and everything is controlled by the natural state. All the world of convention bounded by thoughts is no longer relevant. All thoughts

---

42 This means that if your body is stable and does not move, naturally your lamps will not move.

are inserted into the natural state. It is called 'Without acting to put to the body'. Soon thereafter the practitioner's body will be liberated into the natural state and all the three kayas will appear through the wisdom of the natural state.

Second, the practitioner's speech is like that of a madman and he or she does not care. The practitioner has liberated all the thoughts and is not bound by thoughts, so the speech is not bounded. Thus the nail of the unsayable is fixed to the speech. For such a practitioner the awareness and unification is very clear and he or she is completely controlled by that. There is no thought of what other people think.

Third, the practitioner's mind is like that of a man who has been poisoned—he has no control. The practitioner is completely controlled by his or her awareness and everything spontaneously comes without any planning. All the thoughts are self-liberating. That is the nail without thoughts that fixes to the thoughts.

The Fourth Support—the Signs of Liberation. The signs of liberation are given in two parts. First there is the time of completion, in which the visions become complete. All things are liberated and all the visions become complete. Like the elephant who gets into the mud in the middle of the rice field, they will come out by themselves! The practitioner does not need any special practice. That is called 'without any stopping'.

The result is that the wisdom of the activities will be controlled so whatever the practitioner says is sweet to those who hear his or her voice. The speech has been controlled with awareness, and compassion automatically appears. All that he or she speaks becomes teachings and they will be deep and clear. The mind is like a man who once had smallpox—after he has recovered it never comes back. In the same way when the practitioner has liberated all thought, then obscuring thoughts never return. The practitioner is controlled by wisdom and awareness. This sign is called 'the nails without thoughts fix the remembering thoughts'.[43]

The second sign of liberation has four divisions. Here everything is won. All the visions are won and during that time the practitioner's body is like a corpse. Whatever he or she eats or whatever happens he or she does not care—that is the feeling of the body. This means that the mind is completely liberated into the unification and clarity. The practitioner is without fear; thus 'without fear the nail fixes without focussing'. For example, if the practitioner is surrounded by enemies he or she is not frightened. That is the sign that all the thoughts are liberated into the unchangeable unification.

The practitioner's speech is like echoes in the rocks; whatever others say he or she just repeats, for there is no plan to say anything. This sign shows that all the syllables that normally exist in the channels are liberated into the unification, so the 'nail of the unsayable pins the thoughts' and everything is bright, clear and natural. The practitioner's mind is like a mist that disappears into space—there is no trace of where it is liberated or where it has gone. All that remains is the unification and the liberated wisdom without delusion. Wisdom shines brightly to him or her.

These signs come to the practitioner who has achieved the visions. The practitioner has received four initiations: for the four signs of the body he or she has received the four initiations of the base; secondly he or she has received the four initiations of the path; finally in the mind he or she has received the four initiations of the fruit. That is the sign of liberation.

Recognising the Degree of Achievement Through Dreams. Achievement comes according to the practitioner's determination to practise. The best practitioner stops all dream vision and does not care or learn from them. The dreams are liberated into the clear light. This is the sign

43 Lopon comments that means that all thoughts disappear.

that he or she will take a rainbow body during this lifetime. The practitioner of second capacity recognises the dream visions as dream and controls them; when he or she is able to do this liberation will be achieved during the intermediate state. The third capacity of practitioner has stopped the bad karmic causes of dreams and always has good dreams. He or she will be reborn in the magically emanated realms.[44]

Quote from the *Text of Molten Gold*: "The practitioner has received the empowerment of the visions. By this all the visions of secondary causes are the support for the practice. Also he or she has received the empowerment of the body. By this all material things disappear and only clear lights remain. He or she receives the empowerment of the secret mind and wind. By this all thoughts are liberated into the natural state."

The Four Satisfactions. The first satisfaction is that whether the practitioner hears all the teaching of the Buddhas or not, he or she is neither happy nor sad. The practitioner never expects to hear it or to see it because he or she realises completely that the Buddha is not far from his or her unification—that is known. The second is that the practitioner neither wishes nor doubts. The third satisfaction is that when he or she sees that the lower realms of existence have so much suffering, the practitioner does not fear it. He or she does not wish or pray not to be reborn there because the natural state has been completely achieved. The fourth is that the practitioner will never roam in samsara. There is nothing left of his or her vision to be born or bring suffering.

Four servants are all serving him

These are the four wisdoms. The first is the ability to distinguish clearly (intellect). All existences do not mix; therefore they are clearly distinguished.

44 These are emanated by him in the intermediate state.

The second is the ability to know how things are related. The practitioner sees how all existence is connected with awareness.

The third is the conception of how things are liberated. The practitioner sees that all existences are liberated into the natural state.

The fourth is called the ultimate nature of things. The practitioner sees that all that exists is sent entirely to the pure natural state; nothing exists beyond this nature.

This completes the forty-two methods of Tögel practice.

All the impure visions are liberated into pure nature. The practitioner comes to the permanent place and there is no doubt that he or she will never depart from there.

Book Four
Phowa and Bardo Practices

[Tibetan text 46b, line 6]

THE THIRD CATEGORY OF ESSENTIAL TEACHINGS FOR THE PRACTICE

The Traveller Who Crosses the Mountains and Having Mistaken His Way is Helped to Find the Right Path.[1]

These are the teachings for liberation during the bardo intended for the practitioner of medium capacity. This teaching has three subdivisions, namely the teachings for the intermediate state of life, the instructions just before the moment of death and the instructions of emptiness.

---

1 Lopon comments that this section is for those who have not practised during their lifetime and who therefore have to depend on bardo teachings.

Magyu

THE TEACHINGS FOR THE INTERMEDIATE STATE

All the beings within what spontaneously exists possess two types of alaya.[2] For example, a mirror automatically collects grime, even though no one puts dirt on it. In the same way, if you have not purified all the tough and subtle causes then those previous karmic traces that you have collected become the seeds for future karmic actions. You have collected many causes and so, without being able to choose, you take birth in the six realms of sentient beings and experience the feelings of happiness, suffering or neutral emotions. These traces have the power to do this. When karmic traces are mixed with consciousness it is called 'deluded consciousness'.

Human beings in particular are bounded by the five aggregates.[3] These five limit human experience so we are completely restricted; thus we don't see the visions of the five Buddha Bodies.[4]

So this limitation of the five aggregates and the five consciousnesses restricts our experience and covers the vision of the pure lights. Also we are bound by the emotions and karmic causes. By this the vision of unification, wisdom and emptiness is covered. We are always taking and collecting deluded visions and being bound by them. By this cause we circulate for innumerable lives in samsara.

---

2 Lopon comments that this refers to basic alaya, which is consciousness and those karmic traces dependent on consciousness.

3 These are body, mind, perceptions, emotions and sense organs; other realms have fewer skandhas. For example, the demigods and gods are not bounded by body.

4 Dharmakaya, Sambhogakaya, Nirmanakaya, Nature Body and Perfection Body.

Because we always have these sufferings and miseries we begin to search for nirvana, wanting to be released from these fetters. One who raises this intention must from the beginning listen to and learn the right teachings. In the second place what is learnt must be practised with contemplation. Finally what has been practised should give fruit. During this life you must do this or without any doubt you will remain trapped by samsara. This is the purpose of a worthwhile life.

Quote from the *Text of Molten Gold*: "During the bardo of normal life you must learn and practise."[5]

THE TEACHING FOR THE PERIOD JUST BEFORE DEATH

Now there are three capacities of practitioner. The first dies like a child dying, the second like an old dog dying and the third like a king dying.

For the first, there is no worry about whether one is alive or dying, just as a young child does not know whether it wants to be alive or die.

For the second, there are a further two subdivisions. The first is like a dog who has not prepared for death, but when it realises it is dying, runs from the crowds of people and lies down beside the road outside the town. The second is like a dog who when it realises it is going to die makes time to go away for a long distance to find a cave or an empty valley where it is certain to be undisturbed.

5 Lopon comments that it does not say to go directly into meditation after having only heard a few teachings—you must learn and understand first. This is like when the Fifth Dalai Lama rebuked the Kagyupa order of Tibetan Buddhism on the grounds that there was no learning, only practice for Siddhas in their monastic syllabus. Indeed it was said of those days that half of Tibet were beggars and most of them were Siddhas!

The third is like the king dying. When he is sick everybody is trying to cure him with medicines and pujas, and after his death all the relatives surround him and shed tears for him and hear his will. Then the people make prayers for forty-nine days, and there is an elaborate funeral with a large gathering. This kind of death is for a person who shows the sign of not being a real Dzogpachenpo practitioner.

That is the way of death for ordinary beings.

The real practitioner, who has visions and experiences with wisdom and clear light, chooses the right body posture for death. This is the lion lying down.[6] The mind is transferred through the eye and mixes with the unification without any extending and conclusion. One just remains there in the natural state and takes death without any distractions.

Quote from the *Text of Molten Gold*: "It is important to remember not to be deluded but to be in the natural state just before taking death, which will stop all the elements.[7] The best way is to remain in the unification of clear light. If the practitioner does this then the practice and experience will all help to send him or her to the visions of the intermediate state. The practice will send and the visions of the intermediate state will receive, so one is able to be liberated in a moment."

---

6 Lopon comments that this is like the posture of the Shakyamuni's parinirvana seen in statues.

7 Lopon comments that this refers to the fact that our body is connected with five elements, each supporting the mind. When the elements disconnect the mind starts to lose its support, then the body, having no connection with mind, no longer works. It becomes like a corpse or rock.

THE ESSENTIAL TEACHING

For this purpose from now on you should always practise the gazes in clear space and remain united with your nature without distraction. Sometimes you should think that when you die you will mix only with the unification. That you must practise during this lifetime. From time to time think this way while you are maintaining the gazes in clear space, then breathe out strongly and hold your contemplation in the unification. That is my essential teaching.

In this case, without depending on the teachings, one can keep faith with one's master and friends; they must remind one to keep in the nature. If one realises that one is ready to stop connection with the elements one can eject the mind by saying *HIK* twenty-one times. This practice is part of Phowa,[8] so there are two things one can do. Best of all is not to distract the departing person from meditation or do anything. It is only if he or she is unable to remain continuously in the natural state that this must be done. In this case, one should visualise the mind as the letter *AH* inside the central channel at the heart level. Each time one says *HIK*, the letter *AH* rises the width of a thumb until it leaves the crown of the head, at which point it is liberated into space.

In the *Magyu (ma rgyud)*[9] there is a teaching of Phowa in three stages—Phowa for the Dharmakaya, Sambhogakaya and Nirmanakaya. In this case one should have experience with the Sambhogakaya transference. Quite often in tantric teaching there is the description of the disconnection of the elements one from another. If one is not

8 This is the practice of the transference of conciousness, which is described in the text that follows.

9 The *Magyu* is the teachings of the highest tantra within the Bönpo tradition and is thus a very important text.

dependent on gradual disconnection of the elements from the mind, one can transfer to nirvana.

Another type of practitioner is one who has received detailed teachings on Dzogchen but has not practised them very well. In this case one has to depend on various ways of dying according to the disconnection of the elements from the mind. There are four external elements and five internal descriptions of sky and five different secret energies. Altogether there are twenty lifting winds which are gradually dissolved. The process of their dissolution Shardza commented on in detail in the full two-volume text of which this is a condensed summary.

The Disconnection of the Elements

Here is the very simple explanation of how the mind is disconnected at the time of death.

First a quote from the *Text of Molten Gold*: "When the earth element dissolves into earth and is disconnected with mind, the sign will be that the body feels very heavy, and although the person may be hungry he or she is unable to eat or stand up or move. When the water element dissolves into water and is disconnected with mind the sign is that the person cannot keep water and it flows from the mouth, nose and eyes. When the fire element is disconnected with mind and dissolves into fire the body begins to get cold starting from the feet and moving to the centre. And when the wind element dissolves into wind and is disconnected with mind the person makes a sound automatically and the limbs move involuntarily. During this time the eyes roll up and that is the sign that death has come. If the person has received teachings previously then somebody must remind him or her."

Then in all the branches of the channels and veins the blood comes back to the heart. This blood makes three drops inside the heart where there is a hollow, and three exhalations occur. That is the final breathing. At that time the drop of semen received from the father comes down from the crown to the heart in the central channel, and the drop of blood received from the mother comes up from the solar plexus to the heart in like manner. The dying person sees first a bright white light and then a bright red light. When the two drops meet in the centre of the heart everything goes dark and unconsciousness occurs for an uncertain length of time. The good practitioner who stays in the natural state, if very accomplished, can remember the natural state during this time, but it is very difficult.

The length of the time of unconsciousness depends on many conditions, but afterward the person awakens with a very clear awareness. If one has received these teachings and has realised the natural state then one will be in the natural state like a clear light in a cloudless sky, with no *tsel* or visions appearing. It is very important to realize that this happens to all beings after death. They are all there for a long or short time, although it is not sure how long it will be for any particular individual. But the realisation of it depends on them.

If one realises one's presence during this time and realises the natural state then one will surely obtain Buddhahood.

Quote from the *Golden Spoon (gser gyi thur ma)*: "That is the time of the separation of wisdom and mind. If one who has practised realises this here then he or she will surely become Buddha, and once one has entered this state one will never come back to samsara. *E MA HO*—wonderful!"

The Bardo Visions

The time of clear vision is called the *bonyi (bon nyid)* bardo of emptiness. If one is not liberated during this time when the natural state appears clearly, then one starts to have basic visions of the clear light. There appear five very bright colours. If you realize that this is your own vision at this time then it is also possible to be liberated.

Quote from the *Yangtse (yang tse)*: "Awareness comes out from the eyes, and disappears into space and clear light vision comes. That is the time for one who has received teachings and practised them to be liberated."

If one is not liberated in this time then another state occurs, called 'United with the Clear Light'. Previously one had visions; now they develop much more and one sees the bodies of the Buddhas and hears sounds and sees lights and rays. If one has practised there can be many visions of divinities and forms.

Quote from the fourth section of the *Zhang Zhung Nyengyu* (the *Zerbu*; *gzer bu*): "The light becomes like realms of unlimited divinities—clear as rainbows shining in the sky. And very loud sounds sound as if they are in empty space (like echoes). They come from within themselves without stopping, like dragons roaring. The shapes of the rays are various, like open brocade. The practitioner who has experienced these previously will see the Buddha realms and all the Buddhas there."

In this time one sees rays from one's chest connecting to the Buddhas.

Quote from the *Text of Molten Gold*: "Inside the heart the clear light shines (in a tigle) the size of a thumb; the visions are connected with Buddhas from there. You have to keep in the nature without delusion. For the practitioner who realises that the visions are all his own visions, then these visions are called 'the Awareness is Entered to the Light'."

Automatically one can enter the natural state without thought. Then all the visions dissolve into the rays coming from one's chest; that is called 'the Light Dissolved into Awareness'. If one realises that the visions are all one's own nature, one will liberated into the natural state.

If one does not keep this vision and cannot be liberated into nature then the next stage is called 'Unification Dissolves into Wisdom'. At this time the vision comes from one's chest and fine light rays rise into the sky. The practitioner looks through the rays and they become more extended with five colours and visions.

Quote from the *Text of Molten Gold*: "When one has visions that one's body is light, the five wisdoms can be seen as the five colours, and it is important to realize the natural state. The five lights are blue, white, yellow and red. These four are not separate but fine and clear. Each of these colours and rays have tigle at their end according to the colour of the rays; their size is like mirrors and they are ringed with the five colours. On the top of these tigle there are many coloured lights around like a peacock's feather. That is called the 'Visions of the Four Wisdoms United'."

The text quoted above says four but it should be five colours; the five wisdoms are all coloured and completed.

If at this point the practitioner does not realize that these visions are all self-created visions then the wisdoms dissolve into what spontaneously exists. They dissolve round the lights and the lights extend and become like the clear sky. Under there wrathful deities appear complete with their retinues. All the peaceful divinities with their retinues are completed and all the six realms of beings with the six Buddhas emanated by Tonpa Shenrab can be seen. They are not far from the natural state, and therefore this is called 'the Vision of the Base'.[10]

---

10 Lopon comments that this is called Dzogchen Zhitro but is a naturally appearing vision, not a visualisation. In the practice of zhitro (*zhi khro*), eighty-six wrathful and forty-five peaceful Buddhas are seen with the six realms of beings emanated by the six Buddhas.

In the bardo one has left the physical body but still has the *yilu (yid lus)*, the vision body (*yid*, consciousness; *lus*, body). It is just the same as the body of dreams, the mind body. Even though the physical body is dead there is so much attachment that one has the vision of the body. This body can feel like the ordinary body. For instance, if you

The Eight Visions

After the visions of the peaceful and wrathful deities connected to one's chest there are three stages. First, eight visions come.[11] The first is named the vision of compassion; the second is the vision of light. The third is vision of kayas; the fourth is the vision of wisdom. The fifth is the vision of unification and the sixth is the vision of unending liberation. The seventh is the vision of the impure and finally comes the pure vision.

The Vision of Compassion. This means that one suddenly has compassion for samsara and nirvana equally—there is no preference.

The Vision of Light. One sees that the visions are all from inside one's nature—they spontaneously exist.[12]

The Vision of the Kayas. One sees that the visions cannot change one; whether they are wrathful or peaceful does not matter.

The Vision of Wisdom. This means that the visions cannot be stopped because they are recognised as not material.

---

stay in the bardo for two weeks, then in the first week you are in your old body, and in the second week you feel like the new body you will be reborn into.

The time you are in the bardo depends on your condition—seven weeks is an average. But the situation is just the same as dream. There is a story of a man who died and roamed in the bardo. He went back to his family and no one answered him. He was very upset, as he thought that everyone was avoiding him for some reason. It was only when he saw his body being cremated that he realised he was dead.

11 Lopon comments that the extent of these visions depends on the practitioner. For one who has not practised, only the impure vision is seen.

12 Lopon comments that is like the image inside the offering vessel used earlier to explain the body of light.

The Vision of Unification. This means that in one's consciousness one controls wherever one wants to focus on without any delusion.

The Vision of Unending Liberation. All the visions are liberated into the natural state.

The Visions of the Impure. All the six realms of beings come into vision.

The Pure Visions. Now one can reach the pure state. The eight visions are called the pure visions; the wisdom is connected with mother and son.[13]

---

13 Here Lopon explains that the normal visions are impure and the Tögel visions are pure. In this text it is said that the impure visions are the visions of the six realms of beings; pure visions are like the visions of divinities, mandalas, etc. But in these visions of Tögel the quality is the same whatever vision comes—it does not make any difference. All come from the natural state and so come to the practitioner. Generally normal daily visions are impure whereas Tögel visions are pure. But the important point about Tögel visions is not whether they are pure or not, but that they can be clearly seen to have no inherent existence.

If one has practised enough to liberate one's obscurations one will have pure visions, otherwise not. The visions come from the four lamps, but until one reaches the rainbow body they are still mixed with obscurations. Both Tögel vision and everyday awareness come from the natural state. According the *Zhang Zhung Nyengyu* in the base of the natural state there is *tsel* and unification. The *tsel* is temporary and is the vision we have learnt and understood in this text; it is called the son. It is sometimes said that the awareness is the son and the emptiness is the mother.

If one perseveres in the practice, one day the unification will be stable and for a moment it will be near to the basic nature. But this is only temporary and limited. It is like sailing in the English Channel. However, if one practises to the end it is inseparable and goes back to the real nature; this is like sailing in the deep ocean. Whatever one

If one understands that all the visions are self-originated then one will be liberated into the Dharmakaya.

Quote from the *Text of Molten Gold*: "All the visions of the three kayas spontaneously exist and whatever visions arise must be understood as dreams, illusions. When you realize this you realize that they are not inherent; therefore you must leave all desire for them. Just leave everything as it is, whatever comes, good or bad. Remain stable in the natural unification, as stable as possible. This is very important. Whatever vision comes, do not notice it but remain stable in the unification. There is then no doubt you will be liberated into the Dharmakaya."

Now all the visions dissolve into the nature again. All the visions dissolve in eight different ways, but not one after another—all are dissolved at once.

Quote from the *Text of Molten Gold*: "The first vision of compassion is dissolved into compassion, as when the sun sets and all the rays go back together. There is no difference who is leading or led. The visions of light dissolve into the light in the same way as the rainbow is clear but there is no substantial material in it. In the third, the visions of the kayas, all the visions of forms are dissolved to the forms. They are dissolved externally, into the nature. So there will be clarity inside, like the image that is inside the vessel. The fourth are the visions of wisdom. The visions of wisdom are all dis-

---

practises will develop and ultimately return to the changeless nature.

This must be understood or it can be a source of confusion. The real nature does not develop nor decrease, but the practice must develop. Simply hearing that the natural state exists is not enough, for even though some people realize it, they still circulate in samsara. There is no contradiction here. You can realize Buddhahood in a moment, yet it is said it can take a very long time. It depends on the viewpoint.

solved to wisdom and the son goes to the mother's lap. In this way awareness is liberated into the basic nature."[14]

The vision of unification dissolves to the unification, meaning that all visions dissolve into nature like water pouring into water.

The sixth is the vision of unending liberation. It is dissolved like the sky is dissolved into sky and everything is in Yungdrung Bön (the natural state).

The seventh is the impure visions. They are dissolved into the pure visions like tents collapsing when you cut the guy ropes that support them. Everything is

---

14 Lopon comments that unification means two things are united—awareness and emptiness. Awareness (the son) is dissolved into emptiness (the mother); however, they have always been inseparable. But how can you say that awareness dissolves into nature if they have always been together? What does it mean that awareness dissolves into nature? You must understand that they have always been united; that is the Dzogchen view. So this refers only to the practitioner who has started to realize.

When a person enters the intermediate state, at the beginning there are no visions. Then one comes out of that state and the visions start. They are sounds, rays and lights—and when the visions start the perception starts at the same time. The sounds, rays and lights are all seen as the objects with the perception as the subject.

This first perception is called *yid* (consciousness). At that moment either one realises that these objects come from one's nature and the visions are illusion, or one is deluded and sees them as inherently existent. In this second case the very subtle ignorance, called the 'born together ignorance' arises, and it is the beginning of a new cycle of birth. But if one realises that the visions are self-created, then that is the beginning of Rigpa and one is not led into samsara. In a little while one will dissolve into the natural state. So the unification of mother and son is the realisation that the visions are self-created.

collapsed and you cannot see the tent—in the same way everything enters light without any delusion.

The pure visions are dissolved into purity, into the door of wisdom. It is like the snow lion who runs to the high mountain—he is safe because there is no doubt he will not come back.

After all the eight visions dissolve all that is left is unification, stable and clear forever. Someone who realises the nature and practise up to this point will achieve the place of the Dharmakaya and will never return to samsara at all. It is important to see that the practice during the lifetime is preparation for realization in the bardo when these kinds of visions arise. If you have experienced all these visions you can realize them and remain in the natural state.

The Three Teachings

These visions come during the bardo time. All their conclusions are sounds, rays and lights and this is like a receiver. If you have practised Tögel visions then that is like a transmitter, so in this time when you have these visions you must remember the following three teachings.

First, whatever vision comes everything is your own self-vision. Remember it without any doubt, like when the son sees his mother.

Second, once you realize that the visions are all self-vision, from then on you will never ever be deluded or disturbed. Like a golden spoon you will never change.

Third, once you keep the final stable unification your awareness never comes back to samsara. It is like an arrow shot by a Hero; it goes always straight but never comes back.

These are the three teachings.

The three important teachings are taken from the *Dzogchen Yang Tse (rdzogs chen yang rtse).*[15]

Quote from the *Dzogchen Yang Tse*: "When he [Lishu Taring] was teaching it to his consort he said that the person who has been shown directly in this way during the life takes no more than the next bardo. The three matters will be receiving and three matters will be sending. He or she realises the three important teachings and finally will be liberated."

The Secondary Causes That Make for Liberation

There are six kinds of secondary cause to remind you in the bardo. They are:

1. When the visions start you immediately realize that this is a vision.
2. Once you remember that these are the bardo vision this makes you remember your yidam. Then suddenly the visions will come as the yidam, and you can see the yidam.
3. You realize that you are in the bardo and you are reminded of your lama. Then he comes in front of you and he again teaches you about the bardo visions.
4. You suddenly remember the teachings you have received.
5. You remember your view.
6. You remember to practise the natural state and you remain in it.

Quote from the *Text of Molten Gold*: "Remember lama, remember teaching, remember yidam, remember view, remember emptiness and remember practice."

At this time the practitioner receives the six clairvoyant faculties: (1) The six sense organs become purified and (2) the intelligence is purified. Therefore all the thoughts and doubts are purified. (3) The wisdom is purified and so it is known when all beings are born and where they will be reborn, and (4) the contemplation is purified so it is easy and stable. (5) All the obscurations

15 Lopon comments that this is an important text written by Lishu Taring (*li shu stag ring*), an early eighth-century master.

are purified so the practitioner has achieved his or her own purpose. He or she can see all the six realms clearly and emanate to them and teach them according to their understanding. (6) All knowledge is purified and he or she can see all the Buddhas' knowledge.

Quote from the *Text of Molten Gold*: "All the sense organs and all the knowledge is pure, wisdom and contemplation are pure, all the obscurations are finished and all the knowledge is perfect."

To achieve this stage takes three moments, the second stage takes five moments and the third takes twenty-one moments.

This is the end of the bardo teachings.

Before we said that if you do not realize the visions in the first, second or third stage, but you finally realize them in the fourth stage, you will be born in the magically emanated realms and you will learn and practise Dzogchen there. Before all the visions came and you did not realize the twenty-one levels; you realised them only in the bardo of existence (the fourth stage).

It is like in a dream. If you remember now that all the visions must be the bardo, you will realize that you are in the bardo of existence. If you remember at this time and wish to be reborn in the magically emanated realms, then you will take the magical birth there (i.e. birth not dependent on parents).

Quote from the *Golden Spoon*: "If you realize the sipai bardo (*srid pa'i bar do*) and you practise there, you will liberate all the karmic traces that result in your birth in the realms of sentient beings and you will be reborn in a Nirmanakaya form. The realm in which you will be born is connected to you by prayer and dedication and at the end of that life you will achieve Buddhahood."

Therefore if during this life you judge that you have not practised enough to do this, you should practise Phowa.

Phowa Practice

Imagine the central channel running through your heart and through a hole in the crown of your head. Imagine your mind leaping through this hole like a shooting star. Remember the magically emanated realms and remember your intention to be reborn there. Your mind is visualised as a letter *AH*. Remember the chief Buddha of this realm and imagine that your mind is ejected like a shooting star and dissolves in his heart. If you wish to be born in the east (white) the chief is the 'Self-Originated Clear Tonpa' (Buddha) and the realm the 'Clear Happiest'; to the north (green) the realm is called 'Perfection of Good Actions' and the Tonpa is called Gelha Garchug (*dgel lha gar phyug*); to the west (red) the realm is called 'Heaped Flowers' and the Tonpa is called Jedrag Ngöme (*bye brag dngos med*); to the south (blue) the realm is called 'Excellent Brilliant Place' and the Tonpa is called Gawa Dondrub (*dga' ba don grub*). Finally the central realm is called 'Perfection Exists' and the Tonpa is called Ökar Nedzin (*'od dkar gnas 'dzin*)

Surrounding each Buddha are Bodhisattvas and attendants whom he is teaching. All the realms are made from precious jewels and there are birds and animals. Trees and clean waters and all kinds of fruits and jewelled clothes are there. Above these realms are the realms of the wrathful deities. If you are born there you will live there for five hundred years, and after that you will not have bardo visions but will achieve Buddhahood without doubt. The realms were originally connected with each person's own nature. They are the self-emanated realms.

The beings who have not received Dzogchen but have practised the Yungdrung Bön teachings can be born there without any practice other than prayer, refuge and dedication to be reborn there.

The rest of the beings are driven on by karmic causes and have peaceful, happy, sad and neutral feelings. They take various births and hear nothing and believe nothing.

They are always circulating into the option of misery, and nothing can help them.

What follows is the dedication to the benefit of all beings.

> My place[16] is where all the Dakinis and Siddhas visit and it is called Swastika Mountain. It is wrapped with rainbows like tents in the summer time, in round, straight and semicircular shapes. Flowers of snow come raining during the winter. There are trees which take warmth from the top and damp from the roots and the centre of the trunk is white; the bark is red and their leaves are green like turquoise, and they have golden fruits. When it rains they give a wonderful smell and there are many of them, heaped. Inside there is my hermitage. When the sun shines they look like ladies looking at me and I am very happy and warm. They look as if they are dancing in front of me and many birds are dancing and singing and looking at each other. And tens and twenties of serious practitioners are by the side.
>
> This teaching was written there on paper given to me by my students and copied from the original manuscript by my first student Sherab.
>
> This is the essence of all the Dzogchen methods. If you practise this there will be no doubts nor mistakes and you will not waste your life.

---

16 Lopon comments that Shardza concludes with a poetic description of his hermitage in a juniper grove in the mountains were he went after having abandoned the life of a monk.

Chenlha Migu

Appendix 1
An Eyewitness Account of a Rainbow Body

One of Shardza Tashi Gyaltsen's main students was called Tsewang Gyurme (*tse dbang 'gyur med*). He passed away between 1969 and 1970 in a Chinese jail. This was in Nyarong in Kham; it is not known what became of him. Four young monks went from Khyungpo to see him before he was arrested and they received all the teachings of Dzogchen from him including all of Shardza's works with all the initiations. They were there a long time. These monks were named Tsultrim Tarchen (*tshul khrims thar phyin*), Tsewang Dechen Nyingpo (*tshe dbang de chen snying po*), Tsupu Özer (*gtsud phud 'od zer*) and Sonam Kelsang (*bso nams skal sangs*).

They were with him for nine years, but in 1958/9, when the Chinese started to govern Tibet directly, they came back to Khyungpo. The first monk, Tsultrim, was lost in the chaos of 1969. The second, Tsewang, was hidden by the villagers during the Cultural Revolution in 1969/70, but he was not well and died while in hiding. His body shrank over a ten-day period and was hidden afterwards in a basin; it was the size of a ten-inch plate.

Nege Jampa

Hiding it had been a considerable danger to the villagers but it was displayed in 1984, for at that time the Chinese lifted restrictions on the practice of religion. The third student, Tsupu Özer, died in 1983. After seven days his body also shrunk to a small size but did not get any smaller; this was kept for two months along with Tsewang's body.

Both these bodies were cremated together in a large ceremony. The cremations were attended by two monks, Yeshe Özer (*ye shes 'od zer*) and Sangye Monlam (*sangs rgyas smon lam*), who live in Kathmandu with Lopon Tenzin Namdak.

At least 10,000 people gathered to witness these cremations. Yeshe saw both bodies close up; they were nearly naked sitting in full lotus posture. The bodies were very light, perfect but just small, as everything had shrunk at the same rate. Indeed both monks were in the village when Tsupu Özer died, and witnessed many other stange manifestations, such as rainbows spreading along the ground even though there was a clear sky. This was even more surprising as Tsupu Özer was not thought to be much of a practitioner because he drank chang!

Another student of Shardza called Tsondru Rinpoche (*brtson 'grus rin po che*) passed away in 1985 in the Bönpo centre at Dolanji. Everybody living there saw rainbows, straight as well as round, some white and some five-coloured. They appeared out of the clear sky as he died. Even when it was nearly dark there were white rainbows glowing in the sky. This was seen by many many people in Dolanji. After he was cremated many people searched in the ashes for relics. The officiating monks found many big relic pills; others were seen but when people tried to pick them up they could not catch them—they seemed to disappear. The pills are kept by the Abbot in Dolanji.

Tonpa Shenrab

Appendix 2
A Short History Of Bön[1]

THE ORIGIN OF BÖN

The Bönpos maintain that Bön originated in the land of Olmo Lungring (*'ol mo lung ring*), a part of a larger country called Tazig (*rtag gzigs*). *Ol* symbolizes the unborn; *mo* the undiminishing; *lung* the prophetic words of Tonpa Shenrab (*ston pa gshen rab*), the founder of Bön; and *ring* his everlasting compassion. Olmo Lungring constitutes one third of the existing world and is situated to the west of Tibet. It is described as an eight-petalled lotus under a sky which appears like an eight-spoked wheel. In the centre rises Mount Yungdrung Gutseg (*gyung drung dgu brtsegs*), 'Pyramid of Nine Swastikas'. The swastika is the symbol of permanence and indestructibility. The nine swastikas piled up represent the nine ways of Bön. At the base of Mount Yungdrung spring four rivers, flowing toward the four cardinal directions. The mountain is surrounded by temples, cities

1 Extracted from the pamphlet "Tibetan gYung-Drung Bön Monastery in India," published by the Yungdrung Bön Monastic Center (Solan: 1983); translated by Tadeusz Skorupski.

and parks. To the south is the palace Barpo Sogye (*bar po so brgyad*), where Tonpa Shenrab was born. To the west and north are the palaces in which lived the wives and children of Tonpa Shenrab. A temple named Shampo Lhatse (*sham po lha rtse*) is to the east. The complex of palaces, rivers and parks with Mount Yungdrung in the centre constitutes the inner region (*Nangling; nang gling*) of Olmo Lungring. The intermediate region (*Barling; bar gling*) consists of twelve cities, four of which are toward the cardinal directions. The third region includes the outer land (*Taling; mtha' gling*). These three regions are encircled by an ocean and again by a range of snowy mountains. The access to Olmo Lungring is gained by the so-called arrow way (*Delam; mda' lam*). Before his visit to Tibet, Tonpa Shenrab shot an arrow thus creating a passage through the mountain range.

This very sophisticated description of Olmo Lungring has been tentatively related by some scholars to different geographical locations. Some see it as a description of Mount Kailash (*Ti se*) and the four great rivers that spring from its base—China being the land to the east, India to the south, Orgyan to the west and Khotan to the north. To other scholars the description seems to resemble the geography of the Middle East and Persia in the time of Cyrus the Great. To a believing Bönpo the question of the geographic identification of Olmo Lungring does not come so much to the foreground as does its symbology, which is clearly made use of to indicate the supramundane origin of his religion. Symbolic descriptions which combine history, geography and mythology are well-known phenomena in ancient scriptures. The description of the universe with Mount Meru supporting the sky and the four Chief Continents to the four cardinal points and this earth as the southern continent (Jambudvipa) is another similar example.

THE FOUNDER AND HIS TEACHINGS

The founder of Bön religion is the Lord Shenrab Miwo (*gshen rab mi bo*). In past ages there were three brothers, Dagpa (*dag pa*), Selwa (*gsal ba*) and Shepa (*shes pa*), who studied the Bön doctrines in the heaven named Sipa Yesang (*srid pa ye sangs*), under the Bön sage Bumtri Logi Chechen (*'bum khri glog gi lce can*). When their studies were completed, they visited the God of Compassion, Shenlha Ökar (*gshen lha' od dkar*) and asked him how they could help the living beings submerged in the misery and sorrow of suffering. He advised them to act as guides to humankind in three successive ages of the world. To follow his advice the eldest brother, Dagpa, completed his work in the past world age. The second brother, Selwa, took the name Shenrab and became the teacher and guide of the present world age. The youngest brother, Shepa, will come to teach in the next world age.

The Lord Shenrab was born in the Barpo Sogye Palace to the south of Mount Yungdrung. He was born a prince, married while young and had children. At the age of thirty-one he renounced the world and lived in austerity, teaching the doctrine. During his whole life his efforts to propagate the Bön religion were obsructed by the demon Khyabpa Lagring (*khyab pa lag ring*). This demon fought to destroy or impede the work of Tonpa Shenrab until he was eventually converted. Once, pursuing the demon to regain his stolen horses, Tonpa Shenrab arrived in Tibet; it was his only visit to Tibet. There he imparted some instructions concerning the performance of rituals but, on the whole, found the land unprepared to receive fuller teachings. Before leaving Tibet he prophesied that all his teachings would flourish in Tibet when the time was ripe. Tonpa Shenrab departed this life at the age of eighty-two.

There are three written accounts of Tonpa Shenrab. The earliest and shortest one is known as *Dodu (mdo 'dus)*, 'Epitome of Aphorism.' The second, which is in two volumes, is called *Zermig (gzer mig)*, 'Piercing Eye.' These two accounts date from the tenth and eleventh centuries respectively. The third and largest is in twelve volumes and is known by its shortened title, *Zhiji (gzhi brjid)*, 'The Glorious.' It belongs to the category of scriptures known as 'spiritual transmission' (*bsnyan rgyud*). It is believed to have been dictated to Londen Nyingpo (*blo ldan snying po*) who lived in the fourteenth century.

The doctrines which were taught by Lord Shenrab and recorded in these three accounts are divided into two systems. One classification is called Gozhi Dzönga (*sgo bzhi mdzod lnga*), 'The Four Portals and the Treasury as Fifth.' These are:

1. Chabkar (*chab dkar*): 'White Waters': contains the esoteric or higher tantric practices.
2. Chabnag (*chab nag*): 'Black Waters': includes narratives and various rites, magic and ordinary rituals such as death, funeral, illness and ransom rituals.
3. Panyul (*'phan yul*): 'The Land of Pan': explains the monastic rules and gives exposition of philosophical concepts.
4. Ponse (*dpon gsas*): 'The Lordly Guide': contains the Great Perfection practices (Dzogchen; *rdzogs chen*).
5. Totog (*mtho thog*): 'The Treasury': it comprises the essential aspects of all the Four Portals.

The second classification is called Tegpa Rimgui Bön (*theg pa rim dgu'i bon*), 'The Bön of the Nine Successive Stages,' or simply 'The Nine Ways of Bön.' The first four are the cause (Gyuyi Tegpa; *rgyu yi theg pa*), the next four are the ways of result (Drabui Tegpa; *'bras bu'i theg pa*) and the ninth is the Great Perfection (Dzogchen; *rdzogs chen*). Examined individually their subject matter is as follows:

1. The way of the Shen of Prediction (Chashen Tegpa; *phywa gshen theg pa*): describes four different ways of prediction—sortilege (Mo; *mo*), as-

trology (Tsi; *rtsis*), ritual (To; *gto*) and examination of causes (Che; *dpyad*).

2. The way of the Shen of the Visual World (Nangshen Tegpa; *snang gshen theg pa*): explains the origin and nature of gods and demons living in this world, the methods of exorcism and ransoms of various kinds.
3. The way of the Shen of Illusion (Trulshen Tegpa; *'phrul gshen theg pa*): contains the rites for the disposing of adverse powers.
4. The way of the Shen of Existence (Sishen Tegpa; *srid gshen theg pa*): concerns the state after death (bardo) and methods of guiding living beings towards the final liberation or a better rebirth.
5. The way of the Virtuous Followers (Genyen Tegpa; *dge bsnyen theg pa*): guides those who follow the ten virtues and ten perfections.
6. The way of the Monkhood (Drangsong Tegpa; *drang srong theg pa*): describes the rules of monastic discipline.
7. The way of Pure Sound (Akar Tegpa; *a dkar theg pa*): gives an exposition of higher tantric practices, the theory of realization through the mystic circle (*mandala*) and the rituals which form an integral part of these practices.
8. The way of Primeval Shen (Yeshen Tegpa; *ye gshen theg pa*): stresses the need for a suitable master, place and occasion for tantric practices. Here the layout of the mystic circle is described in detail together with instructions for meditation on particular deities.
9. The Supreme Way (Lame Tegpa; *bla med theg pa*): the highest attainment of the Great Perfection (*rdzogs chen*).

THE PROGAPATION OF BÖN IN ZHANG ZHUNG AND TIBET

The first Bön scriptures were brought to Zhang Zhung by six disciples of Mucho Demdrug (*mu cho ldem drug*), the successor of Tonpa Shenrab. They were first translated into Zhang Zhung language and later into Tibetan. The works included in the Bönpo canon as we know it now are written in Tibetan language, but a number of them, especially the older ones, retain the titles and at times whole passages in the Zhang Zhung language.

Until the seventh century, Zhang Zhung existed as a separate state which comprised the land to the west of the Central Tibetan provinces of U (*dbus*) and Tsang (*gtsang*), generally known now as Western Tibet. The historical evidence is incomplete but there are some reliable indications that it may have extended over the vast area from Gilgit in the west to the lake of Namtso (*gnam mtsho*) in the east, and from Khotan in the north to Mustang in the south. The capital of Zhang Zhung was a place called Khyunglung Ngulkhar (*khyung lung dngul khar*), 'The Silver Palace of the Garuda Valley', the ruins of which are to be found in the upper Sutlej Valley to the southwest of Mount Kailash. The people of Zhang Zhung spoke a language which is classified among the Tibeto-Burmese group of Sino-Tibetan languages.

The country seems to have been ruled by a dynasty of kings which ended in the eighth century when the last king, Ligmirya (*lig myi rhya* or *lig mi rgya*), was assassinated by King Songsten Gampo and Zhang Zhung became an integral part of Tibet. Since the annexation, Zhang Zhung became gradually Tibetanized and its language, culture and many beliefs were integrated into the general frame of Tibetan culture. Through Zhang Zhung, which was geographically situated near the great cultural centres of Central Asia such as Gilgit and Khotan, many religious and philosophical concepts infiltrated Tibet.

With the increasing interest in Buddhist religion, the founding of Samye (*bsam yas*) Monastery in 779 C.E., and the establishment of Buddhism as the principal religion, the Bön religion was generally discouraged and serious attempts were made to eradicate it. However, the adherents of Bön among the nobility and especially among the common people, who for generations had followed the Bön beliefs, retained their religious convictions and Bön survived. During the seventh and eighth centuries which were particularly difficult times, many Bönpo priests fled Central Tibet, having first concealed their scriptures for fear of their destruction and to preserve them for future generations. Drenpa Namkha (*dran pa nam mkha'*), one of the greatest Bönpo personalities of that time, embraced Buddhist religion out of fear of being killed and for the sake of preserving in secret the Bönpo teachings.

From the eighth to the eleventh centuries we know practically nothing of the developments among the Bönpos. The revival of Bön began with the discovery of a number of important texts by Shenchen Luga (*gshen chen klu dga'*, 969-1035) in the year 1017 C.E. With him the Bön religion emerged as a fully systematized religious system. Shenchen Luga was born in the clan of Shen, which is descended from Kongtsha Wangden (*kong tsha dbang ldan*), one of the sons of Tonpa Shenrab. The descendants of this important Bönpo family still live in Tibet.

Shenchen Luga had a large following. To three of his disciples he entrusted the task of continuing three different traditions. To the first one, Druchen Namkha Yungdrung (*bru chen nam mkha' gyung drung*), who was born in the clan of Dru which migrated to Tibet from Drusha (*bru sha* is the Tibetan name for Gilgit), he entrusted the studies of cosmology (Dzopu; *mdzod phug*) and metaphysics (Gapa; *gab pa*). Namkha Yungdrung's disciple founded the monastery of Yeru Wensaka (*gyas ru dben sa kha*) in 1072. This monastery remained a great centre of learning until 1386 when it was badly damaged by floods and later on was abandoned. With the decline of Yeru Wensaka the Dru family continued to sponsor the Bön religion but it came to extinction in the nineteenth century when, for the second time, a reincarnation of the Panchen Lama was found in this family. (The first reincarnation was the Second Panchen Lama, b.1663, and the second the Fifth Panchen Lama, b. 1854.)

The second disciple, Zhuye Legpo (*zhu yas legs po*), was assigned to maintain the Dzogchen teachings and practices. He founded the monastery of Kyikhar Rizhing (*skyid mkhar ri zhing*). The descendants of the Zhu family now live in India.

The third disciple, Paton Palchog (*spa ston dpal mchog*), took responsibility for upholding the tantric teachings. The members of the Pa family moved from Tsang to Kham where they still live.

Meukhepa Palchen (*rme'u mkhas pa dpal chen*, b. 1052), who came from the Meu clan, founded the Zangri (*zang ri*) Monastery, which also became a centre for philosophical studies. Thus during the period from the eleventh to the fourteenth centuries the Bönpos had four important centres of studies, all of which were in Tsang Province.

At the beginning of the fifteenth century, the religious studies were strengthened by the founding of Menri Monastery in 1405 by the great Bönpo teacher, Nyame Sherab Gyaltsen (*mnyam med shes rab rgyal mtshan*, 1356-1415). Menri Monastery and the two mentioned below remained the most important centres of studies until the Chinese takeover of Tibet in 1959. The monastery of Yungdrung Ling was founded in 1834 and, soon afterwards, the monastery of Kharna (*mkhar sna*) both in the vicinity of Menri. With these monasteries as centres of study and religious inspiration, many monasteries were established throughout the whole of Tibet (except the Central Province of U), especially in Khyungpo, Kham, Amdo, Gyarong and Hor. By the beginning of the twentieth century there were three hundred and thirty Bönpo monasteries in Tibet.

Appendix 3
Biography of Lopon Tenzin Namdak

Lopon Tenzin Namdak (*slob dpon bstan 'dzin rnam dag*) was born in 1926 in Khyungpo Karu (*khyung po dkar ru*) in Kham province of Eastern Tibet. At the age of seven (1933) he entered Tingchen Monastery (*steng chen*) in the same district and in 1941 travelled to Yungdrung Ling (*gyung drung gling*), one of the two leading Bönpo monasteries in Central Tibet. Coming from a family famous for its artists, he was largely engaged here in helping to execute a series of wall paintings in the new temple at this monastery. In 1944 he went on pilgrimage to Nepal, including Solu-Khumbu, Kathmandu, Pokhara, and Mustang. In 1945 he returned to Yungdrung Ling to begin his studies in philosophy (tsennyi; *mtshan nyid*). From 1945 to 1950 he lived more or less a hermit's existence with his tutor and master Gangru Rinpoche (*sgang ru tshul khrims rgyal mtshan*) under whom he studied grammar (da; *sgra*), poetics (nyanga; *snyan ngag*), monastic discipline (dulwa; *'dul ba*), cosmology (dzopu; *mdzod phug*), and the stages of the path to enlightenment (salam; *sa lam*). Following his master's advice, in 1950 he went to Menri Monastery (*sman ri*, literally 'the medicine mountain') in Tsang Province in Central Tibet, in order to complete his

Nyame Sherab Gyaltsen

studies in preparation for the Geshe (*dge bshes*) degree examination, the Tibetan equivalent to a Doctor of Philosophy. In 1953 he obtained this degree from Menri.

From 1953 until 1957 he was the teaching master or professor (*slob dpon*) at Menri. He retired from this position in 1957 as conflict between the native Tibetans and the encroaching Chinese Communists increased in Central Tibet. Until 1960 he remained in retreat at Sezhig Monastery on the Dangra Lake in northern Tsang. After the March 10, 1959 Lhasa uprising against the Communist Chinese, many of the most famous lamas of Tibet, including the Dalai Lama and the Gyalwa Karmapa, were forced to flee their homeland. Following them, a flood of Tibetan refugees entered India and Nepal. In 1960 Lopon Rinpoche also sought to flee to India, but he was shot and wounded on the way by Chinese soldiers and was incarcerated in a Chinese prison for ten months. Finally he was able to make an escape and find his way to safety in Nepal, by way of the small principality of Mustang.

In 1961, while in Kathmandu, Lopon Rinpoche met and was befriended by the celebrated English Tibetologist David Snellgrove, who invited him to come to London. Thus Lopon came to serve as a visiting scholar at the University of London, and under a Rockefeller Foundation grant he resided for a time at Cambridge University. A collaboration with Professor Snellgrove resulted in the publication of *The Nine Ways of Bön* (London: Oxford University Press, 1967), which contains translated extracts from the famous *Zhiji* (*gzi brjid*), the most extensive hagiography of the Buddha Tonpa Shenrab. This was the first scholarly study of the Bönpo tradition to be made in the West. Lopon Rinpoche remained in England for three years (1961 to 1964). He made a second visit to Europe in 1969, when at the invitation of Professor Helmut Hoffmann he was a visiting scholar at Munich University, contributing to the monumental Tibetan-German-English dictionary being compiled there.

Among the nearly one hundred thousand Tibetan refugees who had fled the Chinese occupation of Tibet, a number belonged to the Bönpo tradition. Escaping from Tsang Province, the monks of Menri Monastery, which had been totally destroyed by the Communists, found themselves in the Kulu-Mandi district of Himachal Pradesh state in northwestern India. Impoverished, they were forced to secure a livelihood as road workers. Among their number was Sherab Lodro, the thirty-second abbot of Menri (1935-1963). Finding the road work hard and exhausting, many of the monks died or suffered from serious illness.

Lopon Tenzin Namdak consequently undertook the task of raising funds and finding land in order to establish a Bönpo settlement in India. With the financial help of the Catholic Relief Service, he purchased a piece of undeveloped forest land at Dolanji, near Solan in Himachal Pradesh. In 1967 the settlement was formally established and registered with the Indian Government under the name of the Tibetan Bönpo Foundation. About seventy families transferred there from Manali and each received a house and a small piece of land, the size depending on the number of people in the family in question. The Tibetan Bönpo Foundation possessed its own constitution and administration, with the Abbot of Menri acting as president. The new settlement at Dolanji was named Thobgyal Sarpa (*thob rgyal gsar pa*) after the village Thobgyal in Tsang Province which was located near Menri Monastery. Most of the Tibetans in the new settlement came from the Mt. Kailash region and Upper Tsang in the west, and from Hor, Kongpo, Derge, Amdo and Gyarung in the east of Tibet.

After the death in 1963 of the abbot of Menri, Sherab Lodro, the abbot of Yungdrung Ling, became the spiritual head of the Bönpo community in exile. He came to Dolanji with a group of monks and founded a new monastic community, overseeing the erection of some small houses and a small prayer chapel. In 1969 the successor to the deceased abbot of Menri was chosen by lot. The office fell to Lungtog Tenpai Nyima Rinpoche (*lung rtogs bstan pa'i nyi ma rin po che*), who thus became the thirty-third abbot of Menri. Following the death of the Yungdrung Ling abbot, Sangye Tenzin assumed the spiritual leadership of the Bönpos in exile. More houses were erected, as well as a library and an abbot's residence (labrang; *bla brang*). Monastic life was organized around the ordinances of the Vinaya (dulwa; *'dul ba*). The foundation for a main temple was laid in 1969 and completed in 1978. It was given the name of Pal Shentan Menri Ling (*dpal gshen bstan sman ri'i gling*). The whole complex was designated as the Bönpo Monastic Centre and formed part of the Tibetan Bönpo Foundation.

From 1970 to 1979 Lopon Rinpoche continued teaching and writing while residing at the Bönpo Monastic Centre, and in addition he was much engaged in the publishing in New Delhi of a large number of important Bönpo texts. From the time the first monks came to Dolanji in 1967, the teaching had been done by Lopon Sangye Tenzin, the former head teaching master at Menri, assisted by his successor, Lopon Tenzin Namdak, himself the founder of the settlement at Dolanji. When Sangye Tenzin died in 1968, Lopon Tenzin Namdak was assigned the full responsibility for the education of the younger generation of monks. By 1978 a sufficient number of Bönpo texts had been published so that classes could be organized around them in a curriculum. Thus a lama's college (shedrup; *bshad sgrub*) was established in 1978, organized under the guidance of Lopon Rinpoche who served as one of the two professors at the college. The official name of the college is Yungdrung Bön Shedrup Lobnyer Dude (*gyung drung bon bshad sgrub slob gnyer 'dus sde*).

The purpose of the new lama's college at Dolanji was to preserve the tradition of philosophy established and developed at Yeru Wensaka (*gyas ru dben sa kha*), where philosophical analysis and logic were applied to the understanding of *Do Nga Semsum (mdo sngags sems gsum)*, that is, to the teachings of the Sutras, the Tantras and

Dzogchen. Unlike the Nyingmapa tradition, the Bönpos developed a system of logic and debate specifically relating to the Dzogchen teaching. At Menri in Tibet, the monks studied the five scripture systems (Dozhung Nga; *mdo gzhung lnga*) in the philosophy college, but all instruction in Tantra and Dzogchen was done in private. The five scriptures, actually five collections of texts, are:

1. Tsema (*tshad ma*)—pramana or logic;
2. Parchin (*phar phyin*)—prajnaparamita or the Perfection of Wisdom Sutras;
3. Uma (*dbu ma*)—Madhyamaka philosophy;
4. Dzöpu (*mdzod phug*)—Abhidharma or cosmology; and
5. Dulwa (*'dul ba*)—Vinaya or monastic discipline.

However, at the revived Menri at Dolanji, students also study Tantra and Dzogchen in the college, as well as the above five scriptural systems which pertain to the Sutra level of teaching. Also included in the course of studies are the secular sciences (rignai; *rig gnas*), such as grammar, poetics, astrology, and so on. The college has a nine-year program of studies which prepares the student for the Geshe degree examination. The first group of young monks completed the course in 1986. Recently another Bönpo monastery and college has been established under Lopon Tenzin Namdak's direction in Nepal. Known as Triten Norbutse (*khri brtan nor bu rtse*), it is located near the famous hill of Swayambhu, west of Kathmandu.

In 1989, Lopon Tenzin Namdak made his third visit to the West, this time to England, America and Italy, at the invitation of the Dzogchen Communities in those countries. During the course of six months Lopon Rinpoche presented to interested Western students the Dzogchen teachings according to the Bönpo traditions of the Atri (*a khrid*) and the *Zhang Zhung Nyengyu (zhang zhung snyan rgyud)*.

Also, in the beginning of 1991, he visited Germany, England, Holland and Italy. During his visit to these countries, he gave discourses and teachings on various meditation systems and fields of study of the Bön tradition. Later that year he was invited by His Holiness the Dalai Lama to represent the Bön tradition at the Kalachakra Initiation in New York. In this way, Lopon Rinpoche has been spreading the Bönpo teachings in many countries. His permanent residences lie in Kathmandu (Nepal) and Dolanji (India).

Illustrations

1. Sipa Gyalmo *cover*

The central figure is Sipa Gyalmo (*srid pa rgyal mo*), a guardian deity with three heads and six arms who rides on a black mule. She is shown surrounded by flames on a lake of blood that is encircled by snakes moving through rocks. She carries swords, dagger, mirror, skull cup and hook.

There exist four emanations of Sipa Gyalmo. The peaceful rides a white mule; she has four heads and eight hands. The extended Sipa Gyalmo rides on a blue mule; the subduer Sipa Gyalmo rides on a red mule and the wrathful Sipa Gyalmo rides on a black mule. Here, the central figure shows the wrathful form. To the left is the subduer form on a red mule; to the right is an emanation of Sipa Gyalmo called Midrema (*mi dred ma*) riding on a yak. She is the particular protector of a cycle of Dzogchen teachings called Tsewang Bö Yulma (*tshe dbang bod yul ma*).

In front of Sipa Gyalmo is Nyame Sherab Gyaltsen (*mnyam med shes rab rgyal mtshan*), the founder of Menri Monastery.

In general Sipa Gyalmo is a protector of all Yungdrung Bön teachings and of this text.

This thangka is newly drawn by Tsering Yangpel (*tshe ring gyang 'phel*), who is the first cousin of Lopon Tenzin Namdak and is considered to be the foremost thangka painter still living in Tibet.

2. Tonpa Tritsug Gyalwa *frontispiece*

Tonpa Tritsug Gyalwa (*ston pa khri gtsug rgyal ba*) is Tonpa Shenrab in the form of a monk after his ordination at the age of thirty-two.

Drawing by Tsering Yangpel.

3. Shardza Tashi Gyaltsen *page 16*

Here Shardza is shown in his ordinary form. Above the central figure to the viewer's left is Shardza's yidam, Purba Drugse Chempa (*phur pa 'brug gsas chem pa*). At the top centre is the Dharmakaya Buddha Kuntuzangpo, who represents the nature of Shardza's achievement, his three kayas (bodies). At the top right is the emanation of the Siddha Tsewang Rigdzin (*tse dbang rig 'dzin*), the twin brother of Guru Rinpoche, son of Zhang Zhung Drenpa Namkha (*zhang zhung dran pa nam mkh'a*) and the Indian Brahmin girl Öden Barma (*'od ldan 'bar ma*) according to the Bön tradition.

At the bottom left is Shardza's form as a tantric practitioner. The bottom centre figure is the particular guardian for the Dzogchen lineage and practitioners, Yeshe Walmo (*ye shes dbal mo*). At bottom right is Shardza's form as a Dzogchen practitioner, in the style of a yogi. Surrounding Shardza are many animals, signifying his compassion towards all beings.

This image was made in Shardza's monastery of Shardza Ritrö (*shar rdza ri khrod*) in Dege.

4. Gyalyum Sherab Jamma *page 34*

This is the mother of all Buddhas, Gyalyum Sherab Jamma (*rgyal yum shes rab byams ma*), whose name translates as "Loving Goddess of Wisdom".

The figures surrounding Gyalyum Sherab Jamma show the six Na (*na*), which have the function of subduing disturbances. There is a garuda at the top. The upper pair of Na are half human, half bird; the middle pair ride on the mythological animals called *sha ra na*; and the lower pair ride on elephants.

Drawing by Tenzin Namdak.

5. Drenpa Namkha *page 50*

Here Drenpa Namkha (*dran pa nam mkh'a*) appears in the form of an early siddha of Bön.

This was drawn by Tsering Yangpel.

6. Tugkyi Trowo Tsocho Kagying *page 76*

Another of the five essential yidams of Bön, *thugs kyi khro bo gtso mchog mkha' 'gying* has three heads and six arms and stands in union with his consort. He presses down the male and female forms representing ignorance and desire and stands in a flaming fire. In front of him there is an offering in a skull of the five sense organs—eyes, ears, tongue, nose and skin. In general he represents the mind of the Buddha.

This image was copied by Tenzin Namdak from the original drawn by his great-grandfather.

7. Purba Drugse Chempa *page 78*

The uppermost image is a peaceful form of Purba Drugse Chempa (*phur pa 'brug gsas chem pa*) called Mapang Yingchen (*ma pang dbyings chen*) with consort. He has three heads and six arms and sits on a lotus cushion.

Beneath is the image of Trowo Drugse Chempa (*khro wo 'brug gsas chem pa*) with three heads and six arms in union with a consort, flying on a garuda.

The main image is of Purba Drugse Chempa. The upper part of the body is a wrathful deity with three heads and six arms in union with consort. The lower part of the body becomes a three-bladed dagger (*phur pa*). This dagger emerges from the head of a crocodile-like mythological animal. It is decorated with snakes and human heads and entrails. Beside the dagger Purba emanates two attendants. On the deity's right side is a human with the head of a makaru riding on a makaru. On his left side is a human with a boar's head riding on a boar. The dagger impales two figures, male and female, representing ignorance and desire.

The image has three main parts which represent the peaceful, wrathful and extremely wrathful aspects of this deity. Purba is one of the five essential yidams of the Bönpo and represents the activity of the Buddha.

Drawing by Tenzin Namdak.

8. Magyu *page 116*

The main figure of Magyu (*ma rgyud*) has seven heads, sixteen hands and eight legs. The right hands hold skull cups filled with the hearts of the gods. The left hands hold the blood of the eight classes of beings. Magyu is shown in union with his consort, Kyema Wötso (*kye ma 'od mtsho*). Beneath his feet are the eight different objects of desire (the kleshas). He stands on a lotus on a throne supported by snow lions representing anger. Above him is the peaceful form of Magyu called Kang-ying Karpo (*mkh'a 'gying dgar po*). He has four hands and sits in the lotus posture on a lotus cushion. Surrounding Magyu are the four dakinis representing the qualities of compassion, loving-kindness, equanimity and happiness. They have four heads and eight arms. Then there are eight more dakinis; four of them have three heads and eight arms as wrathful forms and the other four have two heads and four arms as peaceful forms. They represent further qualities.

Below the throne are sixteen offerers offering the two cycles of Magyu and other objects.

Altogether the complete cycle of Magyu has five thangkas, representing the base, the path and the fruit of this tantra. This image represents the fruit aspect.

This figure comes from the Gyarong Trochen (*rgya rong khro chen*) Palace. It was carved of wood, but was entirely destroyed in the Cultural Revolution.

9. Chenlha Migu *page 134*

The protector Chenlha Migu (*gcan lha mig dgu*) has three heads—to the right of the central head is a crow's head and to the left of the central head is a boar's head. Chenlha Migu has eight arms and stands on a nine-headed boar. He is the particular guardian of the Namgyal (*rnam rgyal*) cycle emanated by Tonpa Shen-rab. He is also in general a protector of Yungdrung Bön.

This image was recopied by Tenzin Namdak from the original drawn by his great-grandfather.

10. Nege Jampa *page 136*

This image shows Nege Jampa (*ne ge 'byam pa*), the important protector of the Walse (*dbal gsas*) cycle and later the protector of Nyame Sherab Gyaltsen (*mnyam med shes rab rgyal mtshan*), who was the founder of Menri Monastery. The protector rides on an otter and carries an axe in his right hand and a spear and black flag in his left. His function is to protect the Bönpo and the purity of the teachings and to give assistance to serious practitioners.

Drawing by Tenzin Namdak.

11. Tonpa Shenrab *page 138*

This is an image of Tonpa Shenrab (*ston pa gshen rab*) when he was king of the central part of Olmo Lungring. This form shows him after his coronation but before the age of thirty-two when he took vinaya vows.

Drawing by Tenzin Namdak.

12. Nyame Sherab Gyaltsen *page 148*

Nyame Sherab Gyaltsen (*mnyam med shes rab rgyal mtshan*) was the founder of Menri Monastery in Tibet. He was the nineteenth abbot of the monastery of Wensaka (*dben sa kha*), which was founded in the tenth century. After it was destroyed by flood, the monastery was moved higher into the mountains and renamed Menri.

This was drawn by Lopon Tenzin Namdak himself.

13. The Well-Situated Swastika Chorten *page 164*

The Yungdrung Köleg Chorten (*gyung drung bskod legs mchod rten*) is a very popular image for the Bönpo. It is one of the 360 chorten described in the Ziji (*gzi brjid*), the biography of Tonpa Shenrab. Only 120 of these can be made as the others are all chorten of emptiness and awareness and are not physical.

The structure of the chorten represents all the teachings of Sutra, Tantra and Dzogchen. From the perspective of Sutra, at the bottom the five steps represent the five elements of the realms of sentient beings. The square pedestal represents the four kindnesses of the Buddhas. The decorated beam represents the guardians between samsara and nirvana and the upper four steps represent the four kindnesses of compassion, loving-kindness, equanimity and happiness.

The vase represents the nature of the Buddha. The absence of corners shows the nature of equanimity. Above this there are thirteen steps that show the complete knowledge of the Buddha. As an aspect of the path these are known as the thirteen bhumis. The umbrella is protection from the elements of fire, wind and rain and shows the kindness of the Buddhas in protecting all sentient beings. At the very top there is a tigle that shows that everything returns to the natural state. The two horns represent the two truths, *thabs* and *shes rab*—method and wisdom. The flaming sword shows that all the passions are destroyed by this knowledge.

This style of chorten is unique to the Yungdrung Bön and is distinct from the Buddhist style.
Drawing by Tenzin Namdak.

Bibliographic Essay

by Per Kvaerne

The Dzogchen of Bön is dealt with in a very limited number of publications. The most extensive treatment is probably my own study of the Atri (*a khrid*) tradition which goes back to Me'u Gongdzo Ritro Chenpo (*rme'u dgongs mdzod ri khrod chen po*) (1038-1096), in which I translated several short biographies and a substantial part of a basic text by Gongdzo himself ("Bönpo Studies. The *A Khrid* System of Meditation," *Kailash* 1, 1 (1973): 19-50; 1,4 (1973): 247-332). A short summary of the entire text is to be found in my "'The Great Perfection' in the Tradition of the Bönpos," in L. Lancaster and W. Lai, eds., *Early Ch'an in China and Tibet*, Berkeley Buddhist Studies 5 (Berkeley: 1983), 367-392. A short extract from a longer text was published by David Snellgrove in his *The Nine Ways of Bön*, London Oriental Series 18 (London: 1967), 226-255.

Turning to the Buddhist variety of Dzogchen, there is a somewhat larger range of literature. Of prime importance is Samten Gyaltsen Karmay's study, *The Great Perfection. A Philosophical and Meditative Teaching of Tibetan Buddhism* (Leiden: Brill, 1988). This study concentrates on the early, formative centuries of the Buddhist Dzogchen tradition, and only devotes a few pages (201-205) to Dzogchen in Bön. Karmay's book is indispensable to anyone who has a serious interest in Dzogchen. Karmay has also published several articles; the reader is referred to his book for further references. For those who read German, a useful and interesting book is Franz-Karl Erhard, *"Flügelschläge des Garuda". Literar- und ideengeschichtliche Bemerkungen zu einer Liedersammlung des rDogs-chen*, Tibetan and Indo-Tibetan Studies 3 (Stuttgart: Franz Steiner, 1990). This is a translation and detailed study of a collection of spiritual songs by the Dzogchen master Shapkar Tsogdrug Rangdrol (zhabs dkar tshogs drug rang grol) (1781-1851). An important introduction to the doctrine and ritual of Dzogchen has been included by Peter Schwieger in his catalogue of the textual cycle of *Kuntu Sangpo Gongpa Sangtel* (*kun to bzang po'i dgongs pa zang thal*) (*Tibetische Handschriften und Blockdrucke* Teil 9 (Stuttgart: Franz Steiner, 1985), especially pp.lxv-lxxxiv).

A book which contains translations of several Dzogchen texts from the Buddhist as well as the Bönpo traditions is Giacomella Orofino, *Sacred Tibetan Teachings on Death and Liberation* (Bridport: Prism Press, 1990; Italian edition, *Insegnamenti tibetani su morte e liberazione*, Rome: 1985). Orofino's book has a brief but useful introduction.

One of the most important Tibetan scholars and spiritual masters of the Nyingmapa Dzogchen tradition is Longchen Rabjampa (klong chen rab 'byams pa) (1308-1364). A major work of his dealing with Dzogchen is *Ngelso Korsum* (*ngal gso skor gsum*) which has been translated in three volumes by Herbert V. Guenther as *Kindly Bent to Ease Us* (Emeryville, CA: Dharma Publishing, 1975-76). Guenther's erudition and complete mastery of the text are beyond dispute; his hermeneutical method, however, renders his translations controversial. Another impressive study is his *Matrix of Mystery. Scientific and Humanistic Aspects of rDzogs-chen Thought* (Boulder: 1984).

Finally, the numerous publications by Namkhai Norbu, himself an accomplished master of Dzogchen and a lama with a large number of pupils in the West, must be mentioned. His works have an authenticity which can only be imparted by an experienced adept. A particularly interesting work is his spiritual autobiography, edited by J. Shane, *The Crystal and the Way of Light: Sutra, Tantra, and Dzogchen* (New York: 1986).

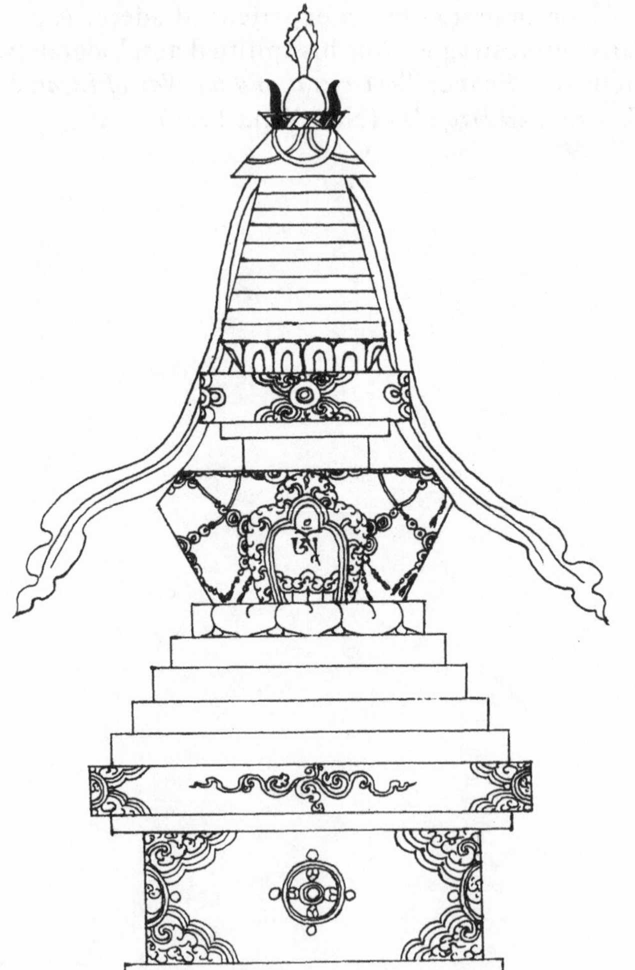

The Well-Situated Swastika Chorten

Tibetan Text

The Teaching of the Progressive Great Perfection Called the Heart Drops of Dharmakaya

ཁ་ གཅིག་

[illegible]

ཀྵྀ། ཨ་རྣ་སྭ་ཏནྟྲ་མ་ཧཱ་ལ་སཾ་པ་ཎ་ཀྵ་ཀྲི་ཡཱཾ་ལ་ལ་སཾ་སྐཧི་ཏེ་ཏྲ་བི་ཛྙ་ན་ཨཿ་བེ་ཛ་ད་རཾ།།

༄། །འོད་གསལ་རྫོགས་པ་ཆེན་པོའི་ལམ་གྱི་རིམ་པའི་ཁྲིད་ཡིག་ཀུན་ཏུ་བཟང་པོའི་སྙིང་ཏིག་ཅེས་བྱ་བ་བཞུགས། །

1

ཁ་ གཉིས་

༄༅།། །འོད་གསལ་རྫོགས་པ་ཆེན་པོའི་ལམ་གྱི་རིམ་པའི་ཁྲིད་ཡིག་ཀུན་ཏུ་བཟང་པོའི་སྙིང་ཏིག་ཅེས་བྱ་བ། །རིག་པ་རང་བྱུང་གི་སྟོན་པ་གཤེན་ལྷ་འོད་དཀར་ལ་ཕྱག་འཚལ་ལོ། བོན་སྐུའི་གནས་ལུགས་ནམ་མཁའི་དབྱིངས་ལྟར་བསམ་མི་ཁྱབ་པའི་རང་བཞིན་ནི། དངོས་དང་མཚན་འཛིན་སྤྲོས་པ་སྤངས་མིན་ཡེ་ནས་མི་མངའ་ཟང་ཀའི་ངང་། སྐུ་དང་ཡེ་ཤེས་རྣམ་ཀུན་འབད་མེད་ལྷུན་གྱིས་གྲུབ་པའི་མཆོག་ལྡན་པ། ཀུན་གྱི་ཐོན་རོལ་མངོན་པར་བྱང་ཆུབ་པ་དེ་བདག་བློའི་པད་མཚོར་རོལ། །གང་དེའི་གནས་ལུགས་མ་གཡོས་དང་ལས་རྩལ་སྣང་རོལ་པ་མངོན་ཤར་པ། མི་འགྱུར་གཡུང་དྲུང་བོན་བཅུར་རྫོགས་པའི་

2

ཁ་ གསུམ་

༄༅། སྐུ་འཕྲུལ་བཀོད་པའི་དཀྱིལ་འཁོར་ནི། ཞི་དང་ཁྲོ་བོ་མ་ངེས་རྣམ་འཕྲུལ་དཔག་མེད་སྟོན་པའི་མདའ་དབང་བདག །འོད་དཀར་འཆང་བ་བསྟན་སོར་བཅས་པས་བདག་གི་སྙིང་ལ་མཆོག་སྦྱིན་མཛོད། ཀུན་བཟང་དང་ལས་མི་གཉིས་གཅིག་ཀྱང་གྲོལ་བ་བཞི་ལྡན་ཉིད་འཛིན་གྱིས། མཐར་ཕྱག་བོན་སྐུའི་འོད་གསལ་མངོན་བྱས་འཕོ་མེད་ཡེ་ཤེས་རྫོགས་པའི་སྐུས། མཁའ་མཐར་གདུགས་ནས་སྲིད་པ་མཐའ་མར་བྱེད་ལ་འཛེམས་མེད་དཔའ་བོ་ཆེ། དྲན་པ་ནམ་མཁས་བདག་གི་སྐྱེ་བ་མ་འོངས་ཀུན་ཏུ་འང་རྗེས་སྐྱོང་ཤིག ཟབ་ཅིང་རྒྱ་ཆེའི་རྒྱུད་དོན་ནམ་མཁའ་རྒྱ་མཚོའི་རང་བཞིན་རྫོགས་དཀའ་བ། བློ་གྲོས་དྲི་མེད་མཁྱེན་རྨོན་ཡངས་པའི་དཔྱོད་ཡུལ་ཉིད་ལས་གཞན་གྱིས་ཅི། དེ་ལྟ་ན་ཡང་ལྷག་བསམ་དགེ་བས་དད་དང་བརྩོན་འགྲུས་རབ་བསྐུལ་ནས། །ཟབ་མོའི་ལམ་འདི་བདག་གིས་

3

ཁ་བཞི

བཤད་བྱ་སྐལ་བ་ལྡན་རྣམས་ཀྱི་ཐོར་ལོང་། །གང་གི་ཚེ་གདོད་མའི་དབྱིངས་ལྷུན་གྱིས་གྲུབ་པའི་ས་བྲང་དུ་ཡང་དག་པར་རྫོགས་པའི་སངས་རྒྱས་དཔལ་ཀུན་ཏུ་བཟང་པོས། །དགོངས་པ་བོན་གྱི་དབྱིངས་
ལས་མ་གཡོས་བཞིན་དུ་ཉིད་ལས་མི་གཞན་པའི་སངས་རྒྱས་ལྔ་དང་རིག་པ་རང་སྣང་གི་འཁོར་བསམ་གྱིས་མི་ཁྱབ་པ་རྣམས་ལ། །དགོངས་པ་ཟབ་མོའི་བརྒྱུད་ནས་གསུངས་པའི་འབྲས་བུའི་བོན་གྱི་
མཆོག་མཐར་ཐུག་པ་ནི་རང་བཞིན་རྫོགས་པ་ཆེན་པོའི་རྒྱུད་སྡེ་རྣམས་ཡིན་ལ། །དེ་ལའང་རྒྱ་ཆེ་བ་བསམ་གྱིས་མི་ཁྱབ་ཅིང་གྲངས་མང་བ་བརྗོད་ཀྱིས་མི་ལོང་བ་ཞིག་ཡོད་མོད་ཀྱང་། །དེ་དག་
གི་སྙིང་པོ་མཆོག་ཏུ་མི་འགྱུར་བའི་གནས་ངེས་པ་ནི་སྡེ་གསུམ་གྱི་རྩ་བ་དང་ཡན་ལག་གི་རྒྱུད་བཞི་བཅུ་རྩ་གཉིས། །མན་ངག་མཐའ་ཡས་པ་དང་བཅས་པ་རྣམས་ལས། །འདིར་སྐབས་ཡང་སྐལ་བ་དང་།
ལྡན་པ་དག་མངོན་པར་རྫོགས་པ་སངས་རྒྱས་པར་བྱེད་པའི་ཐབས་འོད་གསལ་རྫོགས་པ་ཆེན་པོའི་སྒྱུར་ལམ་ཟབ་མོ་བསྟན་པ་ལ་གསུམ། །དབང་རྣོན་ཚེ་གཅིག་ལ་དག་པའི་གཞི་དབྱིངས་སུ་སྒྲོལ་བ།
དབང་པོ་འབྲིང་བར་དོར་འཚང་རྒྱ་བ། །དབང་རྟུལ་རང་བཞིན་སྤྲུལ་པའི་སྐུའི་ཞིང་ཁམས་སུ་རྣམ་གྲོལ་དབུགས་ཆེན་འབྱིན་པའི་ཐབས་ངེས་པའོ། །སྐབས་དོན་དང་པོ་ལའང་གཉིས། །ཐོན་དུ་འགྲོ་

4

༄། །བཞི་རིམ་པ། དངོས་གཞི་གནད་ཀྱི་ཉམས་ལེན་ནོ། །དང་པོ་ལ་གཉིས། སྒོ་གསུམ་འཁོར་བར་འཇུག་པ་བཟློག་པ་འཁོར་འདས་རུ་ཤན་དབྱེ་བ། ཡུལ་ལུས་སེམས་ཀྱི་ཞེན་པ་བཟློག་པ་ལུས་ངག་ཡིད་
གསུམ་སྦྱོང་པའོ། དང་པོ་ལ་ཕྱི་ནང་གཉིས་ལས། དང་པོ་ཕྱི་ལྟར་དབྱེ་བ་ནི། སློབ་དཔོན་ལྡན་པ་ནམ་མཁའི་ཞལ་ནས། རིགས་དྲུག་སྡུག་བསྔལ་སྤྱོད་ཚུལ་ཐམས་ཅད་ནི། སེམས་ཀྱིས་རང་རྒྱུད་སྦྱོང་བ་
ཡིན་སྙམ་ནས། ལུས་ཀྱིས་འཕྱོ་རྒྱུག་འགྲོ་འདུག་རྣམ་འགྱུར་བྱ། ངག་གིས་སྨྲ་སྐད་ཤུགས་འབྱུང་འགག་མེད་སྒྲོགས། ངལ་དུབ་འགྱུ་བ་ཐུར་ཐག་ཆད་པ་རུ། ཡང་ཡང་བྱ་ལ་གནད་རྣམས་གསལ་
ཐེབས་བྱ། ཞེས་མིའི་རྒྱུ་འདུལ་དང་མཐོང་ཆོར་མེད་པའི་གནས་སུ་ཕྱིན་ཏེ། ཡུལ་དེའི་གཞི་བདག་ལ་གཏོར་མ་བྱིན་ནས་གྱ་ཚམ་གྱི་སྤྱོད་པ་ལ་ཀོ་ལོང་མི་བྱེད་པར་ཕྲིན་ལས་བཅོལ། སེམས་ཅན་ཐམས་
ཅད་ཀྱི་དོན་དུ་སྒོ་གསུམ་འཁོར་འདས་རུ་ཤན་དབྱེ་ལ། ཕྱིས་ནས་འཁོར་བར་མི་ལྡོག་པར་བྱ་སྙམ་དུ་སེམས་བསྐྱེད་ནས་ལུས་གཅེར་བུར་བྲུང་ལ། དམྱལ་བ། ཡི་དྭགས། བྱོལ་སོང་། མི། ལྷ་མིན།
ལྷ་སོགས་སོ་སོའི་སྤྱི་རྗེ་སློས་རིགས་རྣམས། ཡས་རིམ་བཞིན་ལྷུང་ཚུལ། མས་རིམ་བཞིན་ཐར་ཚུལ་དང་སྦྱར་ནས་ལུས་ཀྱི་བྱ་བ་གང་ཡིན་བྱེད། ངག་གིས་སྨྲ་སྐད་སྣ་ཚོགས་སྒྲོགས། སེམས་ཀྱིས་རྣམ་

5

ཁ་དྲུག

རྟོག་གང་དྲན་བསྐྱེད་ཅིང་རྩལ་སྦྱོང་བར་བྱའོ། དེ་བཞིན་དུ་སྔ་མ་ལས། ལུས་ཀྱིས་བདེ་གཤེགས་ཞི་ཁྲོའི་རྣམ་འགྱུར་བྱ། ངག་གིས་ཐུགས་ཀྱི་སྒྲ་དབྱངས་གང་དྲན་བརྗོད། ཡིད་ཀྱིས་ཡི་དམ་ལྷ་ཡི་ང་
རྒྱལ་གཟུང་། ཞེས་པ་ལྟར་འོལ་གླིང་དུ་སྟོན་པས་གཡུང་དྲུང་སེམས་དཔའ་རྣམས་ལ་བོན་གྱི་འཁོར་ལོ་རིམ་པ་གསུམ་བསྐོར་ཚུལ། རྩ་གསུམ་དུ་འཆི་མེད་ཀྱིས་ལྷ་ཀླུ་མིའི་རིག་འཛིན་རྣམས་ལ་གསང་སྔགས་ཀྱི་
བསྟན་པ་སྤེལ་ཚུལ། འོག་མིན་དུ་ཀུན་ཏུ་བཟང་པོས་རིགས་ལྔའི་བདེ་བར་གཤེགས་པ་རྣམས་ལ་རྫོགས་པ་ཆེན་པོའི་རྒྱུད་འཆད་ཚུལ་རྣམས་ལས་རིམ་བཞིན་སྒྲུབ་ཅིང་རང་རྒྱུད་ལ་བཀལ། དེ་ནས་འཁོར་
བ་ལྷུན་གྲུབ་ཀྱི་སྒོ་ཐིམ་ཚུལ། ལྷུན་གྲུབ་ཀྱི་སྣང་བ་ཀ་དག་གི་དབྱིངས་སུ་ཐིམ་ཚུལ། ཀ་དག་ལས་སླར་ཡང་འགྲོ་དོན་དུ་ལྷུན་གྲུབ་ཀྱི་ཞིང་ཁམས་བཀོད་ཚུལ་རྣམས་བྱས་ལ་སྣང་བ་གཏད་མེད་དུ་གཏོང་ངོ།
དེ་དག་གི་ཞག་ཚད་ནི། ཟླ་བ་གསུམ་མམ་གཉིས་སམ་གཅིག་ལ་འབད་པར་བྱ་སྟེ། གསེར་གྱི་ཐུར་མ་ལས། ཟླ་བ་གཅིག་གིས་ཡོན་ཏན་སྐྱེ། ཞེས་སོ། དགོས་པ་ནི། རང་གི་ཤེས་པ་སྐད་ཅིག་མ་
འདི་འཁོར་འདས་ཐམས་ཅད་ཀྱི་རྩ་བ་ཡིན་པས། རིགས་དྲུག་གི་ལས་སྤྱོད་རྣམས་བཙན་ཐབས་སུ་སྐྱོང་ནས་སྤྱོད་པ་བྱས་ཏེ་མཁན་པོ་རྩད་གཅོད་པས། སེམས་ལ་གཏུག་གིས་ཐུག་ནས་དེ་དག་ཉམས་ཀྱི་

6

ཞ

༄། ནང་དབྱེན་དུ་ཤེས། དེ་ཤེས་པས་ད་ལྟའི་རིགས་དྲུག་གི་སྣང་ཚུལ་འདི་ཡང་སེམས་ཀྱི་རྣམ་འགྱུར་ཙམ་དུ་ཤེས། དེ་ཤེས་པས་སེམས་ཀྱི་ངོ་བོ་སྟོང་པ་ཡིན་པར་ཤེས་ནས་འཁོར་བའི་རྒྱུ་ལྡོག
དེ་ལྡོག་པས་འབྲས་བུ་འཁོར་བ་རང་སོག་ནས་ཕྱིས་འཁོར་བ་ལ་མི་འདུག་སྟེ། དོན་རྒྱུད་ལས། ཕྱིས་ནས་འཁོར་བར་ཕྱི་མི་ལྡོག་པར་འགྱུར། ཞེས་སོ། །གཉིས་པ་ནང་ལྟར་དབྱེ་བ་ནི། རིགས་དྲུག
རང་སྦྱོང་གི་གདམས་པ་སྟེ། ལག་ལེན་ཟུར་དུ་ཡོད་པ་ལྟར་ཉམས་སུ་བླང་ངོ་། གཉིས་པ་སྒོ་གསུམ་སྦྱང་བ་ལ་གསུམ་ལས། དང་པོ་ལུས་སྦྱང་བ་ནི། གསེར་གྱི་ཐུར་མའི་རྒྱུད་
ལས། ལུས་ནི་རྡོ་རྗེའི་གདམས་པ་བྱ། མིག་འབྲས་མ་ཡེངས་མཁའ་ལ་གཏད། ཞག་གསུམ་དོས་པའི་ཚད་དང་ལྡན། ཡོན་ཏན་གནས་སྐབས་མཐར་ཐུག་གོ། ཞེས་ལངས་ལ་ཁང་མཐིལ་གཉིས
བྲད་ཅིང་པུས་མོ་བསྐྱོད། སྒྲིད་པ་དྲང་པོར་བསྲང་། ལག་པ་གཉིས་སྤྱི་བོར་རྒྱངས་བཞིན་དུ་ཐལ་མོ་སྤྱི་བོར་མ་རེག་པར་སྦྱར། མཁྲིན་པ་ཨོལ་མདུད་ནོན་པར་བྱས་ཏེ་ལུས་རྡོ་རྗེ་སྟོན་པོ་རྩེ་གསུམ་པ
མི་འབར་བ་ཞིག་ཏུ་སྒོམ་ལ་ཅི་ནུས་འདུག མི་ནུས་པར་གྱུར་ཚེ་རྒྱབ་ཏུ་འགྱེལ་བཙུག་ཅིང་དག་ཏུ་ཏ་ཞེས་དབུགས་ཐག་ཆད་པ་ལྟར་བྱ་ལ་ཡང་ཡང་སྦྱོང་ངོ་། དེ་ལྟར་བགྱིས་པ་ལ་དགོས་པ་གསུམ་སྟེ། །

7

ཐུན་མོང་དུ་ངལ་དུབ་ཀྱིས་ལུས་སྒྲིབ་འདག ཁྱད་པར་ལ་ལུས་རྡོ་རྗེ་མི་འབར་བར་མཐོང་བས། གདོན་བགེགས་ཀྱི་བར་ཆད་ཞི། མཐར་ཐུག་ལུས་ཀྱི་མངོན་ཞེན་ལྡོག་སྟེ་སྤྲུལ་སྐུར་འགྲུབ་པར
འགྱུར་བ་ནི། ཡབ་སྲས་དོན་རྒྱུད་ལས། ཡང་ཡང་སྦྱང་པས་ཐུན་མོང་ལུས་སྒྲིབ་དག བར་ཆད་ཞི་ཞིང་ལུས་ཀྱི་མངོན་ཞེན་ལྡོག མཐར་ཐུག་སྤྲུལ་པའི་སྐུ་དང་གཉིས་མེད་འགྱུར། །ཞེས་སོ།
གཉིས་པ་ངག་སྦྱོང་བ་བསྟན་པའི་ཕྱིར་རྒྱུད་ཀྱི་རྒྱལ་པོ་ལས། ངག་ནི་ཧཱུྃ་ཞེས་གནས་པ་ལ། རྒྱས་གདབ་པ་དང་རྩལ་སྦྱོང་དང་། མཉེན་བཙལ་ལམ་དུ་གཞུག་པ་ཡི། དེ་ལྟར་ངག་སྦྱངས་སེམས་ལ
ཕན། ཞེས་རྣམ་པ་བཞིར་བསྟན་པ་ལས། དང་པོ་རྒྱས་གདབ་པ་ལ་གསུམ། ངེས་པའི་ཚིག་ནི། མ་དག་པའི་སེམས་རང་ལ་སྣང་བའི་སྣང་བ་དང་ལུས། སངས་རྒྱས་ཀྱི་ཐུགས་གསང་བ་ཡེ་ཤེས་ཀྱི་ངོ་
བོ་ཧཱུྃ་གི་རྣམ་པར་གནས་པའི་ཡི་གེའི་བྱིན་གྱིས་དག་པའི་སྣང་བར་རྒྱས་གདབ་པས་ན་རྒྱས་གདབ་ཅེས་བྱའོ། གཉིས་པ་ཉམས་ལེན་ལ་ཕྱི་ནང་གཉིས་ལས། ཕྱི་སྣང་བ་ལ་རྒྱས་གདབ་པ་ནི། ལུས་གནད་
འདུག་ལ་སྔ་ལྟར་བྱ་བའམ་ཡང་ན་སྐྱིལ་མོ་ཀྲུང་བཅས་ཏེ། མིག་བར་སྣང་ལ་གཏད། སྙིང་གར་ཧཱུྃ་སྔོན་པོ་བསམས། དག་ཏུ་ཧཱུྃ་ཧཱུྃ་ཧཱུྃ་ཞེས་གདངས་འགྱུར་འཕྲུལ་རིང་པོས་བརྗོད་པའི་སྙིང་གའི་ཧཱུྃ་ལས

8

ཞ

༄། ཧཱུྃ་གྲངས་མེད་པ་འཕྲོས་ཏེ་སྣ་བུག་གཡས་ནས་ཐོན། ཕྱིའི་སྣང་བ་བརྟན་པ་སྣོད་གཡོ་བ་བཅུད་ཐམས་ཅད་ཧཱུྃ་དུ་ལམ་ལམ་སོང་བར་བསམ་ཞིང་། རླུང་སེམས་སྣང་གསུམ་གཅིག་ཏུ་བསྲེ
སྟེ། སེམས་ཧཱུྃ་གི་རྣམ་པར་ཤར་བ། རླུང་སྒྲ་ཧཱུྃ་དུ་གྲགས་པ། སྣང་བ་ཧཱུྃ་གི་རང་བཞིན་དུ་སོང་བར་བསམ་པའོ། གཉིས་པ་ནང་ཕུང་པོ་ལ་རྒྱས་གདབ་པ་ནི། དག་ཏུ་ཧཱུྃ་ཧཱུྃ་ཞེས་སྒྲ་ཕྱུང་
བཟློད་པས་ཕྱི་རོལ་གྱི་ཧཱུྃ་རྣམས་སྣ་བུག་གཡོན་ནས་ཞུགས་ཏེ་ཁོང་པའི་ནང་དུ་ཚུད་ནས། ནང་ཁྲོལ་ཤ་ཁྲག་གང་ཡང་མེད་པ་ལུས་ཕྱི་ནང་ཀུན་ཧཱུྃ་གིས་མེར་མེར་གང་བར་བསམ་མོ། གསུམ་པ་དགོས
པ་ནི། ཡུལ་སྣང་རང་བཞིན་མེད་པར་གྲོལ་བ་དང་། ལུས་ཀྱི་འབྱུང་བ་དག་སྟེ་ནོས་བཅས་ཟག་པ་མེད་པར་གྲོལ་བའོ། འབྱོངས་པའི་ཚད་ནི་གསེར་གྱི་ཞུན་མ་ལས། ཕྱིའི་སྣང་བ་ཐམས་ཅད་ཧཱུྃ་དུ
ལམ་ལམ་འཆར་བ་དང་། །ནང་གི་ཕུང་པོ་ཧཱུྃ་གིས་རེང་ངེ་བ་སྐམ་བྱེད་ན་རྒྱས་གདབ་པ་འབྱོངས་པའི་རྟགས་ཡང་དག་པའོ། ཞེས་སོ། གཉིས་པ་རྩལ་སྦྱོང་ལ་གསུམ་ལས། ངེས་ཚིག་ནི། སེམས
རང་ལ་སྣང་བའི་སྣང་བ་རང་གི་རྩལ་གྱིས་བཤིགས་ཤིང་རྩལ་སྦྱོང་བས་རྩལ་སྦྱོང་ངོ་། གཉིས་པ་ཉམས་ལེན་ལ་གཉིས་ཀྱི། ཕྱི་སྣང་བ་ལ་སྦྱོང་བ་ནི། དག་ཏུ་ཧཱུྃ་ཧཱུྃ་ཧཱུྃ་ཞེས་དྲག་ལ་གཏུམ་པར་བརྗོད་

9

པས། རིག་པའི་ཧཱུྃ་ལས་ཧཱུྃ་མཐིང་ནག་དྲག་པོའི་ཚད་ཐོག་ལྟ་བུ། རྩུབ་པའི་ཚད་བསྐལ་མེ་ལྟ་བུ། རྣོ་བའི་ཚད་མཚོན་ཆའི་འཁོར་ལོ་ལྟ་བུ། མྱུར་བའི་ཚད་གློག་ལྟ་བུ་མང་པོ་ཐོལ་ཐོལ་བྱུང་ནས་རི་དང་ཁང་ཁྱིམ་ཐོགས་རེག་གི་སྣང་བ་ཤར་བ་མཐའ་དག་ཕར་ཐལ་ཚུར་ཐལ་དུ་ཞུག་ནས་ཁྲལ་ཁྲོལ་ཁལ་ཁོལ་མེད་པར་བསམ་མོ། གཉིས་པ་ནང་ཕུང་པོ་ལ་སྦྱོང་བ་ནི། དག་ཏུ་ཧཱུྃ་ཧཱུྃ་ཞེས་བརྗོད་པས་ཧཱུྃ་མགོ་གང་བ་ཁ་དོག་སྔོ་བའི་མཚན་ཉིད་བཻ་ཌཱུརྻའི་མདོག་ལྟ་བུ། །ཤུགས་དང་ལྡན་པའི་མཚན་ཉིད་གནམ་ལྕགས་ཐོག་ལྟ་བུ། རེག་བྱ་ཚ་བའི་མཚན་ཉིད་བསྐལ་པའི་མེ་དཔུང་ལྟ་བུ། གང་ཡང་འཇོམས་པའི་མཚན་ཉིད་རྡོ་རྗེ་ཕལ་ལམ་ལྟར་བུ། མཚན་ཉིད་བཞི་ལྡན་གྱིས་ལུས་ཕྱིར་ཐལ་ནང་ཐལ་ཁོལ་རྩེ་མེད་པར་ཞུག་པས་རྡུལ་ཕྲན་དུ་དག་པར་བསམ་མོ། གསུམ་པ་དགོས་པ་ནི། སྣང་བ་བདེན་མེད་དུ་དག་པ་དང་། ནད་གདོན་ཞི་ཞིང་ལུས་འོད་གསལ་དུ་ཡལ་བར་བྱེད་དོ། འབྱོང་བའི་ཚད་ནི་གསེར་ཞུན་ལས། སྣང་བ་ལ་རྩལ་སྦྱངས་པས་སྣང་བ་ཁྲལ་མ་ཁྲོལ་དུ་འདུག་པའི་ཉམས་འཆར་ཞིང་ ཕུང་པོའང་ལྷུག་ཆགས་ལྟ་བུའི་སྣང་བ་འཆར་བ་བྱུང་ན་རྩལ་སྦྱོང་འབྱོངས་པའི་རྟགས་ཡིན་ནོ། ཞེས་སོ། གསུམ་པ་མཉེན་བཅལ་ལ་གསུམ་ལས། ངེས་ཚིག་ནི། སེམས་རང་ལ་རང་

10

༄། གིས་མཉེན་བཅལ་ཅིང་དབང་བསྒྱུར་བས་མཉེན་བཅལ་ལོ། གཉིས་པ་ཉམས་སུ་ལེན་ཐབས་ནི། མདུན་དུ་ཤིང་བུ་ལ་སོགས་དམིགས་རྟེན་རིང་བ་བཙུགས། དག་ཏུ་ཧཱུྃ་ཧཱུྃ་ཞེས་སྐད་ལ་རིང་བར་བརྗོད་པས་སྙིང་གའི་ཧཱུྃ་ལས་ཧཱུྃ་གི་ཕྲེང་བ་ཞུ་གུ་རྒྱུད་དུ་འབྲེལ་བ་དམིགས་རྟེན་གྱི་རྩ་བ་ནས་རིམ་པར་དཀྲིས་ཤིང་རྩེ་མོར་སླེབ་པ་དང་ཧཱུྃ་ཕྱུ་མ་དེ་མདུན་ཚུགས་སུ་གནས་པ་ལ་ཤེས་པ་གཏད་དེ་ཧཱུྃ་གི་ཕྲུ་དལ་པོས་ལེན། རྣམ་རྟོག་ལྷང་བ་ན་གཅིག་ལ་གཅིག་ཐིམ་དུ་སྙིང་གའི་ཧཱུྃ་ལ་ཐིམ་པར་བསམ་མོ། གསུམ་པ་དགོས་པ་ནི། ཡང་ཡང་སྦྱངས་པས་ཕྱི་ནང་རྣམ་རྟོག་གི་འགྲོ་ཕྱོག་ལམ་དུ་ལོངས་ནས་སེམས་ལ་ཤིན་ཏུ་སྦྱངས་པའི་ཡོན་ཏན་ཐོབ་སྟེ་དམིགས་པ་གང་དུའང་བསྒྱུར་ཐུབ་པ་འོང་ངོ། བཞི་པ་ལམ་གཞུག་ལ་གསུམ་ལས། ངེས་ཚིག་ནི། ཡུལ་ལུས་སེམས་གསུམ་སྦྱངས་ནས་འོད་གསལ་གཉུག་མ་ཉིད་ཀྱི་ཐོག་ཏུ་ཕྱིན་པས་ན་ལམ་གཞུག་ཅེས་བྱའོ། གཉིས་པ་ཉམས་སུ་ལེན་ཐབས་ནི། རང་ལུས་རླུང་སེམས་གཅིག་ཏུ་བྱས་པའི་ཧཱུྃ་སྔོན་པོ་གྲུ་གང་བ་ཞིག་ཕར་འཕྱོག་ཚུར་འཕྱོག་སྲིན་བུའི་འགྲོས་ཀྱིས་མཐོང་ཡུལ་གྱི་རི་དང་ཡུལ་སྤྱོངས་ནས། མི་མཐོང་ཞིང་རྒྱུས་ཡོད་པའི་ཡུལ་དང་གཞན་ཡང་རི་ལུང་མཐའ་མེད་དུ་སོང་བར་བསམ་ཞིང་། འགྲོ་ལུགས་དང་མཐུན་པའི་ཧཱུྃ་དལ་བུས་

11

བརྗོད། སྐབས་སུ་ཕཊ༔ སྒྲས་བཅད་ལ་དམིགས་མེད་དུ་བཞག་ཅིང་གཉུག་མ་ཉིད་ངོས་བཟུང་། སླར་ཡང་ཧཱུྃ་ཧཱུྃ་ཞེས་བརྗོད་ཅིང་འོལ་མོའི་གླིང་དང་ཤར་ཕྱོགས་མངོན་དགའ་ལ་སོགས་པ་དག་པའི་ཞིང་ཁམས་རྣམས་སུ་ཡང་དཔག་ཆེན་གྱིས་མདའ་འཕེན་པ་བཞིན་དུ་ཕྱིན་པར་བསམ་ལ་དམིགས་མེད་དུ་ལ་བཟླའོ། དེས་ཡུལ་གྱི་བག་ཆགས་སྦྱོང་ཞིང་རྣམ་རྟོག་རང་ཤུགས་ཀྱིས་འགགས་ནས་བདེ་གསལ་མི་རྟོག་པའི་ཉམས་སྐྱེའོ། གསེར་གྱི་ཞུན་མ་ལས། མཉེན་བཅལ་བ་དང་ལམ་དུ་ཞུགས་པ་ལ་སོགས་ལ་སྦྱངས་པས། ཤེས་པ་གཏོང་ན་འགྲོ་ཞིང་གཏད་ན་ལམ་ལམ་སྡོད་པ་འབྱུང་། གཟུང་འཛིན་འཕྲོ་རྟོག་གི་དབང་དུ་སོང་ན་མཉེན་བཅལ་ལམ་ཞུགས་མ་འབྱོང་པའི་རྟགས་སོ། ཞེས་རྟགས་ཚད་སྔར་ལ་ཉམས་སུ་བླང་ངོ། དག་སྦྱོང་གི་དགོས་པ་ནི། ངག་གི་སྒྲིབ་པ་འདག་ཅིང་རྫོགས་སྐུར་འགྲུབ་པ་ནི། དོན་རྒྱུད་ལས། །དེ་ཡིས་ངག་གི་སྡིག་དག་བར་ཆད་ཞི། ངག་གི་མངོན་ཞེན་ཕྱོག་ནས་མཐར་ཐུག་ཏུ། ལོངས་སྤྱོད་རྫོགས་པའི་སྐུ་དང་གཉིས་མེད་འགྱུར། ཞེས་སོ། གསུམ་པ་སེམས་སྦྱོང་བ་ལ་གཉིས། སེམས་བཟུང་ཐབས་དཀྱུས་སེམས་ཉིད་གཏན་ལ་ཕབ་པ། བྱུང་གནས་འགྲོ་གསུམ་གྱིས་

12

ཀ

༄། སེམས་ཀྱི་གཞི་རྩ་བཅད་པའོ། དང་པོ་ནི། གསེར་གྱི་ལུང་དོན་ཆེ་བ་ལས། གང་ཞིག་ལས་འཕྲོ་དང་ལྡན་པ་དེས། རང་གི་སེམས་སྟོང་པར་བརྟག་ལ་བཙལ། སྣང་བར་བརྟག་ལ་བཙལ། སྣང་ལ་རང་བཞིན་མེད་པར་བརྟག་ལ་བཙལ། སྣང་སྟོང་མཐའ་ལས་འདས་པར་བརྟག་ལ་བཙལ། ཡོད་པར་བརྟག་ལ་བཙལ། མེད་པར་བརྟག་ལ་བཙལ། །གཉིས་ག་མ་ཡིན་པར་བརྟག་ལ་བཙལ། གཞི་ལ་བརྟག་ལ་བཙལ། གཞི་སྟོར་བྲལ་མེད་པས་བཙལ་མི་བཙལ་གཉིས་ཀྱི་ཐ་སྙད་མེད་པར་བཞག་པ་དང་དགུས་བཙལ་བར་བྱའོ། ཞེས་སེམས་ཉིད་མ་རྟོགས་པའི་དུས་ན་བཙལ་དུ་ཡང་ཡོད་པར་སྟོན་ཏེ། དེ་ཡི་དང་པོ་ནི། ལུས་ཆ་ལུགས་ལྷ་ལྡན་དུ་བྱས་ལ་བསམ་དྲན་གྱི་རྩ་བ་རང་གི་སེམས་འདི་དངོས་པོ་དང་མཚན་མ་ཅན་དུ་འདུག་གམ་མི་འདུག་ཁ་ནང་དུ་ཕྱོགས་ནས་བརྟག་པས། བརྟག་བྱ་བརྟག་བྱེད་ཀྱི་སེམས་གཉིས་ཀ་ལ། ཅི་ཡང་མེད་པ་ནམ་མཁའ་བཞིན་སྟོང་ཧར་གྱིས་སོང་བ་ནི་ངོ་བོ་སྐྱེ་མེད་ཀྱི་སེམས་ཟིན་པའོ། གཉིས་པ་ནི། ཅིར་ཡང་མེད་པ་དེ་ན་དེ་ལས་ཕྱིས་མེད་པར་བྱེད་དུ་འདུག་གམ་མི་འདུག དེ་སྐད་བའམ་གཞོམ་དུ་ཡོད་མེད་བརྟག་པས་གཉེན་པོས་བཤིག་ཅིང་དགག་ཏུ་མ་བཏུབ་པའི་དྭངས་གསལ་གྱི་སྙིང་པོ་ཅན

བདུན

གསལ་གསལ་ཧྲིག་ཧྲིག་ཕྱུག་ཕྱུག་ཏུ་བྱུང་བ་དེ་ནི་རང་བཞིན་འགག་མེད་ཀྱི་སེམས་ཟིན་པའོ། གསུམ་པ་ནི། དེ་ལྟར་བརྟགས་པས་སེམས་སྟོང་སྟེ་དངོས་མཚན་མ་གྲུབ། གསལ་ཏེ་བསྒྲིབས་པ་མེད་པའི་ཡེ་ཤེས་ཉིད་ལ་ཉིད་ཤར། གསལ་སྟོང་གཉིས་ཀའི་མཐའ་ལས་འདས་པ། འདི་ཞེས་མིང་འདོག་ཏུ་མེད་པའི་དོན་ཉམས་སུ་མྱོང་བ་ནི་མཚན་ཉིད་གཉིས་མེད་ཀྱི་སེམས་ཟིན་པའོ། བཞི་པ་ནི། སྣང་བ་འདི་གདོད་ནས་མ་གྲུབ་སྟེ། ད་ལྟ་དངོས་སུ་སྣང་བ་འདི་ནི་འཁྲུལ་པའི་སྣང་བ་ཡིན་ཅིང་ཡང་དག་དོན་ལ་མེད། དཔེར་ན་རྨི་ལམ་གྱི་རྣམ་བཞིན་ནོ། གལ་ཏེ་བདེན་པར་གྲུབ་པ་ཡོད་ན་རྟུལ་ཕྲན་དུ་བཤིག་ནས་མཁའ་ལ་ཐིམ་པའི་རྗེས་སུ་དེ་ཡོད་དགོས་ཀྱང་མེད་པའི་ཕྱིར་རོ། དེ་ལྟར་བརྟག་པའི་སྣང་ཡང་བདེན་མེད་སྒྱུ་མ་ལྟ་བུའི་ཉམས་ཤར་བ་ནི་རོལ་པ་འགག་མེད་ཀྱི་སེམས་ཟིན་པའོ། ལྔ་པ་ནི། སེམས་འདི་མེད་ན་སྣང་བ་འདི་སུ་ལ་སྣང་། སྣང་བའི་མཁན་པོ་སུས་བྱེད། མིང་སུས་འདོག བདེ་སྡུག་སུས་མྱོང་དེ་ཀུན་སེམས་ཀྱིས་བྱེད་པས་ཁོ་ཡོད། མེད་མ་མྱོང་། ཁོ་ཡོད་པས་ཐམས་ཅད་ཡོད་པ་ཡིན། ཁོ་མིན་གཞན་དུ་འགྱུར་པ་རྡུལ་ཙམ་ཡང་མེད། ས་ས་མིན། རྡོ་རྡོ་མིན། སྣང་

ཁ

༄། བ་སྣང་བ་མིན། སེམས་ཀྱི་འཁྲུལ་སྣང་ཡིན། དེ་ལྟར་རྟོགས་པ་ནི་ཀུན་བྱེད་རྒྱལ་པོའི་སེམས་ཟིན་པའོ། དྲུག་པ་ནི། སེམས་འདི་ཡོད་ན་དངོས་སུ་སྣང་རུང་བ་ལ་མི་སྣང་སྟེ། ཁོ་ཡོད་མ་མྱོང་། ཡོད་ནས་མངོན་དུ་འབྱུང་བའི་དུས་མེད། དུས་གསུམ་དུ་མེད་པ་འདི་ཀ་རང་ཡིན། མེད་པའི་སྙིང་པོ་རིག་པ་ཡོད། རིག་པ་ལ་མིང་ཚིག་ཡི་གེ་གང་གིས་ཀྱང་མཚོན་ཀྱང་ཁོའི་ཐོག་ཏུ་མི་ཕྱིན། ཕྱིན་པ་མེད། དེ་ལྟར་བརྟག་པས་ཀླུགས་པས་བུ་རམ་གྱི་རོ་མྱོང་བ་ལྟ་བུ་རྟོགས་ན་བསམ་བརྗོད་དང་བྲལ་བའི་སེམས་ཟིན་པའོ། བདུན་པ་ནི། སེམས་ཡོད་པ་འང་མིན་ཏེ་དངོས་པོ་མེད། མེད་པ་འང་མིན་ཏེ་སྟོང་ཐབས་དང་བྲལ། གཉིས་ཀ་འང་མིན་ཏེ་ཡོད་མེད་གཉིས་སུ་མེད། གཉིས་ཀ་མ་ཡིན་པའང་མིན་ཏེ་གང་ཡང་ཁས་ལེན་མེད་པའི་བཞག་ས་ལས་འདས། དེ་ལྟར་བརྟག་པའི་ཐྲོས་པའི་མཐའ་གཅིག་གིས་གཅིག་ཆོད་ནས་མཐའ་ཐམས་ཅད་དང་བྲལ་བ། གང་དང་ཡང་ཐུན་མོང་དུ་མ་གྱུར་པའི་དོན་རྟོགས་པ་ནི། ཐྲོས་མེད་མཐའ་འདས་ཆེན་པོའི་སེམས་ཟིན་པའོ། བརྒྱད་པ་ནི། འོ་ན་ཁྱོད་ཀྱི་སེམས་དེ་ལ་མིང་ཅི་སྐད་ཟེར་བྱས་པས་བརྟགས་པས། སྔ་མ་ལས། མི་རྟོག

བརྒྱད

16

ཨཱ་ཀ་ཨཱ་ཐ

བཏག་ཏུ་མེད་དེ་རྟོག་པའི་སྤྱོད་ཡུལ་མིན། ཞེས་ཅིའང་རྟོག་ཏུ་མེད་པས་མིང་འདོག་ཏུ་ཟད། དཔེས་མཚོན་པས་ཀྱང་མཚོན་མ་ནུས། འོ་ན་སྨྲར་ཐོག་ཧེ་ཁོ་རང་གིས་ཁོ་རང་ལ་ཅར་
ཐོག་ཏུ་དཔྱད་དང་དཔྱད་པས་ཉམས་སུ་མྱོང་ཡང་མིང་དོན་འདི་ཞེས་བྱ་བ་མེད་པར་རྟོགས་པ་ནི། མིང་མེད་བློ་འདས་ཀྱི་སེམས་ཟིན་པའོ། དགུ་པ་ནི། སེམས་ཉིད་ལ་རང་བཞིན་
མེད་པས་བཙལ་ཀྱང་རྙེད་པའི་རྒྱུ་མེད། མ་བཙལ་ཀྱང་སྟོར་བྲལ་མེད། ཡེ་ནས་རང་ལ་ཡོད། རང་ལ་གནས། རང་རང་ཡིན། རང་སྟོར་རྒྱུ་འདུག་གམ། རང་གིས་
རང་བཙལ་བས་རྙེད་སྲིད་དམ། །དེས་ན་སེམས་ཉིད་ལ་རང་བཞིན་མེད་པས་བཙལ་མི་བཙལ་གྱི་ཐ་སྙད་མེད། དུས་གསུམ་དུ་རང་དང་བྲལ་མ་མྱོང་བ་ནི། ཡང་དེ་ཉིད་ལས། མ་འོངས་
མི་འགྲོ་ཡེ་ནས་དབྱིངས་ན་འདུག མ་སྟོར་མ་བྲལ་ཡེ་ནས་རང་ལ་ཡོད། མ་བཙལ་ ི་ཚོལ་བཙལ་བའི་ཐ་སྙད་མེད། མི་འགྱུར་སྐུ་ལ་མ་བསྒྲིབས་ཡེ་ཤེས་ཤར། བལྟས་པས་
བདག་ཞལ་བདག་གིས་མཐོང་བ་ལ། གཞན་གྱིས་མཐོང་བའི་རྒྱུ་ནི་ཅང་ཡང་མེད། ཅེས་པས་སེམས་ཉིད་ཡེ་ནས་རང་ལ་རང་བྱུང་དུ་ཡོད་པར་རྟོགས་པ་ནི། བཙོལ་མེད་ལྷུན་གྲུབ་ཀྱི་སེམས་

17

ཁ

༄། ཟིན་པའོ། དེས་ན་སེམས་དགུ་ཡོད་པ་མ་ཡིན་ཀྱང་ཐོག་ཆ་ནས་དེ་ལྟར་བརྟག་ཅིང་བཙལ་བས་སེམས་ཉིད་ཐིག་ལེ་ཉག་གཅིག་གི་གཞི་དང་རྩ་བ་ཆོད་ནས་རིག་པ་ཟང་ཀ་བོན་སྐུ་རྗེན་པ་རྟོགས་པའོ།
གཉིས་པ་ནི། དེ་ལྟར་བློ་འདས་ཀྱི་རིག་པ་ཟང་ཀ་མ་གཏན་ལ་ཕེབས་ནས་རིག་པའི་རྩལ་སེམས་སུ་འཕྲོ་བའི་གཞི་དང་རྩ་བ་བཅད་པའི་ཕྱིར་སེམས་བྱུང་གནས་འགྲོ་གསུམ་ལ་བརྟག་པ་ནི། གསེར་
གྱི་ཕུར་མའི་རྒྱུད་ལས། སེམས་ནི་བྱུང་གནས་འགྲོ་གསུམ་བརྟག བརྟགས་པས་མ་རྙེད་ཇོ་བོ་སྟོང་། གཏད་པ་མེད་པར་ཏད་དེ་ཡུས། ཞེས་པས། ཐོག་མ་བྱུང་ས་བྱུང་
ཁུངས་ལ་བརྟག་པ་ནི། སེམས་རྟོག་ཕལ་གྱིས་ཤར་ནས་བྱུང་ན་གང་ནས་བྱུང་། ཡོད་པ་དངོས་པོའི་ནང་ནས་བྱུང་ངམ། མེད་པ་སྟོང་པའི་ནང་ནས་བྱུང་། །དངོས་པོའི་ནང་
ནས་བྱུང་ན་ཕྱི་ས་རྡོ་རི་བྲག་ཡུལ་ཁམས། ནང་རང་གི་ལུས་སོགས་དངོས་པོར་སྣང་བ་ཐམས་ཅད་རེ་རེ་ནས་རྡུལ་ཕྲ་རབ་ཀྱི་ཆ་ཤས་ཙམ་དུའང་བཤིག་ནས་བཙལ་བས་བྱུང་ས་རྙེད་དམ། གལ་
ཏེ་སྟོང་པའི་ནང་ནས་བྱུང་ངམ་སྙམ་ན། སྟོང་པ་ནམ་མཁའ་ལྟ་བུ་ལ་བྱུང་ས་མི་རྙེད་དེ། ནམ་མཁའ་ལ་འབྱུང་བཞིའི་བྱུང་ས་བཙལ་བས་རྙེད་དམ་རྟོགས་ཤིག དེ་ལྟར་བརྟགས་པས་

18

ཨཱ་ཀ་ཨཱ་ཐ

བྱུང་ས་མ་རྙེད་ཀྱང་བྱུང་མཁན་གྱི་ཤེས་པ་ཤར་རེ༔འོལ་ལེ་བ་ནམ་མཁའ་ལས་ལྷུང་པོ་བཞིན་བྱུང་སྙམ་ན། འོ་ན་བྱུང་མཁན་གྱི་ཤེས་པ་ཁོ་རང་ཅར་གྱིས་ངོས་བཟུང་ཞིག་དང་། དེ་ལ་དངོས་པོ་
འདུག་གམ། ཁ་དོག་འདུག་གམ། གཅིག་དང་དུ་མ་ལ་སོགས་གང་འདྲར་འདུག་རྟོགས་ཤིག བརྟགས་ཤིང་བཙལ་བས་བྱུང་མཁན་མ་རྙེད་ན་འཚོལ་མཁན་གྱི་སེམས་ལ་ལྟུར་ལྟོས་ཤིག
བལྟས་པས་ཀྱང་གང་ཡང་མཐོང་དུ་མེད་པས་བྱུང་ས་བྱུང་མཁན་དུ་སྣང་བའི་གཟུང་འཛིན་ཡུལ་མེད་ཤེས་པ་རྗེན་བྲལ་སྨྲ་བསམ་བརྗོད་འདས་ཆེན་པོའི་སྙིང་དུ་ཐ་སྙད་དེ་ཡུས་པ་ནི། ལམ་གྱི་དུས་ན་
ལྟ་བ་མཐའ་བྲལ། འབྲས་བུའི་དུས་ན་སྐྱེ་མེད་བོན་སྐུ་ཞེས་བྱ་སྟེ། ཇི་སྐད་དུ། རྫོགས་ཆེན་དོན་རྒྱུད་ལས། སེམས་ཀྱི་ཇོ་བོ་བྱུང་བའི་ས་མེད་དེ། རང་བྱུང་སྟོང་ཉིད་
དང་དུ་དངས་སང་ངེ་། མ་བལྟས་རྗེན་པ་དེ་ལ་ལྟ་བ་ཟེར། བོན་སྐུ་སྤྲོས་བྲལ་དེ་དང་ངོ་འཕྲོད་དོ། ཞེས་སོ། གཉིས་པ་གནས་ས་གནས་མཁན་ལ་བརྟག་པ་ནི། སེམས་ཞེས་
བྱ་བ་ཁོ་ཡོད་ན་ད་ལྟ་གང་ན་གནས། དངོས་པོའི་ཕྱོགས་ཐམས་ཅད་ནི་རྡུལ་ཕྲ་རབ་ཏུ་བཤིག་སྟེ་ནམ་མཁའ་ལ་ཐིམ་ནས་སོང་ན་གནས་ས་མེད། གནས་ས་མེད་ཀྱང་གནས་མཁན་ཀྱི་དྲན་པ་གསལ་

༄། །གསལ་ཧྲིག་ཧྲིག་ཏུ་འདུག་ན་དེ་ཙར་གྱིས་ངོས་ཟུངས་ཤིག །བཟུང་བས་གནས་ས་གནས་མཁན་གཉིས་ཀ་མ་གྲུབ་པས་ཕར་བལྟས་སྟོང་སྦ་ལེ། །ཚུར་བལྟས་ཟང་ཐལ་ལེ། །བར་མེད་དུ་ཏ་རེ་བ། །རང་གསལ་དུ་ཡེ་རེ་བ་དེ་ནི། །ལམ་གྱི་དུས་ན་སྒོམ་པ་རང་གསལ། །འབྲས་བུའི་དུས་ན་འགག་མེད་རྫོགས་སྐུ་ཞེས་བྱ་སྟེ། །ཐ་མ་ལས། །གནས་པའི་ཡུལ་ལ་ཅེར་བལྟས་པས། །རང་གསལ་རང་དངས་ངང་དུ་གནས། །དེ་ནི་ཡོངས་སྒྱུར་ངོ་འཕྲོད་དོ། །ཞེས་སོ། །གསུམ་པ་འགྲོ་ས་འགྲོ་མཁན་ལ་བརྟག་པ་ནི། །སེམས་རྟོག་ཕལ་གྱི་ཤར་ནས་ཡལ་ནས་སོང་སྐམ་བྱེད་པ་འདི་གང་དུ་འགྲོ་བརྟགས་པས། །ཕྱི་ཡུལ་དངོས་མེད་སྟོང་པ་ལ་དང་པོ་འོང་ས་མ་རྙེད་པས་ཐ་མ་འགྲོ་ས་མ་རྙེད། །གལ་ཏེ་རྙེད་ན་འགྲོ་མཁན་གྱི་བྱད་བཞིན་ལ་སོགས་པའི་མཚན་ཉིད་ཀྱང་ཤེས་དགོས་པས་བརྟགས་པའི་ཚེ་དེ་ལྟར་མི་འདུག་པར་རང་ཡལ་དུ་ཡལ། །རང་དག་ཏུ་དག་ནས། །འཁྲུལ་པ་མ་སྣངས། །གྲོལ་བ་མ་བླངས། །རང་ཤར་རང་གྲོལ་དུ་སྟོང་སངས་སངས་སོང་བ་ནི། །ལམ་གྱི་དུས་ན་སྤྱོད་པ་རྗེས་མེད། །འབྲས་བུའི་དུས་ན་གཉིས་མེད་སྤྲུལ་སྐུ་ཞེས་བྱ་སྟེ། །དེ་ཉིད་ལས། །སེམས་རྟོག་གར་སོང་ཅེར་བལྟས་པས། །སེར་བུ་རང་སར་ཡལ་བ་ལྟར། །རང་གྲོལ་ངོས་མེད་རྗེན་པར་གྲོལ། །འཛིན་མེད་སྤྲུལ་སྐུའི་རང་ཞལ་མཇལ། །ཞེས་སོ། །དེ་ལྟར་བདག་འཛིན་གྱིས་ང་ཡི་སེམས་ཞེས་ཡོད་པར་གཟུང་བ་དེ་སྡུད་གནས་འགྲོ་གསུམ་གྱིས་བརྟགས་པས་མེད་ཐག་ཆོད་པ་ནི། །སེམས་ཀྱི་ཁང་བུ་རྡིབ་པ་ཞེས་བྱ་སྟེ། །འགྲོ་འོང་དང་བྲལ་བའི་སེམས་ཉིད་བདག་མེད་ཡེ་སྟོང་མཐའ་བྲལ་ཆེན་པོའི་ཐོག་ཏུ་སླེབ་ཡང་སླེབ་ཚུལ་ཡང་བློས་བཞག་ས་དང་བཞག་མཁན་དུ་བྱས་པ་མ་ཡིན་པར། །རང་བཞིན་རྫོགས་པ་ཆེན་པོའི་གཤིས་འོད་གསལ་གཅུག་མ་ཉིད་ཀྱི་དོན་མངོན་སུམ་རྗེན་ཅེར་དུ་མཐོང་བ་ལ་སླེབ་པ་ཞེས་སྐྱོ། །སེམས་སྦྱོང་གི་དགོས་པ་ནི། །སྐུ་གསུམ་དོན་རྒྱུད་ལས། །དེ་དག་གིས་ཀྱང་ཡིད་ཀྱི་རིག་སྒྲིབ་དག །བར་ཆོད་ཞི་ཞིང་ཡིད་ཀྱི་མངོན་ཞེན་ཟློག །མཐར་ཐུག་བོན་གྱི་སྐུ་དང་གཉིས་མེད་འགྱུར། །ཞེས་སོ། །དོན་གཉིས་པ་དངོས་གཞི་གནད་ཀྱི་ཉམས་ལེན་ལ་གཉིས། །དང་པོ་དངོས་གཞིའི་ལམ་ལ་འཇུག་སྔོའི་ཐོག་མ་རྒྱུད་སྨིན་པར་བྱེད་པའི་དབང་གི་དཀྱིལ་འཁོར་ཆེན་པོར་འཇུག་པའི་བྱ་བ་རྣམས་ནི་སྐབས་འདི་ཉིད་དུ་དོན་གྱིས་ཐོབ་པ་ཡིན་ནོ། །གཉིས་པ་ལམ་དངོས་ལ་འཁྲིད་ཚུལ་གྱི་འབྲེལ་དགོད་པ། །ཉམས་ལེན་དངོས་རྒྱས་པར་བཤད་པ་གཉིས་ལས།

༄། །དང་པོ་ནི། །ནམ་མཁའ་འཕྲུལ་མཛོད་ལས། །གོལ་ས་ལ་བཟླ་བའི་རྫོགས་པ་ཆེན་པོ། །གོལ་ས་མན་ངག་ཏུ་བསྟུན་པའི་རྫོགས་པ་ཆེན་པོ། །གོལ་ས་ཤུགས་ལས་ཆོད་པའི་རྫོགས་པ་ཆེན་པོ་དང་གསུམ་དུ་གསུངས་པ་ལས། །འདི་ནི་ཕྱི་མ་ལྟར་ཁྲིད་པའི་ལུགས་ཡིན་ལ། །གོལ་ས་ལ་བཟླ་བའི་རྫོགས་ཆེན་པ་ནི། །ཐེག་པ་རིམ་པ་བརྒྱད་སྤང་བྱ་དང་གོལ་སར་བཞག་ནས། རང་གཞུང་བཟང་པོར་བསྒྲུབ་པར་འདོད་དེ། །མཉམ་པ་ཉིད་ཀྱི་རིག་པའི་དོན་ལ་འགལ་བས། །འདི་ནི་རིམ་པ་བརྒྱད་པོ་རང་གི་ངང་དུ་གྲོལ་བས་གོལ་སར་མི་འཛིན་ཏེ། །ཡེ་ཁྲི་མཐའ་སེལ་ལས། །རྫོགས་ཆེན་ཐེག་པ་ཡང་རྩེ་ནི། །ཐམས་ཅད་མི་སྤོང་ཆེར་མི་འཛིན། །ས་ལམ་འབྲས་བུ་རྗེས་མི་བཅད། །ཕྱི་ནང་གྲུབ་མཐའི་འཛིན་པ་གྲོལ། །སྤང་ཐོབ་འབྲས་བུའི་ཡུལ་ལས་འདས། །དབང་པོ་ཡང་རབ་སྤྱོད་ཡུལ་ཡིན། །ཞེས་སོ། །གོལ་ས་མན་ངག་ཏུ་བསྟུན་པའི་རྫོགས་ཆེན་པ་འདི་ཡང་གསལ་གསལ་པོའམ། །སྟོང་སྟོང་པོའམ། །ཡིན་ཡིན་པོ་མང་པོ་བསྒྲུབས་པའི་ཞེ་འདོད་ཀྱིས་བཅིངས་པས། །འདི་ནི་བཤད་བཤད་མང་པོའི་ཁ་ན་མེད་དེ། །བསལ་བཞག་མེད་པའི་དོན་ལ་ཅེར་བཞག་གིས་གོལ་སྒྲིབ་ཤུགས་ལས་ཆོད་དེ། ། །

ཀྲང་ཁྲིད

བསྒོམ་བསྒྲུབ་ཀྱི་ཚོལ་བ་ལས་འདས་པའི་ཟུར་མེད་ཀྱི་གཤིས་ཟང་ཐལ་ལ་དུས་གསུམ་དུ་འཕོ་འགྱུར་མེད་པའི་རང་བཞིན་ཡེ་དག་ལས་མི་གཡོ་བས་གོལ་ས་དང་། རང་ས་དཀྲུག་གིས་འདྲིས་ཏེ་གོལ་བ་
གཏན་མེད་དེ། །དཔེར་ན་རི་མགོ་ནས་རྒྱ་བརྫོལ་བས་རྩྭ་ཤིང་ནགས་ཚལ་ཐམས་ཅད་རྒྱས་གླུང་དུ་ཤུངས་ཀྱིས་འཁྱེར་བ་ལྟ་བུའོ། ཡང་ན་ཁྲིད་ཀྱི་ལུགས་དང་། ངོ་སྤྲོད་ཀྱི་ལུགས་དང་།
མགྲོན་པོ་ལ་བཀྲལ་བ་ལ་ཚང་སྤྲུགས་སུ་གདབ་པ་གསུམ་ལས་འདི་ནི་ཁྲིད་ཀྱི་ལུགས་སུ་གདབ་པ་ཏེ། ངོ་སྤྲོད་པ་ཁྲིགས་ཆོད་དང་ཐོད་རྒལ་གྱི་གདམས་ངག་ཅར་ཐོག་ཏུ་དབོག་པ་དང་། ཚང་
སྤྲུགས་སུ་གདབ་པ་བར་དོའི་གདམས་ངག་སྟེ། དེ་གཉིས་འདིའི་ཁོངས་སུ་ཤུགས་ཀྱིས་འདུའོ། དེ་ལའང་དབང་རྩལ་རྣམས་ལམ་ལ་རིམ་གྱིས་འཁྲིད་དེ། རྟོགས་བྱ་རང་རིག་ཡེ་ཤེས་
ཁད་ཀྱིས་འཆར་ནས། དག་བྱ་ཀློ་ཡི་དྲི་མ་རིམ་གྱིས་དག་སྟེ། འཁོར་བ་ལས་གྲོལ་བར་བྱེད་པའི་ཐབས་ཟབ་མོ་རྫོགས་པ་ཆེན་པོ་སྐུ་གསུམ་རང་ཤར་ཞེས་པ་ཤིན་ཏུ་རྒྱ་ཆེ་བར་བསྟན་ནས་
ཡོད་དོ། འདི་ནི་དབང་རྣོན་རྣམས་ལ་གདམས་པ་ཐོག་བབ་ཅིག་ཅར་སྤྱི་བླུགས་སུ་གདབ་པ་སྟེ། གཞི་ཡེ་གྲོལ་གྱི་སྙིང་དུ་ལམ་རྩོལ་བྲལ་དུ་ངོ་ཅར་ཐོག་ཏུ་སྤྲོད་པས་ཐག་ཆིག་ཐོག་ཏུ་ཆོད་

22

ཁ

བཅུ་གཉིས

༄། ནས་སངས་རང་ས་ན་རྒྱས་ཏེ། འབྲས་བུ་མངོན་གྱུར་དུ་ཚེ་འདི་ཉིད་ལ་གདོད་མའི་གཞི་ཐོག་ཏུ་བཙན་ས་ཟིན་པའོ། གཉིས་པ་ལ་གཉིས། དབང་རྣོན་སྒོམ་དུ་མེད་
ཀྱང་ལ་བཟླ་བས་གྲོལ་བ་ཁྲིགས་ཆོད་ཀྱི་གདམས་པ་དང་། བརྩོན་འགྲུས་ཆེན་པོས་ཐོད་རྒལ་དུ་སྒོམ་པས་སྐུ་གསུམ་ལམ་སྣང་ལ་རྫོགས་ཏེ་ཕུང་པོ་ལྷག་མེད་དུ་གྲོལ་བའི་གདམས་པའོ། དང་པོ་
ལ་དབང་པོའི་ཁྱད་པར་གྱི་གཉིས་ལས། དང་པོ་དབང་ཐ་རྣམས་ལ་ངོ་སྤྲོད་པའི་ལུགས་ནི། འབྲིང་པོ་སོར་གཞག་ལས། སྣང་བ་སེམས་སུ་ངོ་སྤྲོད་དོ། སེམས་སྟོང་པ་ངོ་
སྤྲོད་དོ། སྟོང་པ་འོད་གསལ་དུ་ངོ་སྤྲོད་དོ། འོད་གསལ་ཟུང་འཇུག་ཏུ་ངོ་སྤྲོད་དོ། ཟུང་འཇུག་བདེ་བ་ཆེན་པོ་ངོ་སྤྲོད་དོ། ཅེས་སྣང་བ་སེམས་སུ་ངོ་སྤྲོད་པས་དངོས་པོ་རང་
མཚན་པ་ཞིག སེམས་སྟོང་པར་ངོ་སྤྲོད་པས་བདེན་འཛིན་རང་རྒྱུད་པའི་རྟོག་པ་ཆད། སྟོང་པ་འོད་གསལ་དུ་ངོ་སྤྲོད་པས་བོན་ཉིད་གཤིས་ལ་ཤོར་བའི་གོལ་ས་ལས་གྲོལ། འོད་གསལ་
ཟུང་འཇུག་ཏུ་ངོ་སྤྲོད་པས་དབྱིངས་རིག་ཟུང་དུ་ཆུད། ཟུང་འཇུག་བདེ་བ་ཆེན་པོར་ངོ་སྤྲོད་པས་རིག་སྟོང་རྗེན་པའི་ངོ་བོ་སྐྱེ་འགག་གནས་གསུམ་དང་བྲལ་བར་རྟོགས་པ་ལ་དགོངས་པ་ཅམ་མོ།

23

ཀྲང་ཁྲིད

དེ་ལས་ཕྱོགས་དང་པོའི་འདོད་ལུགས་འདི་ལ་ཁོ་བོའི་མན་ངག་གིས་ཟིན་དགོས་པས་ན་འདི་ལྟར་ཡིན་ཏེ། དེའང་སྣང་བ་འདི་སེམས་མ་ཡིན་ཏེ་སེམས་ལ་དེ་ལྟར་མི་སྣང་བའི་ཕྱིར་རོ། འོ་ན་གང་
ཡིན་ཞེ་ན་བག་ཆགས་ཀྱི་སྣང་བ་ཡིན་ཏེ། སེམས་ལ་བག་ཆགས་བརྟས་པའི་སྨྱོ་བུར་བའི་རྐྱེན་ལས་སྣང་བ་དཀར་དམར་བྱུང་བའི་ཕྱིར་རོ། དེ་ལྟར་བྱུང་ཞིང་སྣང་ནའང་ངོ་བོ་ཉིད་བདེན་པ་མ་
གྲུབ་པ་ནི་རྨི་ལམ་གྱི་སྣང་བ་ལྟ་བུ་སྟེ། རྨི་ལམ་གྱི་སྣང་བ་ཡང་རྨི་ལམ་གྱི་ཤེས་པའི་ངོར་དངོས་པོ་ལྟར་སྣང་ན་ཡང་དོན་ལ་དངོས་པོ་མེད་པ་ལྟར་རོ། བག་ཆགས་ཀྱི་སྣང་བའང་འཁྲུལ་པའི་
སེམས་ཀྱི་ངོར་བདེན་པར་གྲུབ་པ་ལྟར་སྣང་ཡང་དོན་དམ་པར་གཞི་ནས་བདེན་པར་གྲུབ་མ་མྱོང་བ་ཅིག་སྟེ། ཡུན་རིང་བྱུང་ཙམ་མིན་གཞི་མེད་པའི་ཕྱིར་མི་སྣང་བའི་སྣང་བ་རྨི་ལམ་གྱི་སྣང་བ་དང་
སྣང་ཚུལ་གཅིག་པའོ། ཡང་ན་རྫོགས་ཆེན་སེམས་སྡེ་བ་ལྟར་ངོ་སྤྲོད་པའི་ལུགས་ནི། བྱང་ཆུབ་ཀྱི་སེམས་གང་གིའང་འཆར་གཞིར་གྱུར་པ་རྒྱ་མཚོ་ལྟ་བུ། དེའི་རྩལ་གང་ཡང་འཆར་
ཙང་དུ་གནས་པ་རྒྱ་མཚོའི་དངས་ཆ་ལྟ་བུ། དེའི་རོལ་པ་སྣ་ཚོགས་སུ་སྣང་བ་རྒྱ་མཚོ་ལ་གཟའ་སྐར་ཤར་བ་ལྟ་བུར་ཤེས་དགོས་ལ། འདི་གསུམ་ཡང་གཞི་བྱང་ཆུབ་སེམས་ཀྱི་ངོས་ནས་ཕར་

24

ཁ

བཅུ་གསུམ

༄། དཔྱད་ན་དེ་ལྟར་མི་ཟུང་ངོ༔ སེམས་ཉིད་ལ་དེ་ལྟར་མི་སྣང་བའི་ཕྱིར་རོ། དཔེར་ན་རྒྱ་མཚོ་དང་དངས་ཆ་དང་དེ་ལ་ཤར་བའི་གཟའ་སྐར་གསུམ་པོའང་ངོ་བོ་ཆུ་གཅིག་ལས་
གཞན་དུ་བརྗོད་དུ་མེད་པ་བཞིན་ནོ། རོལ་པའི་ངོས་ནས་རྩར་དཔྱད་དུས་དེ་ལྟར་མི་འགལ་ཙམ་སྟེ། སྣང་ཚུལ་ལ་རྒྱ་མཚོ་དང་དངས་ཆ་དང་གཟའ་སྐར་གསུམ་དུ་དབང་པོའི་ཡུལ་དུ་ཟུང་
བ་བཞིན་ནོ། ཡང་དག་པར་གཞི་མེད་ཀྱི་སྣང་བ་ཡིན་པས་སྣང་སེམས་གཉིས་སུ་སྒྲོ་འདོགས་མེད་པ་ནི། །ལུས་རྒྱུད་དང་འདྲ་བའི་གདམས་པ་ལས། སྣང་དང་སྟོང་པའི་སྒྲ་མི་འཇུག
གཉིས་ག་གང་ལའང་གཞི་མེད་དོ། ཅེས་སོ། དེ་བས་ན་འདི་ནི་ཕྱག་ཆེན་པའི་ལུགས་ཀྱིས་དབང་རྩལ་རྣམས་རིམ་གྱིས་ལམ་ལ་བགྲོ་བའི་ཐབས་ཙམ་སྟེ། བྲུ་རྒྱལ་གྱི་ཕྱག་ཁྲིད་དང་།
དེའི་རྗེས་འབྲེང་པ་དག་གི་མན་ངག་རྣམས་སུ་དྲངས་པ་འདུག་སྟེ། རིགས་པ་ཚད་མས་དཔྱད་མི་བཟོད་པའི་ཕྱིར་ན་རྫོགས་པ་ཆེན་པོ་འདིའི་དགོངས་གཞི་ལ་གནམ་ས་ཙམ་དུ་མཐོ་དམན་དུ་སོང་
བ་ཞིག་གོ། གཉིས་པ་དབང་རྣོན་རྣམས་ནི། ངོ་སྤྲོད་པས་གྲོལ་དགོས་པས་ན། དེ་ལའང་གཉིས། ངོ་སྤྲོད་པ་དངོས་དང་། ཁྱད་མེད་ཆེན་པོར་ལ་བཟླ་བའོ། 25

དང་པོ་ལ་གསུམ། གནད་བཀྲོལ་བ། འགག་བསྡམ་པ། ཆིངས་སུ་བཅིང་བའོ། དང་པོ་ལ་གཉིས། རྩ་བ་ཡེ་རིག་ངོ་སྤྲོད་པ། དེ་ལས་འཕྲོས་པའི་ལྟ་སྒོམ་སྤྱོད་འབྲས་
བཞི་ངོ་སྤྲོད་པའོ། དང་པོ་ལ་གསུམ། ཁྱབ་རིག བསམ་རིག ཡེ་རིག་གོ། དང་པོ་ནི། །བདེ་གཤེགས་སྙིང་པོས་འགྲོ་བ་ཡོངས་ལ་ཁྱབ་པ་ཙམ་ལ་འདོད་པའོ། །
གཉིས་པ་ནི། ཐེག་པ་འགའ་ཞིག་ནས་བསྒོམ་ན་རིག མ་བསྒོམ་ན་མི་རིག་པར་འདོད་པའི་གསལ་འགྲིབ་ཅན་དེའོ། གསུམ་པ་འདི་རྫོགས་པ་ཆེན་པོའི་རིག་པ་ཡེ་རིག་ཡིན་ཏེ། ཤེས་
མ་ཤེས་བསྒོམ་མ་བསྒོམ་མེད་དེ་རིག་པ་ནི་ཡེ་ཤར་ཡེ་རིག་པའོ། ཅི་ལྟར་རིག་ན། ཕྱི་སྣང་བ་དངོས་མེད། ནང་སེམས་ཉིད་བདག་མེད། བར་ནམ་རྟོག་ཡེ་ཤེས་སུ་མཉམ་ཤར་མཉམ་
སྟོང་མཉམ་ཉིད་དུ་ཡེ་ནས་རིག་པའོ། དེའི་དོན་ངོ་སྤྲོད་པ་ནི། སློབ་མ་ལུས་གནད་བདུན་དང་ལྡན་པར་བྱས་ལ་རིག་པ་བཅོས་བསླད་མེད་པར་ཐད་ཀར་ཞོག་ཅིག་བྱས་ལ། བླ་མས།
ཀྱེ་ཀྱེ་སྐལ་ལྡན་རིགས་ཀྱི་བུ། ཁྱོད་ཀྱི་བསམ་དྲན་གྱི་མཁན་པོ་ཁོ་རང་ལ་ཅེར་གྱིས་ལྟོས་དང་། ལྟ་མཁན་དང་ལྟ་ཡུལ་གཉིས་སུ་འདུག་གམ། གཉིས་སུ་མེད་པའི་ཤེས་པ་ཁ་ནང་དུ་ལོག 26

ཁ

བཅུ་བཞི

༄། པས་རང་གཤིས་ནམ་མཁའ་བཞིན་ཕྱམ་གྱིས་སོང་དུས། དེ་ཉིད་ལ་བསྒྱུར་བཀོད་སྤྱི་ཙམ་མ་བྱེད་དང་། དེའི་རང་བཞིན་ལ་བརྗོད་དུ་མེད་པས། དེ་ལ་གསལ་སྟོང་སྣང་
སེམས་ཟུང་འཇུག་སོགས་གང་གིའང་མིང་མི་ཐོགས་པ། །དཔེ་བརྗོད་དང་རྟོག་དཔྱོད་གང་གིས་ཀྱང་གཏན་ལ་མི་ཕེབས་པའི་ཤེས་པ་ཟང་ཀ་མ་སྤྱང་ཐབས་དང་བྲལ་བ་འདི་གཞི་རྩ་མེད་པར་སྟོང་
ཕྱལ་ཕྱལ། མ་འགགས་པར་གསལ་ཧྲིག་ཧྲིག ཡེ་གྲོལ་དུ་ཟང་ཐལ་ཐལ། རང་བྱུང་དུ་དངས་གསལ་གསལ། གཉེན་པོ་མེད་པར་བདེ་ཆམ་ཆམ། ཡེ་ཤར་དུ་རྗེན་ཅེར་
ཅེར། ཡེངས་མི་ཤེས་པའི་རིག་པ། མཐོང་བ་མེད་པའི་འོད་གསལ། རྒྱུན་ཆད་མེད་པའི་གཉུག་མ། སྒྲར་མི་བཏུབ་པའི་གཤིས་ལུགས། སྤྱང་མི་ཤེས་པའི་ཡེ་ཤེས། བདག་
མེད་ཀྱི་སྣང་བ་ཡེ་རེ། རྟོག་མེད་ཀྱི་ཤེས་པ་ཁྲོལ་ལེ། ཡུལ་ཤེས་མི་ཕྱེད་པའི་ཡེ་ཤེས། ངོ་བོ་མེད་པའི་ཤེས་པ་ཧྲར་སངས་ཕྱལ་ཡས་འདི་རྫོགས་པ་ཆེན་པོའི་གསང་ལམ། མ་དང་མཁའ་
འགྲོའི་སྙིང་ཁྲག དྲན་པ་ནམ་མཁའི་ཐ་ཐོག རིག་པ་རང་ཤར་གྱི་གདམས་ངག་ཡིན་ནོ། གོ་འམ། རྟོགས་སམ། ཨ་ལ་ལ་ཨེ་མ་ཧོ། དེ་ལ་ལུང་གིས་སྒྲོ་བ་བསྐྱེད་པ་ནི། 27

ཨཱ་ཏ་ཁྲི

ཀུན་བཟང་ཐུགས་ཀྱི་བརྟག་པ་ལས། ཨེ་མ་གསུང་དབྱང་རིན་པོ་ཆེ། །ཨེ་མ་སྒྲ་བ་སྒྲོག་གི་མཁར། ཨེ་མ་བརྟན་པ་འགྱུར་ལྡོག་མེད། ཨེ་མ་གསལ་བ་ཡོངས་ལ་ཁྱབ། ཨེ་མ་མ་སྐྱེས་ལྷུན་གྱིས་གྲུབ། ཨེ་མ་ཡེ་ནས་རྣམ་པར་དག རང་ལ་ཤར་བས་གོལ་ས་མེད། དབྱིངས་དང་ཕྲད་པས་སྐྱར་མི་ལྡོག དོན་དམ་རྟོགས་པས་བདེ་བའི་སྐུ། དཀར་ཉེམ་འཆེར་བ་དག་པ་སྟེ། མཐའ་ཡས་སེམས་ཅན་སྲུས་མ་རྙེད། ཕུང་པོ་བཞིགས་པས་རང་ལས་འབྱུང་། དམ་པ་བྱང་ཆུབ་སེམས་ལ་གནས། བྱང་ཆུབ་སེམས་ཆེན་གདལ་པ་ལ། རང་གི་ཡེ་ཤེས་ལྷག་གིས་ཤར། སྐྱེ་འཆི་མེད་དེ་དངས་རེ་སྒྲོ། འདུ་འབྲལ་མེད་དེ་དངས་རེ་སྒྲོ། ཞེས་དང་། ཡེ་ཁྲི་མཐའ་སེལ་ལས། གསུང་དབྱང་སེམས་ལ་འགྱུར་བ་མེད། གསུང་དབྱང་སེམས་ལ་འཛོ་བ་མེད། གསུང་དབྱང་སེམས་ལ་སྐྱེ་ཤི་མེད། གསུང་དབྱང་སེམས་ལ་འདུ་འབྲལ་མེད། གསུང་དབྱང་སེམས་ལ་ཕྱོགས་རིས་མེད། གསུང་དབྱང་སེམས་ལ་རྟོག་པ་མེད། གསུང་དབྱང་སེམས་ལ་དགག་སྒྲུབ་མེད། གསུང་དབྱང་སེམས་ལ་ཕྱི་གང་མེད། གསུང་དབྱང་སེམས་ལ་རྩོལ་སྒྲུབ་མེད། ཅེས་དང་། སྨྲ་མེད་བརྡལ་པའི་རྒྱུད་ལས།

28

༄། དོན་ལ་ཛོ་བོ་འདི་ཞེས་མེད། བྱུང་ཐིམ་ཀུན་གྱི་རྩ་བ་མེད། རྩ་བ་མེད་པའི་རྩེ་མོ་གང་། །མཐོ་རིས་ངན་སོང་ཅིའི་ཕྱིར་ཡོད། རིག་པ་ཟང་ཐལ་དབྱིངས་སུ་ཤར། ཉིན་དང་མཚན་དུ་གསལ་འགྲིབ་མེད། ཀུན་ལ་སྙོམས་ཏེ་མཉམ་པར་གནས། །གནས་དང་གཞན་དུ་ཕྱེ་བྲག་མེད། མ་བཅོས་ཐིག་ལེ་གཅིག་ཏུ་རྫོགས། ཞེས་དང་། སེང་གེ་སྒྲ་བསྒྲགས་ལས། ཕྱི་དང་ནང་མེད་ཐམས་ཅད་ཀུན། མ་བཅོས་གདོད་ནས་ཀ་དག་ཉིད། རང་བཞིན་ཉིད་ནི་ཡེ་སངས་རྒྱས། ཐིག་ལེ་ཆེན་པོ་བོན་གྱི་སྐུ། ནམ་མཁའ་ལྟ་བུ་མཚོན་དང་བྲལ། འདི་ནི་སེང་གེ་སྒྲ་བསྒྲགས་ལྟ་བའི་མཆོག ཅེས་སོ། །གཉིས་པ་ལ་ལྟ་སྒོམ་སྤྱོད་འབྲས་བཞི་ལས། དང་པོ་ནི། དེ་ལྟ་བུའི་རིག་པ་དེ་ནི་འཁོར་འདས་ཀུན་གྱི་དངོས་གཞི་ཡིན་ཏེ། དངོས་པོ་ལྟར་སྣང་བ། དངོས་མེད། གཉིས་ཀ། གཉིས་མེད་གང་ཡང་མ་གྲུབ་སྟེ། དངོས་པོ་ལྟར་སྣང་བ་ཡང་རྨི་ལམ་དང་སྒྱུ་མའི་རོལ་པ་ཙམ་ལས་དོན་ལ་ཛོ་བོ་ཉིད་མ་གྲུབ་པས་དངོས་མེད་ལས་མ་འདས་ཤིང་། དངོས་པོ་དངོས་མེད་གཉིས་སུ་མི་སྣང་བས་གཉིས་སུ་མེད་འདོགས་ས་ཟད། གཉིས་སུ་མེད་པ་དེ་ལ་ཡིན་མིན་གང་ཡང་ཁས་

29

ཨཱ་ཏ་ཁྲི

ལེན་དང་བྲལ་བས་བོན་ཉིད་སྤྲོས་བྲལ་ལས་འདའ་མི་ཤེས། དེ་ལ་ཁྱད་དུ་བལྟས་ཀྱང་ཡུལ་དང་མཁན་པོ་གཉིས་ག་མ་གྲུབ། རང་བཞིན་མེད་པས་བལྟ་བྱ་དང་ལྟ་བྱེད་ལས་འདས། མ་བལྟས་ཀྱང་དེ་ལས་གཞན་དུ་འགྲོ་ས་དང་འགྱུར་ས་མ་རྙེད་པ་དེ་ནི་ཡེ་གྲོལ་ཆེན་པོ་ལྟ་བའི་ཀློང་ཞེས་བྱ་སྟེ། ནམ་མཁའ་དབྱིངས་ཡངས་རྒྱུད་ཀྱི་ལེའུ་དགུ་པ་ལས། ཀུན་གྱི་དངོས་གཞིར་ཤར་བ་ཡི། རིག་པ་བྱང་ཆུབ་སེམས་ཉིད་ནི། རྒྱུ་ཀྱེན་ཡེ་བྲལ་རྣམ་པར་དག །ཁ་དོག་དབྱིབས་བྲལ་སྒྲོ་སྐུར་འདས། ཀུན་ཏུ་སྣང་ལ་དེ་མི་གནས། ཀུན་བྲལ་ཉག་གཅིག་ཅི་མ་ཕྱང་། ཀུན་སྤངས་ལྷུན་རྫོགས་དངོས་གཞིར་ཤར། བོན་དངོས་ཐམས་ཅད་གཞི་པོ་འདི། བྱང་ཆུབ་སེམས་ཀྱིས་ཀུན་ཁྱབ་ཕྱིར། དངོས་པོ་མ་གྲུབ་ཀུན་གཞིར་ཤར། ཞེས་སོ། འོ་ན་དེ་གདམས་ངག་ཏུ་ཅང་འགྲོའམ་ཟེར་ན། འགྲོ་སྟེ་ལྟ་བ་བཞག་ས་མི་ཚོལ་བས་གཤིས་ལས་གྲོལ། གོ་བ་འཛིན་པ་མེད་པས་གཉེན་པོ་ལས་གྲོལ། ཉམས་སུ་བླང་རྒྱུ་མེད་པས་སྒོམ་པ་ལས་གྲོལ། ། ཐ་མལ་གྱི་སྣང་བ། ཐེག་པའི་ཕྱོགས་ཞེན། ཉམས་མྱོང་གི་རོ་ལ་ཆགས་པ། རེ་དོགས་ཀྱིས་བཅིངས་པ་ལ་སོགས་པའི་འཛིན་པ་ཐ་དག་ལས་གྲོལ་བ་ཡིན་ནོ། གཉིས་པ་ནི།

30

31

ཁ་ བཅུ་དྲུག

༄། དེ་ལ་བསྒོམ་ཀྱང་སྒོམ་བྱེད་མཁན་པོ་མ་རྙེད་བསྒོམ་རྒྱུའི་ཡུལ་མ་རྙེད། སྒོམ་པ་བློས་མ་བྱུད་པའི་ཤེས་པ་ཟང་ཀ་མ་ཧ་ར་སངས་རྒྱ་ཡན་དེ་ཉིད་བློ་བྲལ་གྱི་སྒོམ་པ་རང་ཤར་བ་ཅེས་བྱ།
མ་བསྒོམ་ཀྱང་ངོ་བོ་མེད་པས་ཤོར་བ་མེད་པར་གང་གིས་ཀྱང་བྱར་མི་བཏུབ། དེ་ལ་དུས་གསུམ་མིང་གི་བྱེ་བྲག་མེད་པས་རང་གྲོལ་ཆེན་པོ་སྒོམ་པའི་ཀློང་ཞེས་བྱ་སྟེ། ཡེ་ཁྲི་མཐའ་སེལ་ལས།
བོན་ཉིད་ཕྱོགས་ལྷུང་མེད་པར་གདལ་བ་ཡིན། སེམས་ཉིད་ཁྲི་གང་མེད་པར་གནས་པ་ཡིན། །ཉམས་ལེན་རྒྱ་ཡན་ཆེན་པོ་ཤར་བ་ཡིན། སྒོམ་པ་སྣ་ཚོགས་རང་གསལ་ཆེན་པོ་ཡིན།
ཞེས་སོ། འོ་ན་དེའི་དུས་ན་སྣང་བ་སྲིད་ངམ་སྣང་ཟེར་ན། །སྣང་བ་ཐི་ལམ་གྱི་སྣང་བ་དང་འདྲ་བ་ལ། མ་འགགས་པར་ཡེ་རེར་ཡོད་ཀྱང་སྟར་གྱི་འཁྲུལ་སེམས་རང་ཁ་མའི་མཚང་རིག་
ནས་བོན་ཉིད་དུ་དག་པས་ཡུལ་ལ་རྟོག་མི་ཤེས་ལ། གཉིད་སད་པས་ཐི་ལམ་གྱི་སྣང་བ་རང་སངས་སུ་འགྲོ་བ་ལྟར་སང་རྒྱས་པ་ན་འཁྲུལ་སྣང་རང་དེངས་ལ་འགྲོ་བས་སྣང་བ་སྲིད་ཞྭང་གང་ཡང་
མི་བྱ་སྟེ། སྒྲ་མེད་བརྡལ་པའི་རྒྱུད་ལས། སྣང་བ་ཡོད་པར་མཐོང་བ་ནི། རྟག་འཛིན་དངོས་པོ་ལྟ་བས་གོལ། སྣང་བ་མེད་པར་མཐོང་བ་ནི། བྱུལ་ཞིང་ཆད་པར་ལྟ་བས་

32

ཀྲ་ཁྱི

གོལ། ཞེས་དང་། ཤེང་གི་སྒྲ་བསྒྲགས་ལས། སྣང་དང་མི་སྣང་དཔྱད་ལས་འདས་པར་བཞག ཅེས་སོ། འོ་ན་དེའི་ཚེ་ཡུལ་ལ་རྟོག་པ་མི་ཤར་བ་ཡིན་ནམ་ཞེ་ན། ཡུལ་
ལ་ཤེས་པ་ཤར་དུས་ནས་ཤར་མཁན་མེད་པར་ཤེས་པའི་ཡེ་ཤེས་རང་ལ་ཤར་ནས། ཉི་མ་དང་ཉི་ཟེར་བཞིན་རང་མལ་གྱི་རང་བྱུང་གི་ཡེ་ཤེས་ལ་འདུས་ཤིང་། དོན་དུ་ངོ་བོ་དང་རྩལ་འདུ་
འབྲ་གཉིས་སུ་མེད་པའི་འདྲེ་གཉིས་མེད་རང་བྱུང་གི་ཡེ་ཤེས་སྦྲོས་བྲལ་བོན་གྱི་སྐུའི་ངང་དུ་གནས་པའོ། ཁ་ཅིག་གིས་རྣམ་རྟོག་རང་བྱུང་གི་ཡེ་ཤེས་བོན་སྐུར་བཤད་པ་ནི། ངོ་བོ་དང་རྩལ་གྱི་དབྱེ་
བ་མ་ཕྱེ་བ་སྟེ། ཡུལ་ལ་ཤར་བའི་ཤེས་པ་དེ་ཉིད་ཡུལ་ཡོད་མེད་ཀྱི་རྗེས་སུ་བྱེད་པས་རང་བྱུང་གི་ཡེ་ཤེས་མ་ཡིན་ལ། ཤར་དུས་ནས་རང་བཞིན་མ་གྲུབ་པས་རྩལ་གྱི་ཡེ་ཤེས་སུ་ཤར་བ། མ་རྟོགས་པ་
རྟོག་པ་རང་ཁ་མ་འཁོར་བར་བརྒྱུད་པའི་རྒྱུ་མཚང་བའོ། དེས་ན་ཐེག་པ་འདིའི་ལུགས་ལ་གང་ཡང་རིག་པ་ཁྲུབ་བརྡལ་བས་རྩལ་ཅི་ལྟར་གཡོས་ཀྱང་། ཤར་ས་དེ་ཉིད་དུ་ཤར་བ་མེད་པར་
རང་དག་པས། གཞན་དག་དེ་ལ་ལྟ་བའམ་སྒོམ་པའམ་ངོས་འཛིན་ཏེ། རྣམ་རྟོག་བར་ལག་སྲིལ་བའི་ཐུགས་དམ་ཅི་ལྟར་བཟང་ཡང་འཁོར་བའི་ས་བོན་ཀོ་ནར་ཟད་དོ། དེས་ན་རྣམ་

33

ཁ་ བཅུ་བདུན

༄། རྟོག་ལ་མི་ལྟ་མི་དཔྱད་པས་རང་ཡལ་གཏད་མེད་ལ་སོང་བ་ལ། རྣམ་རྟོག་གི་གྲོལ་ཚུལ་གསུམ་ལས་རྣམ་རྟོག་ཕན་གནོད་མེད་པར་གྲོལ་བ་ཁང་སྟོང་གི་ཀུན་མ་ལྟ་བུའི་ཐ་སྙད་བྱེད་དེ་
ཐབ་ཤོར་གང་ཡང་མེད་དོ། དོན་དུ་གནས་འགྱུ་གང་ཡིན་ཡང་ངོ་ཤེས་མཁན་པོ་རང་གཞི་མེད་མཐའ་བྲལ་དུ་མ་སོང་ན་ཐེག་མཆོག་འདིའི་དགོངས་པ་མ་ལོན་པ་ཡིན་ནོ། དེའི་དུས་ན་
ཡུལ་ལ་རྟོག་པ་མི་འཕྲོ་བར་རང་མལ་ན་སྟོད་ཆགས་པར་གནས་ན་མི་རྟོག་པའི་ཉམས་ཡིན། དེ་དུས་ཀྱི་རིག་ཆ་ས་ལེ་ལྷང་ངེ་བ་བོན་སྐུར་ཤེས་པར་བྱ། ཡང་སྟོང་ཐུལ་ཐུལ་གནས་པ་དེ་སྟོང་
ཉམས་ཡིན། དེ་དུས་ཀྱི་རིག་ཆ་ས་ལེ་ཧྲིག་གེ་བ་དེ་བོན་སྐུར་ཤེས་པར་བྱ། ཡང་དགའ་ཡལ་ཡལ། བདེ་ཆམ་ཆམ་གནས་པ་དེ་བདེ་ཉམས་ཡིན། དེ་དུས་ཀྱི་རིག་ཆ་སང་ངེ་ཧར་རེ
བ་དེ་བོན་སྐུར་ཤེས་པར་བྱ། ཡང་གསལ་སང་ངེ་གནས་པ་དེ་གསལ་ཉམས་ཡིན། དེ་དུས་ཀྱི་རིག་ཆ་ཟང་ངེ་ཐ་ལེ་བ་དེ་བོན་སྐུར་ཤེས་པར་བྱའོ། དེ་བས་ན་གང་གི་དུས་ནའང་རིག་པ་
གཞི་མེད་རྗེན་ལ་འབུད་ལ་གསལ་ལེ་རིག་གེར་སྐྱོང་བ་ནི་ཐེག་མཆོག་འདིའི་ཉམས་ལེན་གྱི་མཐིལ། ལྟ་བའི་བཅུད་ཕུར། སྒོམ་པའི་སྙིང་རྡོ་ཡིན་ནོ། གསུམ་པ་ནི། སྤྱོད་ལམ་རྣམ་བཞི

གང་གི་ཚེ། ཕྱི་སྣང་བ་སྣང་དུས་ནས་རང་བཞིན་མ་གྲུབ་པས་བློས་ཕར་དངོས་པོར་མི་འཛིན། །ནང་ནམ་རྟོག་ཤར་དུས་ནས་ངོ་བོ་མེད་པས་ཞེན་པའི་འཁྲིས་མི་གདགས། སྣང་སེམས་ཡེ་གྲོལ་ལྷུག་པ་ལ་འཁྲུལ་པའི་བ་རླབས་མི་སྐྱེད། རིག་པ་ཟང་ཐལ་རྗེན་པ་ལ་རྟོག་པའི་གོས་མི་བསྒོན་པར་ཕྱལ་ཡས་ཁྱབ་བརྡལ་ཆེན་པོར་བཞག་ལ། སྒོ་གསུམ་ལྷུག་པ། སྣང་བ་རྒྱ་ཡན། སྤྱོད་པ་རང་ཡན་ལ། ཡང་བག་ཚ་མེད་པ། དགག་སྒྲུབ་བླང་དོར་མེད་པར་གང་དགར་སྤྱོད་པ་ནི་ཅེར་གྲོལ་ཆེན་པོ་སྤྱོད་པའི་ཀློང་ཞེས་བྱ་སྟེ། ཡེ་ཁྲི་མཐའ་སེལ་ནས་མཁའ་དཀར་པོའི་རྒྱུད་ལས། ཅི་ཡང་མ་འགགས་རང་ཤར་ལ། མ་སྤྱོད་དགག་རྒྱ་ག་ལ་ཡོད། ཡེ་ནས་རང་སྤྱོད་ལྷུག་པ་ལ། སྤྱོད་པས་བོགས་དབྱུང་ག་ལ་སྲིད། གཉེན་རབ་མ་འགགས་ཡན་དུ་འཆིར། དེ་ནི་སྤྱོད་པའི་ཀློང་ཆེན་ཡིན། ཞེས་སོ། ། ཕོ་ན་འཁྲུལ་སྣང་ལ་རང་ཡན་དུ་བཏང་ན་ཐ་མ་བཞིན་དུ་མི་འགྲོའམ་ཞེ་ན། ཐ་མལ་པས་བདག་ཏུ་བཟུང་བས་འཁྲུལ་ཡང་། རྣལ་འབྱོར་པ་ལ་རིག་པ་ཤར་བས་གང་ཡང་གཞི་མེད་དུ་ཤེས་པ་དང་། འཁྲུལ་པ་ཐམས་ཅད་རིག་པས་སེལ་བ་ཡིན་ཏེ། ཐ་མ་ལས། རིག་པ་རང་

༄། ཤར་མཚན་ཉིད་ནི། གཉིས་མེད་ཡིན་པས་གཉིས་སྣང་སེལ། རང་བྱུང་ཡིན་པས་རྒྱ་རྐྱེན་སེལ། ལྷུན་གྲུབ་ཡིན་པས་རེ་དོགས་སེལ། དག་པ་ཡིན་པས་དྲི་མ་སེལ། གསལ་བ་ཡིན་པས་ཆད་པ་སེལ། དངོས་མེད་ཡིན་པས་རྟག་པ་སེལ། ཞེས་དང་། གསེར་གྱི་ཏུས་སྦལ་ལས། ཡང་དག་དོན་གྱི་རིག་པ་ཤར་བའི་ཚེ། ཐམས་ཅད་མ་བཙྲིབས་ངོ་བོ་ཉིད་དུ་གསལ། ཞེས་སོ། བཞི་པ་ནི། ལྟ་སྒོམ་སྤྱོད་པ་གང་ཡིན་ཀྱང་དེ་ཀར་འབྲས་བུ་ལྷུན་གྲུབ་ཡིན་ཏེ། དཔེར་ན་སེམས་གར་ཕྱིན་ཀྱང་ས་སྟེང་ལས་མ་འདས་བཞིན་དུ། ལྟ་སྒོམ་སོགས་ཅི་བྱེད་ཀྱང་འབྲས་བུའི་རང་ས་ནས་མི་འདའ་བོ། དེ་བས་ན་སངས་ལ་རྒྱ་ས་མེད་པས་རེ་བའི་ལྟོས་ཟད། འཁོར་བ་ལྷུང་ས་མེད་པས་དོགས་པའི་ལམ་ཆད། འཁོར་འདས་ཀྱི་བོན་ཐམས་ཅད་རང་བྱུང་གི་ཡེ་ཤེས་སུ་ཡེ་དག་ཡེ་སངས་ཆེན་པོར། ལ་ཡེ་སློས་འབྲས་བུ་ཡེ་ཐོབ་ནི་མཐའ་གྲོལ་ཆེན་པོ་འབྲས་བུའི་ཀློང་ཞེས་བྱ་སྟེ། སེང་གེ་སྒྲ་བསྒྲགས་ལས། ཐིག་ལེས་ཀུན་བསྡུས་ཀུན་ལ་ཁྱབ། ཐམས་ཅད་མ་ལུས་བདེ་བའི་ཀློང་། སྡུག་བསྔལ་བྱ་བའི་མིང་ཡང་མེད། ཐམས་ཅད་མ་ལུས་ཡེ་སངས་རྒྱས། ཞེས་སོ། ཕོ་ན་སེམས་ཅན་ནམ་མཛོད་སྤྲུས་དུ་འཁྲུལ་པ་འདི་

མི་རིགས་སོ་སྙམ་ན། དེ་ལྟར་མ་རྟོགས་ནས་འཁྲུལ་པ་ཡིན་ཏེ། གབ་པ་དགུ་བསྐོར་ལས། དེ་རྟོགས་མ་རྟོགས་ཁྱད་པར་ཆེ། དེ་ཉིད་མ་རྟོགས་སྒྲིབ་པ་ནི། རྒྱ་ལྷའི་སྙིང་པོ་ཕྱིན་ཅི་ལོག ཅེས་སོ། གཉིས་པ་འགག་བསྟམ་ནི། ལྟ་བ་ཐམས་ཅད་ཀྱི་འགག་བོན་ཉིད་ཐོག་བབས་ལ་བསྟམ། དེ་ཅིའི་ཕྱིར་ན། སྣང་ཤེས་གང་ཡང་མ་བཅོས་རང་ལུགས་སུ་ལྷུངས་ཀྱིས་ཤར་བ་དེ། བོན་ཉིད་འཁྲུལ་མེད་དུ་ཡེར་གྱིས་མཐོང་བ་ལྟ་བ་ཐོག་བབས་ཡིན་ནོ། ནམ་མཁའ་འཕྲུལ་གྱི་མཛོད་ཆེན་ལས། སྣང་བ་ཤེས་པ་ད་ལྟ་བ་ས་ལེ་ཕལ་ལེ་ཁྱུག་གེ་སྣང་བ་རྒྱ་རྐྱེན་མེད་པར་རང་ཤར་བས་ན་ཐོག་བབས། འཕོ་འགྱུར་མེད་པར་རང་ཤར་བས་ན་ཐོག་བབས། དགག་སྒྲུབ་མེད་པར་རང་ཤར་བས་ན་ཐོག་བབས། རང་བྱུང་ཆེན་པོར་རང་ཤར་བས་ན་ཐོག་བབས་སོ། ཞེས་སོ། སྒོམ་པ་ཐམས་ཅད་ཀྱི་འགག་རིག་པ་ཅེར་ཐོག་ལ་བསྟམ། དེ་ཅིའི་ཕྱིར་ན། རྣམ་རྟོག་གྲོལ་གྱིས་སྐྱེས་པ་དེ། རང་བྱུང་གི་རིག་པ་ཅེར་གྱིས་གྲོལ་བ་སྒོམ་པ་ཅེར་ཐོག་ཡིན་ནོ། ཐ་མ་ལས། རྣམ་པར་རྟོག་པ་སྐྱེ་ས་མེད་པས་ན་ཅེར་ཐོག ཅི་ཤར་དེ་ཉིད་རང་ཤར་བས་མ་རིག་པ་ལ་གབ་ས་མེད་པས་ན་ཅེར་ཐོག རིག་པ་དང་སྣང་བ་ཇི་ཙམ་ཤར་པས་ཅེར་ཐོག

༄། དེ་ཉིད་བཅིངས་གྲུ་མེད་པས་ན་ཅར་ཕོག ད་ལོགས་ན་སྒོམ་རྒྱུ་མེད་པས་ན་ཅར་ཕོག་གོ། སྤྱོད་པ་ཐམས་ཅད་ཀྱི་འགག་ཡེ་ཤེས་ཤུགས་འབྱུང་ལ་བསྟུམ། དེ་ཅིའི་ཕྱིར་ན། སྤྱོད་ལམ་རྣམ་བཞི་གང་སྤྱོད་ཡང་མ་བཅོས་སོ་མ་རང་ལུགས་སུ་སྤྱོད་པ་ཡེ་ཤེས་ཤུགས་འབྱུང་ཡིན་ནོ། ཐ་མ་ལས། གང་ཡང་ཁྱད་དུ་མ་བཀག་པས་ཤུགས་འབྱུང་། ཅི་ཡང་མི་བྱེད་པས་ཤུགས་འབྱུང་། བྱེད་པས་མི་འགལ་བས་ཤུགས་འབྱུང་། ཅི་སྤྱོད་བོན་ཉིད་རོལ་པར་ཤར་བས་ཤུགས་འབྱུང་། སྤང་སྤྱད་ཞེན་གསུམ་མེད་པས་ཤུགས་འབྱུང་། ཐམས་ཅད་བོན་ཉིད་ཀྱི་ཀློང་འབབ་ཞིག་མཐུན་མི་མཐུན་གཉིས་སུ་མེད་པས་ཤུགས་འབྱུང་། ཐམས་ཅད་ནས་ཐམས་ཅད་དུ་སྒོ་གསུམ་ལྷུག་པ་ལ་གཉེན་པོ་མེད་པས་ན་གྲོལ་བ། ཡན་པ། ཧར་བར་གནས་སོ། ཀློ་བདེ་བོ། ཞེས་སོ། འབྲས་བུ་ཐམས་ཅད་ཀྱི་འགག་སྐུ་གསུམ་ཀློང་བརྡོལ་ལ་བསྟུམ། །དེ་ཅིའི་ཕྱིར་ན། ཅི་ཤར་ཅི་སྣང་ལ་རྩིས་བཏབ་ཚོགས་རིས་ཟད་པ་སྐུ་གསུམ་ཀློང་བརྡོལ་གྱི་འབྲས་བུ་ཡིན་ནོ། ཐ་མ་ལས། བོན་སྐུ་ཀློང་བརྡོལ་བ་ནམ་མཁའ། ལོངས་སྐུ་ཀློང་བརྡོལ་བ་ས་རྒྱ་མི་ཆུང་། སྤྲུལ་སྐུ་ཀློང་བརྡོལ་བ་འགྲོ་དྲུག་སེམས་ཅན། ཡེ་ཤེས་ཀློང་བརྡོལ་བ་དྲུག

37

༄། རིག་པ་ཀློང་བརྡོལ་བ་དེ་དག་ཐམས་ཅད་ཡིན་པས་གང་ཡང་མི་སྤང་བར་ལམ་དུ་བྱེད་དོ། ཅེས་སོ། འོ་ན་དག་བྱ་དང་བཅས་པའི་འཁོར་བ་འདི་ཁོ་ན་མཐར་ཐུག་ཏུ་སོང་བས་འགལ་བ་མ་ཡིན་ནམ་ཞེ་ན། མ་ཡིན་ཏེ་རྫོགས་ཆེན་གྱི་རྣལ་འབྱོར་ལ་ཡེ་རིག་ཤར་བས་དེ་ལྟར་སྣང་བ་ཡིན་ཏེ། མེ་ལོང་དགུ་འདུས་འོད་གསལ་གྱི་རྒྱུད་ལས། དཀྱུང་ལས་ཐོག་བབས་གང་ལ་ཐོགས་ཆགས་མེད་པ་ལྟ་བུ་ལྟ་བའི་དོན། མཐོང་ནས་ཁྲི་གཏུགས་ཤར་བས་མུན་སྨག་ཐོག་བབས་ཡལ་བ་ལྟ་བུ་སྒོམ་པའི་དོན། ཤ་ཚ་ལུང་དུ་བྲུགས་པའི་རྩི་ཤིང་ས་རྡོ་དབང་མེད་ལྷག་པ་ལྟ་བུ་སྤྱོད་པའི་དོན། ནོར་བུ་རིན་ཆེན་རྙེད་པས་དགོས་འདོད་ཕུན་སུམ་ཚོགས་པ་ལྟ་བུ་འབྲས་བུའི་དོན། ཞེས་སོ། གསུམ་པ་ཆིངས་སུ་བཅིང་བ་ནི། དེ་ལྟར་ལྟ་སྒོམ་སྤྱོད་འབྲས་དེ་དག་ཐམས་ཅད་ཀྱི་ཐག་དེ་ལྟར་གྱི་སྣང་བ་གཞི་མེད་འགག་མེད་ཀྱི་སྙིང་དུ་བཅད། མདོར་བོན་ཉིད་ཀྱི་རིག་པ་ཐིག་ལེ་ཉག་གཅིག་ལ་བསྡུ། །འགག་རྩོལ་བྲལ་མཐའ་ལས་འདས་པས་བསྟུམ། གནད་འཁོར་འདས་དབྱེར་མེད་དུ་བསྒྲིལ། ལ་བོན་ཉིད་ཀྱི་དབྱིངས་སྐྱེ་འགག་མེད་པར་བཟླ་སྟེ། དོན་རྣམ་པ་ལྔས་ཆིངས་སུ་བཅིང་བའོ། །དོན་གཉིས་པ་བྱར་མེད་ཆེན་པོར་ལ་བཟླ་བ་ལ་གསུམ།

38

༄། སྐྱོན་སེལ་གྱིས་དོན་སྤྱིར་བསྟན་པ། །བྱར་མེད་ཀྱི་རང་བཞིན་བྱེ་བྲག་ཏུ་བཤད་པ། ཉམས་ལེན་གདིང་གིས་བཅད་པའོ། དང་པོ་ནི་ འོ་ན་དུས་གསུམ་མཉམ་པ་ཉིད་དུ་རྒྱུན་ཆད་མེད་པའམ། སྔ་འཕྱི་ཐོག་མཐའ་མེད་པར་རྟོགས་ཙང་མ་རྟོགས་ཙང་འཁོར་འདས་ཐམས་ཅད་གྲོལ་ནས་འདུག་པས། ད་ཅི་ཡང་བྱ་མི་དགོས་པའི་སྐྱོན་དུ་ཐལ་ལོ། ཞེ་ན། བྱ་བ་མེད་པའི་བོན་བཅུ་གཉིས་ཀྱིས་བྱར་མེད་རྩོལ་འདས་ཆེན་པོར་ལ་བཟླས་པ་ཡིན་ཏེ། བྱ་བྱེད་མངས་ན་འཁོར་བར་འཁྱམས་པ་ནི། སྒྲས་བྲལ་ནམ་མཁའ་དང་མཉམ་པའི་རྒྱུད་ལས། བྱ་བྱེད་མངས་ན་ཡང་དཀ། དོན་ལ་མི་གནས་ཤིང་། རྩོལ་སྒྲུབ་དྲག་ན་གཤེན་རབ་བདུད་ཀྱི་གཡམ་ལ་རྒྱུག །བྱ་བྱེད་རང་གྲོལ་དོན་ལ་མ་ཡེངས་རྐྱོང་ངེ་ཤིགས་སེ་ཞོག ཅེས་སོ། ཐལ་འགྱུར་འདོད་ཐོག་ཏུ་བསྒྲུབ་པ་ཡིན་ནོ། འགལ་བ་ལམ་དུ་སློང་བ་ཡིན་སྐད། སྣང་བ་གྲོགས་སུ་ཁྱེར། ཅི་བྱས་དགེ་སྦྱོར་དུ་འགྲོ་བ་ཞེས་བྱའོ། གཉིས་པ་གསུམ། དགོས་པ་བཞི། གདིང་ཚད་གསུམ། བྱ་བྲལ་དུ་ལ་བཟླ་བའི་བོན་ལྔའོ། དང་པོ་ནི། བསྒྲུབ་བྱ་གོ་ཟློག་ཐུས་པ། གཞན་གྱི་སྒོ་སྒྲུར་ལ་ཉལ་མི་ང་བ། མཚན་མའི་བྱ་བ་ལ་བློ་མི་འཇུག་པ། སྒྲ་དང་ཟ་སྐད་ཕྱིར་མི་འབྲང་བ་

39

40

དང་བཞི་དགོས་སོ། གཉིས་པ་ནི། འཕྲུལ་གྱི་མངོན་པར་ཤེས་པའམ། རྫོད་རྟགས་ཕྲ་མོ་དག་ཨ་ཙང་ཡང་ཆེས་ཏེ། ཀུན་ཏུ་བཟང་པོ་རང་འོད་ཀྱི་ཞིར་མཐོང་ཡང་། རང་
སེམས་ལས་གཞན་ན་མེད་པར་ཐག་ཆོད་ནས། དཀའ་སྤྱོད་མི་སྐྱེ་ན་གོལ་སར་མི་འགྲོ་བའི་གདིང་ཚད་ཡིན། རྨིན་ན་ཚ་ཐུག་བསྔལ་སྒྲོ་བུར་བ་དག་ཨ་ཙང་ཡང་ཆེས་ཏེ། རྨྣ་དམྱལ་བའི་རྒྱལ་
པོས་ཞུགས་ཀྱི་ཁྲོ་ཆུ་ཁོལ་མ་ཁ་ཏ་བླུགས་ཤིང་། སྲིན་པོ་འབར་བ་རང་མཐོང་ཡང་རང་སྣང་ལས་མི་གཞན་པར་ཐག་ཆོད་ནས། ཉམ་ང་བག་ཚ་མེད་ན་གཡང་སར་མི་ལྷུང་བའི་གདིང་ཚད་ཡིན།
བསྟན་པའི་བོན་དང་སྙན་གྲགས་དང་སྨྲ་ཚད་མ་དག་ཨ་ཙང་ཡང་ཆེས་ཏེ། བདེ་གཤེགས་གཡུང་དྲུང་དཔའ་བོའམ། སྟོན་པ་གཤེན་རབ་རང་གདུགས་ཕྱི་ལོ་བོན་གསུངས་ནའང་། རང་གི་
སྣང་ཚུལ་ཡིན་པར་ཐག་ཆོད་ནས། ཚིག་ཕྱིར་མི་འབྲེང་ན་རྫོགས་པ་ཆེན་པོའི་གྲུབ་མཐའ་ལ་བློ་མི་ཕྱོག་པའི་གདིང་ཚད་ཡིན་ནོ། དེ་ལྟར་འཁོར་འདས་ཀྱི་བོན་ལ་རེ་དོགས་ཀྱི་སྤྲོས་ཆད།
ཉམ་ང་བག་ཚ་མེད་ན་བོན་བྱ་མི་དགོས་སོ། དེ་ལྟ་བུའི་གདིང་ཚད་དང་མི་ལྡན་ནས་ཉམ་ང་ན་གཡང་ས། ཐེ་ཚོམ་ཟ་བ་ན་སླར་ཕྱོག་གོ། གསུམ་པ་ལ་ལྔ་ལས། དང་པོ་དྲུས་པའི་བོན་

41

༄། ཀྱི་མ་སངས་མི་རྒྱ་བ་ནི། བྱས་པ་ཐམས་ཅད་འདུས་བྱས་ཡིན་པས། འདུས་བྱས་ཐམས་ཅད་མི་རྟག་པ་དང་། བྱར་མེད་ནམ་མཁའ་ལྟ་བུའི་དོན་བྱ་རྩོལ་གྱིས་མི་འགྲུབ་པས་བྱ་བྲལ་རྩོལ་འདས
ཆེན་པོར་ལ་བཟླ་སྟེ། ཐུ་མ་ལས། བྱ་བྲལ་རྩོལ་འདས་བསྒྲུབ་མེད་དོན་ལ་སུ་ཞིག་གནས། འགྲོ་བ་རྒྱུ་དྲུག་ལུས་དང་ལྷ་མི་གང་སྣང་ཀུང་། སེམས་ཉིད་ཡང་དག་བོན་ཉིད་ཀློང་དུ་ཡེ་
སངས་པས། སུ་ཞིག་བསྒྲིད་དྲང་དོན་ལ་འཇུག་འདོད་ན། རྩོལ་སྒྲུབ་མི་བྱ་དོན་ལ་གནས་པར་གྱིས། ཞེས་སོ། གཉིས་པ་སྤང་བྱ་མི་མཐུན་པའི་ཕྱོགས་གང་ཡང་མེད་པས་གཉེན་པོ་
རྒྱུད་ལ་མི་བརྟེན་པ་ཐམས་ཅད་དག་པ་འོད་གསལ་གྱི་ཞིང་ཁམས་བདེ་བ་ཆེན་པོར་ལ་བཟླ་སྟེ། ཀུན་བཟང་བདེ་བའི་ལུང་ལས། རྒྱལ་བའི་དཀྱིལ་འཁོར་གསེར་གྱི་གདན། ཕྱི་རོལ་ནང་གི་བསྡུས་པ་
ཀུན། བདེ་ཆེན་ཉིད་ལས་གཞན་མ་ཡིན། སངས་རྒྱས་ཉིད་ལས་མ་གཡོས་སོ། ཞེས་སོ། གསུམ་པ་ཅི་ལྟར་ཤར་ཤར་རང་བྱུང་ཡེ་ཤེས་ཀྱི་རོལ་པར། བོན་ཉིད་ཀྱི་རྒྱན་རང་ལ་
རང་ཤར་བ་ཡེ་ཤེས་ཀློང་བརྗོལ་བས། ཐམས་ཅད་རོ་གཅིག་མཉམ་པ་ཉིད་ཀྱི་དབྱིངས་སུ་ལ་བཟླ་སྟེ། བདེ་གཤེགས་དགོངས་པ་འདུས་པའི་རྒྱུད་ལས། རྟོག་པའི་རླུང་གིས་གཡོ་བསྐྱོད་

42

ཀུང་། རང་བྱུང་ཡེ་ཤེས་དབྱིངས་མི་ཉམས། ལྷུན་གྲུབ་ཆེན་པོར་ཞུབས་ཀྱིས་ཁྱབ། རྣམ་དག་ཡོངས་གྲོལ་འབྲས་བུ་ཆེ། དྲི་མེད་ཡེ་ཤེས་འོད་གསལ་བ། སྣ་ཚོགས་སྣང་བ་རོལ་
པའི་རྒྱན། ཞེས་སོ། བཞི་པ་འཁོར་འདས་ཀྱི་བོན་ཐམས་ཅད་ཤར་ཡང་བོན་ཉིད་ཀྱི་དབྱིངས་ནས་ཤར། གྲོལ་ཡང་བོན་ཉིད་ཀྱི་དབྱིངས་ནས་ཤར་དུས་ནས་གྲོལ་བས་སླར་གྲོལ་བ་གཏན་ལ་
ཕབ་མི་དགོས་པ་ཡེ་གྲོལ་ཆེན་པོར་ལ་བཟླ་སྟེ། དེ་ཉིད་ཀྱི་ལྡེའུ་བཅུ་པ་ལས། གོལ་སྒྲིབ་གདར་ཤ་དང་གིས་བཅད། རྟག་ཆད་ཚིག་ལས་ཡེ་ནས་འདས། མ་གྲུབ་མ་འགག་ཡེ་ནས་གྲོལ།
རྣམ་དག་རང་གྲོལ་ཆེན་པོའོ། ཞེས་སོ། ལྔ་པ་རང་བྱུང་གི་རིག་པ་རྟོགས་པས་བཟང་དུ་མ་སོང་མྱ་ངན་ལས་འདས་པའི་མཐའ་ལས་གྲོལ། མ་རྟོགས་པས་ངན་དུ་མ་སོང་འཁོར་བའི་མཐའ་
ལས་གྲོལ། བལྟས་པས་ཕྱོགས་རེ་ལས་མ་རྟོགས་པའི་རིས་ཆད་དུ་མ་སོང་ཐིག་པ་བརྒྱད་པོའི་མཐའ་ལས་གྲོལ། ཇི་ལྟར་བྱས་ཀྱང་ཡེ་ནས་གྲོལ་ཟིན་པས་ད་བལྟ་རུ་མེད་བསྒོམ་དུ་མེད་བསྒྲུབ་དུ་
མེད། བྱར་མེད་རྩོལ་མེད་པས་ཀུ་ཡངས་སློ་བདེར་གནས་པས་ཆོག་གོ། གསུམ་པ་ཉམས་ལེན་གདིང་གིས་བཅད་པ་ནི། འོ་ན་བོན་ཐམས་ཅད་བྱར་མེད་ཡིན་ན། རིམ་པ་བརྒྱད་པོའི་

ཁ ཞེར་གཉིས

༄། །ཀྱཻ་སྤྱོད་ཐམས་ཅད་དོན་མེད་དམ། ཞེ་ན། དེ་དག་རྩོལ་བ་དང་བཅས་པས་རྩོལ་མེད་ཀྱི་དོན་མི་ཐུབ་པས་དེར་མི་འཇུག་ཀྱང་དེ་དག་གི་ཡོན་ཏན་ཤུགས་ལས་ཐོབ་ཅིང་རང་
གི་རོལ་པར་ཤེས་པས་གོལ་ས་ཐམས་ཅད་ཆོད་པ་སྟེ། ཐ་མ་ལས། དཔེར་ན་ཤུགས་ཆེན་ཉ་བརྒྱུགས་ན། རྩེ་ཐོག་ཤུགས་ཀྱིས་འདོར་བ་ལྟར། རྩོལ་བ་བཅས་པའི་ཐེག་པ་རྣམས།
རིག་པ་རྒྱལ་པོ་དབང་ཆེན་གྱིས། ཤུགས་ཀྱིས་འདོར་ཞིང་རྩད་ནས་སྐྱེལ། བཙལ་མེད་འབྲས་བུ་རང་བྱུང་ཉིད། བསྒྲོད་མེད་དགོངས་པ་རང་ལ་རྫོགས། །གདོད་ནས་འཛིན་མེད་ལྷུན་
གྱིས་གྲུབ། ཅེས་སོ། དེ་བས་རང་བཞིན་རྫོགས་པ་ཆེན་པོ་ལ་ཅི་ཡང་བྱར་མེད་པས། བྱར་མེད་རང་ལ་ཉིན་ཞལ་མཚན་ཞལ་ལ་ཉམ་མི་ང་བ་ལྟ་བ། དེ་ལ་སོ་སྣ་འབྱམས་པ་སྒོམ་པ།
རང་བྱུང་དགག་ཏུ་མེད་པ་སྤྱོད་པ། རིག་པ་གང་དགར་གཏོང་བ་དགོངས་ཉམས། རྣམ་རྟོག་ལ་དཀྲུར་མི་ལྟ་བ་བློའི་བཅོས་ཐབས། དུག་ལྔ་མདོག་མི་བསྒྱུར་བ་གདམས་ངག དགེ་
སྡིག་ལ་སྤང་བླང་མི་བྱེད་པ་རྟུལ་ཤུགས། མི་མཐུན་པ་གྲོགས་ཏུ་མི་འདོར་བ་འབྲས་བུ། གཉེན་པོ་རྒྱུད་ལ་མི་བསྟེན་པ་དམ་ཚིག བྱ་བ་ཅི་དང་ཅི་བྱེད་པ་ཐམས་ཅད་ཤུགས་འབྱུང་དུ་གཏོང་བ་

43

ཕྲིན་ལས། གྲོལ་ས་དང་རང་ས་ན་ཡོད་པས་རེ་དོགས་མེད་པ་ལམ། རྟོགས་ཙང་མ་རྟོགས་ཙང་ཐམས་ཅད་རང་གྲོལ་དུ་ཡོད་པ་གོ་ཚད་ཡིན་ནོ། བོན་ཐམས་ཅད་བྱར་མེད་གཅིག་པུར་འདུས་སོ།
འོ་ན་དེ་མེད་པ་ཕྱོགས་གཅིག་པར་མ་སོང་ངམ་ཞེ་ན། བྱར་མེད་ཀྱི་དོན་རྟོགས་པས། བྱེད་པ་ལྟར་མ་འགགས། བྱེད་པ་ལྟར་མ་ཞེན། མི་བྱེད་པ་ལྟར་མ་འགགས། མི་བྱེད་པ་
ལྟར་མ་ཞེན། མ་འགགས་ཏེ་རང་ཤར། མ་ཞེན་ཏེ་རང་གྲོལ། ཇི་ལྟར་བྱས་ཀྱང་རང་ཤར་རང་གྲོལ་གྱི་ཀློང་ལས་མ་འདས་པས་གོལ་ས་དང་ལྷུང་ས་མེད་དོ། དོན་གཉིས་པ་བསྒོམ་
པས་གྲོལ་བ་ཐོད་རྒལ་གྱི་ལམ་བཤད་པ་ལ་གཉིས། ཁྲིགས་ཆོད་ལས་འཕགས་ཚུལ། །ཁྱད་པར་ཅན་གྱི་ལམ་དངོས་བཤད་པའོ། དང་པོ་ལ་ཡེ་ཁྲི་ལས་འཕགས་ཚུལ་བཏུས་བཤད་པ་ཡོད་
ཀྱང་འདིར་བསྡུ་ནས་བཤད་ན་རྣམ་པ་བདུན་ལས། །དང་པོ་བཟུང་འཛིན་དག་པའི་ཁྱད་པར་ནི། ཁྲིགས་ཆོད་དུ་རི་ཐག་སོགས་ཡུལ་གཞི་མེད་དང་། འཛིན་སེམས་རང་གྲོལ་དུ་རྒྱས་
འདེབས་བྱེད་པ་ཙམ་ལས། རྟོས་བཅས་རང་དག་བྱེད་མི་ནུས་པ་ཉིད། ཐོད་རྒལ་དུ་དབྱིངས་འོད་ལྔའི་སྣང་བ་ལ་བརྟེན་ནས། ཕྱི་ཡུལ་འོད་དུ་དག་པས་གཟུང་འཛིན་ལས་དངོས་སུ་གྲོལ་

44

ཁ ཞེར་གསུམ

༄། བ་ནི། ཡེ་ཁྲི་ལས། གཟུང་འཛིན་མི་གནས་རྣམ་པར་དག དེ་ཡི་ངང་དུ་སངས་རྒྱས་ཆེ། ཞེས་སོ། གཉིས་པ་ཕུང་པོ་རང་སྣང་གི་ཁྱད་པར་ནི། ཁྲིགས་ཆོད་འབྱོངས་པ་ན་
ལུས་རྡུལ་ཕྲན་ཆ་མེད་ཙམ་ལས་འོད་དུ་མི་འགྱུར་ལ་འོད་དུ་མ་སོང་ན། རེས་འགའ་བའི་སྐུ་ལུས་དང་ཟད་པར་གྱི་སྐྱེ་མཆེད་སོགས་ཀྱིས་མཐར་ཐུག་གིས་མི་ཆོད་པ་དང་། འོད་ལུས་མ་ཐོབ་ན་སྤྱན་
དང་མངོན་ཤེས་རྫུ་འཕྲུལ་རླབས་ཆེའི་བདག་ཉིད་འཕོ་ཆེན་གྱི་སྐུ་མི་འཐོབ་པས། རྟེན་དེས་འགྲོ་དོན་རྒྱ་ཆེ་མི་འགྲུབ་པ་ལ། ཐོད་རྒལ་དུ་གཟུགས་ཕུང་རང་སྣང་རང་འོད་དང་ཕུང་གཞན་རང་
སར་དག་སྟེ། གཡུང་དྲུང་གི་སྐུར་གྲུབ་པས་འཁོར་བ་མ་སྟོངས་ཀྱི་བར་དུ་བཞུགས་ནས་འགྲོ་དོན་མཛད་པ་ནི། ཐ་མ་ལས། ཕུང་པོ་ལྔ་རྣམས་སྣང་བ་ཡང་། མ་སྲུངས་རང་སྣང་དག
པས་ཆེ། ཞེས་སོ། གསུམ་པ་རྣམ་ཤེས་དག་པའི་ཁྱད་པར་ནི། ཁྲིགས་ཆོད་དུ་འཁྲུལ་སྣང་མ་འགགས་པས། འཁྲུལ་ཤེས་མི་འགགས་ལ་ཡུལ་ཡུལ་ཅན་གྱི་བོན་ལ་བརྟེན་པས་སླར་དུ་གྲོལ་དཀའ་
བ་ཉིད། ཐོད་རྒལ་དུ་ཡུལ་དག་པས་རྣམ་ཤེས་རང་སོག་ནས། ཡུལ་ཡུལ་ཅན་དུ་རྟོག་པ་མེད་པས་འཁྲུལ་སྣང་མེད་མེད། ཡུལ་སེམས་རང་དག་སེམས་དཔའ་སེམས་མ་རུ་གྲོལ་བའི་ཁྱད་

45

46

ཨཱ་ཏི་ཞེ

ཞུགས་པ་ནི། དེ་ཉིད་ལས། ཉམས་ཤེས་བརྒྱད་ཀྱི་ཡུལ་བརྒྱད་ཀྱང་། རང་ལས་སྣང་བའི་སེམས་མ་བརྒྱད། །མ་བཙལ་དང་ལས་ལྷུན་གྱི་གྲུབ། ཡེ་ཤེས་རང་སྣང་བདག་ཉིད་ཆེ། །
ཞེས་སོ། བཞི་པ་འོད་གསལ་མངོན་མཐོང་གིས་རང་ལས་གཞན་དུ་འགྲོ་དོན་བྱེད་དུ་མེད་པ་ནི། རིག་པ་འོད་ཀྱི་ལུས་སུ་ཡེ་ནས་ཡོད། གསུངས་པ་དེ་ཁྲིགས་ཆོད་དུ་སྟོང་པར་མཇལ་བ་ལས་རང་
འོད་མ་མཐོང་བས། ཡུལ་སྣང་རང་སྣང་འོད་གསལ་དུ་མ་གྲོལ་ཏེ་གཞན་དུ་ལྟ་བ་མ་སྤྲངས་པས་འགྲོ་དོན་ཡང་གཞན་དུ་བྱེད་པ་ལ། ཐོད་རྒལ་དུ་གནད་གཅུན་པས་ཛ་ཐའི་རིག་པ་ནང་དུ་ཟིན
དུས་ལྷག་མཐོང་གི་རིག་པ་འོད་གདངས་ཕྱིར་གསལ་ནས་ཐམས་ཅད་རང་སྣང་འོད་གསལ་དུ་གྲོལ་བས། རང་ལས་གཞན་དུ་འགྲོ་དོན་བྱེད་དུ་མེད་པ་ནི། དེ་ཉིད་ལས། རང་ལས་འབྱུང་
ཞིང་རང་ལ་སྣང་། ངང་དྭངས་ཡིན་པས་ཡུལ་བྲལ་དང་། ཡུལ་མེད་རང་སྣང་ཆེན་པོ་ལ། འགྲོ་དོན་གཞན་དུ་མེད་པས་ཆེ། ཞེས་སོ། འོ་ན་སེམས་ཅན་རང་སྣང་དུ་ཤེས་ནས་འགྲོ་དོན་མི་བྱེད་པ་མ་ཡིན་
ནམ་ཞེ་ན། རང་སྣང་དུ་ཤེས་བཞིན་དུ་འགྲོ་དོན་ཡང་མཛད་པའོ། ལྔ་པ་འབྲས་བུ་བཙལ་དུ་མེད་པའི་ཁྱད་པར་ནི། ཁྲིགས་ཆོད་དུ་འཁྲུལ་སྣང་རགས་པས་བཀག་ནས་འབྲས་བུ་རྐྱག་ཏུ

47

ཞ

ཨར་བཞི

༄། ཕྱུར་པ་ལ། ཐོད་རྒལ་དུ་སྣང་བ་ཚད་དུ་ཕྱིན་པས་ན་མངོན་དུ་བྱེད་ནས་འབྲས་བུ་ཕྱིའི་དུས་ལ་མི་འཛོག་པར། ཚེ་འདིའི་ཐོག་ལ་འབྲས་བུ་ཐོབ་པ་ནི། ཐ་མ་ལས། འབྲས་བུ་རང་ཆེ་བཙལ་
དུ་མེད། མ་བཙལ་ལྷུན་གྱིས་གྲུབ་པས་ཆེ། ཞེས་སོ། དྲུག་པ་རང་སྣང་མངོན་སུམ་དུ་གཟིགས་པའི་ཁྱད་པར་ནི། ཁྲིགས་ཆོད་དུ་དབང་དྲུག་གི་སྒོ་མ་དག་པ་ལ། །སེམས་ཀྱི་དྭངས་འཚོལ་དགོས་པ་བྱུང་ལ།
ཐོད་རྒལ་དུ་འོད་གསལ་གྱི་སྒོ་ཡེ་ཤེས་ཀྱི་རླུང་གིས་ཕྱེ་བས་སྒྲོན་མ་བཞིའི་སྣང་བ་འཆར་བས་འཁྲུལ་སྣང་རང་དག་གིས་ཐམས་ཅད་རང་སྣང་དུ་རྟོགས་ནས་བོན་ཉིད་ཟེར་གདང་ལ་མཇལ་བས་དོན་ལ་འདུ
འབྲལ་མེད་པ་ནི། དེ་ཉིད་ལས། རང་གི་སྣང་བའི་དོན་རྟོགས་པས། དོན་ལ་འདུ་འབྲལ་མེད་པས་ཆེ། ཞེས་སོ། བདུན་པ་ས་ཡི་ཁྱད་པར་ནི། ཁྲིགས་ཆོད་དུ་སེམས་ཙམ་ལས་སྣང་ལུས་གཉིས་ཚད་དུ
བསྐྱལ་མ་ནུས་ལ། འདི་སྦྱོང་དུ་མེད་པའི་དོན་ལ་བསྐྱལ་ནས་མི་འགྱུར་གཡུང་དྲུང་གི་ས་ཆེན་པོ་ཐོབ་པ་ནི། དེ་ལས། མི་འགྱུར་གཡུང་དྲུང་ས་འདི་ལ། དོན་ལ་སྦྱོང་དུ་མེད་པས་ཆེ། ཞེས་སོ། གཉིས་པ་མན
ངག་གི་གནད་དེས་པ་གཏན་ལ་ཕབ་པ་ནི། རིག་པ་ཁྲོ་རྒྱུག་གི་ཡན་ལག་བཞི་པ་ལས། རང་ཤེས་རིག་གི་རྒྱལ་པོ་བྱང་ཆུབ་ཀྱི་སེམས་དེ་ཉིད་འགྲོ་བ་སེམས་ཅན་གྱི་དོན་ལ་རྫུ་འཕྲུལ་གྱི་སྤྲུར་སྦྱང་ཙམ་ཉིད་ན།

48

ཨཱ་ཏི་ཞེ

དབང་གི་བྱིའུ་འཕར་མ་མཆུ་རིང་ཞེས་བྱ་བ་སྒྲོ་བ་མ་བཞི་བུ་བཞི་བྲག་དམར་མཚལ་དཀར་དང་འདྲ་བའི་ཚང་ནས་བྱུང་ནས། ཧ་དེ་ལ་ཞོན་ནས་འགྲོ་བ་སེམས་ཅན་གྱི་དོན་རྒྱ་ལག་ཕྱུད་པར་མཛད་དེ། ཅང་
ཤེས་སྤྲུལ་པའི་ཧ་དེས་ནི་བསྐྱོད་ཅིང་འགྲོ་བའི་ཚེ་ན། རྒྱལ་པོ་ཆེན་པོ་བཞིས་ནི་ཞབས་ནས་འདེགས་སོ། དུས་བཞིའི་རྒྱལ་མོ་བཞིས་ནི་མཐའ་རྟེན་ནོ། སྤྲུལ་པའི་རླུང་བཞིས་ནི་བསྐྱོད་ཅིང་
འདེགས་སོ། ཆུ་བོ་ཆེན་པོ་བཞིས་ནི་བསོད་ནམས་ཀྱི་རྒྱུན་བསྲིང་ངོ་། སྤྲུལ་པའི་མེ་བཞིས་ནི་དྲོད་སྐྱོམས་སོ། གསེར་གྱི་ས་གཞི་ལ་ནི་གནས་བཅས་སོ། གསལ་བའི་མེ་ལོང་བརྒྱད་ནི
སྐུ་ལ་བརྒྱན་ནོ། གསང་བའི་ཡི་གེ་འབྲུ་གསུམ་ནི་ཐུགས་ལ་བཀོད་དོ། གསལ་བའི་སྒྲོན་མ་ལྔ་ལ་ནི་དབུ་ཡི་གཙུག་ནས་སྐྱེས་སོ། གཟའ་དང་རྒྱུ་སྐར་ནི་སྐྱེད་ནས་འཆར་རོ། འཁོར་རྣམ་པ
བཞིས་ནི་བཀའ་ཉོན་བྱེད་དོ། འགྲོ་བ་སེམས་ཅན་གྱི་དོན་མ་འགགས་ཤིང་རྣམ་པར་འབྱེད་པ་ནི། ཧ་དེའི་ཡོན་ཏན་ཡིན་ནོ། ཞེས་སོ། འདི་ནི་འོད་གསལ་ཐོད་རྒལ་གྱི་གནད་དེས་པ་
དག་ཀུན་ཏུ་བཟང་པོས་གསུངས་ནས་མཁའ་འགྲོ་མ་རྣམས་ཀྱིས་བརྡ་ཚིག་གིས་བཅིངས་པ་ལྷ་ཐོག་གི་མཁས་གྲུབ་དུ་མ་ཐོན་པ་དག་གིས་བརྡ་མ་བཀྲོལ་བར་ཁོ་བོའི་བགོ་སྐལ་དུ་བཞག་པ་ཞིག་དེས་པའོ།

ཀ ཤེར་ཞེ

༄༅། །དེས་ན་དབང་ཕྱིའུ་མཆུ་རིང་ནི་རིག་གདངས་ལ་ཟེར་ལ། སྙིང་དབུས་སུ་རིག་པ་བཞུགས་པས། སྙིང་ནས་རྩ་གྲུ་སོག་གི་ཕྲུབས་ཙམ་གཅིག་སྒོ་བར་ཟུག་པ་དེའི་ནང་རླུང་གིས་གང་བས། རླུང་དེས་རིག་གདངས་བསྐྱོད་པ་ལས་རྣམ་རྟོག་ཐམས་ཅད་འབྱུང་བ་ལ་སེམས་ཞེས་བྱ་ལ། རླུང་ནི་རྟ་ཞར་བ་རྐང་ཅན་ལ་སེམས་སྐྱེས་བུ་འཕྱེ་བོ་མིག་ཅན་བསྐྱོན་པ་དང་འདྲ་བ་ལ། རླུང་ཞི་བ་དང་གདངས་རིག་པ་ལ་ཐིམ་ནས་མི་འགྱུ་དགུ་འགྱུའི་རྟོག་པ་དག་པའི་རིག་པ་ངོ་བོ་རང་བཞིན་ཐུགས་རྗེ་གསུམ་གྱིས་མཚོན་པའི་འོད་གསལ་གྱི་འཆར་གཞི་མ་འགགས་པར་བཞུགས་པ་ལ། ཐོད་རྒལ་གྱི་གནད་ཟབ་མོས་གཟུན་པས་གདངས་ཡེ་ཤེས་ཀྱི་རླུང་གིས་བསྐྱོད་ནས་འོད་རྩ་དག་པ་ནས་མིག་རྒྱང་ཞགས་ཀྱི་སྒོར་ཤར་བ་དེ་ཉིད་ཚད་དུ་བསྐྱལ་བས་འཁོར་བའི་སྒོ་དག་ནས་ཡེ་ཤེས་ཀྱི་སྣང་བ་ལ་སོངས་སྐྱོད་པའོ། དེའི་ཕྱིར་ན་ཐོད་རྒལ་གྱི་གནད་ཟབ་མོ་བཞི་བཅུ་རྩ་གཉིས་སུ་བསྟན་པ་དེ་དག་གོ་རིམ་དང་བསྟུན་ནས་བཤད་པ་ནི། རྒྱལ་པོ་ཆེན་པོ་བཞིས་ནི་ཞབས་ནས་འདེགས་སོ། ཞེས་པ་ནི། གནད་རྣམ་པ་བཞི་སྟེ། ལུས་ངག་སེམས་ཀྱི་གནད། འཆར་བྱེད་སྒོ་ཡི་གནད། འཆར་གཞི་ཡུལ་གྱི་གནད། རླུང་རིག་དལ་བའི་གནད་དོ། དེས་ན་དམུ་རྒྱལ་ 49

ཤེར་ང

ཕྲུས་པོ་ཉིད་བསྟན་འཛིན་གྱི་རྒྱལ་པོ་ཆེན་པོ་བཞིས་བཏེག་པའི་དུས་ན་འཛིག་རྟེན་གསུམ་ན་དབང་བསྒྱུར་བ་ལྟར། རིག་པའང་གནད་རྣམ་པ་བཞིས་བཏེག་པས་ཡེ་ཤེས་ཀྱི་སྣང་བ་ལ་དབང་བསྒྱུར་བའོ། དེའི་དང་པོ་ལའང་ནང་གསེས་གསུམ་གྱི་དང་པོ་རྟེན་ལུས་གཟུན་པས་རྩ་རླུང་ལས་སུ་རུང་ནས་འོད་གསལ་མངོན་དུ་འཆར་བས་ལུས་གནད་གཟུན་པ་གལ་ཆེའོ། དེའང་གསེར་གྱི་ཕྲེང་བ་མཛེས་པ་ལས། བོན་སྐུ་སེང་གེའི་འདུག་སྟངས་དང་། ཡོངས་སྐུ་གླང་པོ་ཆེའི་འདུག་སྟངས། སྤྲུལ་སྐུ་དྲང་སྲོང་ཙོག་པུས་འདུག ཅེས་རང་རང་གི་བཅའ་ཐབས་དང་། དགོས་པ་གཉིས་རིས་བསྟན་པ་ལ། །དང་པོ་བོན་སྐུའི་བཞུགས་སྟངས་སེང་གེ་འགྱིང་བ་ལྟ་བུ་ནི། འགྱིང་ཚུགས་ཙོག་པུའི་རྐང་པའི་བྲང་བ་གཉིས་ས་ལ་བཙུགས། རྐང་པ་བསྐྱང་ལ་འོག་སྒོ་ཅུང་ཟད་བསྡམ། མགོ་རྩལ་མཛིང་པ་ལ་བསྐུར། ལག་སོར་གཉིས་ནང་དུ་སྒོངས་ཏེ་རྐང་པ་གཉིས་ཀྱི་བར་དུ་ས་ལ་བཙུག་གོ། འདི་ཁ་ཅིག་རྐང་མཐིལ་ས་ལ་ཐབ་པར་འདོད་དེ། རང་གི་ལུང་དོན་དང་མཐུན་མ་རྣམས་ཀྱི་ཕྱག་ལེན་ལ་ཅུང་ཟད་འགལ་བར་སྣང་ངོ། དགོས་པ་ནི། གཡོ་བྱེད་ཀྱི་རླུང་དོན་ནས་དབུ་མ་བྱང་ཆུབ་ཀྱི་རྩ་ཁ་ཕྱེ། ཕྱི་རུ་སྣང་བ་འཕྲུལ་ལ་འཆར། ནང་དུ་བོན་སྐུ་སྐྱོ 50

ཀ ཤེར་ངཀ

༄༅། །འདས་ཀྱི་དགོངས་པ་འཆར་རོ། གཉིས་པ་ཡོངས་སྐུའི་བཞུགས་སྟངས་གླང་ཆེན་ཉལ་བ་ལྟ་བུ་ནི། པུས་བྲང་སྦྱར་ལ་གྲུ་མོ་གཉིས་ས་ལ་བཙུགས་པའི་ཐལ་མོས་ཨོལ་མགོ་བརྟེན། པུས་མོ་ས་ལ་མ་རེག་ཙམ་གྱི་ལྟེད་གྲུ་མོ་དང་རྐང་པའི་བྲང་བ་གཉིས་ལ་བསྒྱུར་རོ། འདིའང་རྐང་སོར་ཕྱིར་འཕྱལ་བར་འདོད་པ་གཞན་ལུགས་ཡིན་པས་རང་ལུགས་ལ་ཅུང་ཟད་མི་མཐུན་ནོ། དགོས་པ་ནི། འགྱུ་བྱེད་ཀྱི་རླུང་དོན་ནས་ཆགས་སྡང་གི་རྟོག་པ་འགག གླང་ཆེན་བཞིན་དུ་སྟོབས་རྒྱས། ཕྱི་རུ་ཞིང་ཁམས་རྫོགས་པ་འཆར། ནང་དུ་ཉམས་རྟོགས་ལ་བོག་ཅིག་ཅར་དུ་སྐྱེའོ། གསུམ་པ་སྤྲུལ་སྐུའི་བཞུགས་སྟངས་དྲང་སྲོང་ཙོག་པུ་ནི། ལུས་ཙོག་འདུག་གི་རྐང་མཐིལ་གཉིས་ས་ལ་ཐབ་ཤ། པུས་མོ་གཉིས་གྲུ་མོའི་ཁུགས་སུ་ཚུད་པར་བྱས་ལ་པུས་བྲང་སྦྱར། ལག་པ་གཉིས་བར་ལྷུ་ལ་བཟུང་ཞིང་རྐལ་ཆིགས་བསྲང་ལ་སྐྲ་མཛིང་ཅུང་ཙམ་བསྡུད་དོ། དེ་ལས་གྲུ་མོ་གཉིས་པུས་མོའི་སྟེང་དུ་བཙུག་པའི་ཐལ་མོས་འགྲམ་པ་གཡས་གཡོན་བསྐྱོར་བ་ལུས་གནད་གཅིག་ཆོག་གོ། དགོས་པ་ནི། སྨིན་བྱེད་ཀྱི་མེ་དྲོད་འབེབས་ཤིང་རྣམ་རྟོག་ཕྲ་རགས་ཐམས་ཅད་ཞི། ཕྱི་རུ་སྤྲུལ་སྐུའི་སྣང་བ་འཆར། ནང་དུ་གསལ་སྣང་ཁྱད་པར་ཅན་སྐྱེའོ། འདུག་སྟངས 51

རྣམས་གང་ཡང་ཏ་ཙང་གཙུམ་པའི་བསྒམས་པ་མ་ཡིན་པར་ཆ་ཆ་ནས་རྟོད་ཆགས་པས་གཙུན་པས་གེགས་མི་འཇུག་ཅིང་ཡོན་ཏན་སྐྱེ་བོག་ཆེའོ། འདི་དག་ལས་གཞན་དུ་དང་མོ་དང་གནའ་བོའི་འཇུག་སྟངས་ཀུང་ཡོད་པ་ལས་དང་མོའི་ཟུར་འཁྲོས་ཀྱི་འདུག་སྟངས་འདི་ལས་དང་པོ་བས་དབྱིངས་སྣང་མཇལ་བ་ལ་སྟབས་བདེ་བ་ལྟ་བུར་འདུག་པས། གྲུ་མོ་གཡས་པ་ས་ལ་བཙུག་པའི་ཐལ་མོས་འགྲམ་པ་གཡས་བརྟེན། ལག་པ་གཡོན་པ་དབྱི་འཁོར་བརྐྱང་ལ་བྲུག་མཛེར་མནན། རྐང་པ་གཉིས་ཙུང་ཟད་སྐྱིད་ཁྲུགས་བྱས་ལ་ཉ་ཤ་གཉིས་བསྒེགས་པ་ལྟར་བྱའོ། དགོས་པ་ནི། རླུང་དབུ་མར་ཚུད་ནས་རྩ་འཕྲུལ་ཡ་མ་ཟུང་དུ་འབྱུང་། དབྱིངས་སྣང་གི་འཕེལ་ཆེའོ། །གཉིས་པ་དག་གི་གནད་ནི། རྟགས་ཚད་སྒྲོན་མ་ལས། དེ་ནས་རྟག་ཏུ་ངག་མ་བཅད་ན། བརྗོད་དུ་མེད་པའི་དོན་མི་མཐོང་བས། ཐིག་ལེ་ཉག་གཅིག་མངོན་དུ་མི་འཆར་རོ། ཞེས་པས། གླེང་བ་ཇེ་ཉུང་ལ་བཏང་ཞིང་མཐར་བརྗོད་པ་ཐམས་ཅད་སྤང་ལ་སྨྲ་བཅད་ལ་གནས་པར་བྱའོ། གསུམ་པ་སེམས་ཀྱི་གནད་ནི། སེམས་ཞེས་རིག་པའི་སྙིང་པོ་ཅན་དེ་ཉིད་ལྟ་སྟངས་དང་བསྟུན་ནས་ཕྱིའི་ནམ་མཁའ་ལ་མདུད་ཚུགས་སུ་གཏད་པས་གཡོ་བྱེད་རླུང་ཞི་ནས་དབྱིངས་རིག་དབྱེར་མེད་ཀྱི

༄། དགོངས་པ་ཟབ་མོ་ངང་གིས་འཆར་བར་འགྱུར་ཏེ། སྒྲ་མ་ལས། མིག་གིས་ལྟ་སྟངས་ཀྱིས་རིག་པ་མ་གཙུན་ན། རིག་པ་ཉིད་མངོན་སུམ་དུ་མི་འཆར་རོ། ཞེས་སོ། ། གཉིས་པ་སྒོའི་གནད་ནི། ཐ་མལ་གྱི་ལྟ་ཕྱུགས་ཀྱིས་ཡེ་ཤེས་མི་འཆར་བས་མིག་ལྟ་སྟངས་དང་བསྟུན་དགོས་ལ། ལྟ་སྟངས་དེའང་བཞུགས་སྟངས་གསུམ་དང་འབྲེལ་པར་བྱ་སྟེ། གསེར་གྱི་ཕྲེང་བ་ལས། བོན་སྐུའི་གཟིགས་སྟངས་གྱེན་དུ་བལྟ། སྤྲུལ་སྐུའི་གཟིགས་སྟངས་ཐུར་དུ་ཕབ། ལོངས་སྐུའི་གཟིགས་སྟངས་ཟུར་བལྟར་ཟུར་ཁྲིད་གཅེས། ཞེས་སོ། སྒོའི་གནད་དེ་ལྟར་གསུམ་དུ་ངེས་ནའང་དེའི་དོན་པོ་དབྱིངས་མཇལ་བ་གཙོ་བས་ན། སྒྲ་མ་ལས། ཉི་མའི་འོག་ནས་ཙུང་ཟད་ཕབ། ཟིམ་བུའི་མིག་གིས་མ་ཡེངས་བལྟ། ཞེས་པས། མིག་བྱེད་བཙུམས་ཟིམ་བུས་ཉི་མ་ལ་ཡིན་ན་ཁྲུ་གང་ཙམ་གྱིས་མ་རེག་པའི་སར་བལྟ་བ་ནི་གནད་དོ། སྒོའི་གནད་འཛིངས་པས་ཡུལ་ལ་ཇི་ཙམ་བལྟས་ཀྱང་ཚོགས་པ་ཡིན་ནོ། གསུམ་པ་ཡུལ་གྱི་གནད་ནི། རྐྱེན་མེད་པའི་གནས་མཐོ་ཞིང་དངས་སངས་བྱེད་པ་ནས་སྨུན་དང་བྲལ་བའི་ཆུའི་སྒྲོན་མས་ནམ་མཁའ་གཡའ་དག་པ་ལ་བལྟས་པས་འོད་གསལ་གྱི་སྣང་བ་འཆར་ལ། ལས་དང་པོ

བས་སྔ་དྲོ་དང་ཕྱི་དྲོའི་ཟེར་གཉིས་དང་སྦྱར་ཞིང་། དབྱིངས་རིག་སྐྱིན་མཚམས་ནས་བྲལ་བ་ན་ནམ་མཁའ་དངས་པར་བལྟ་ལ་དེའང་མཐིང་ཤོག་ལས། སྔ་དྲོ་ནུབ་དབང་ཕྱོགས་སུ་བལྟ། དགོངས་ཀ་དྲི་ཟའི་ཕྱོགས་སུ་བལྟ། ཞེས་སྔ་དྲོ་ནུབ་དང་དགོངས་ཀར་ཤར་ཕྱོགས་ཀྱི་ནམ་མཁའ་ལ་བལྟའོ། བཞི་པ་རླུང་རིག་དལ་བའི་གནད་ནི། ཁ་ཅིག་རླུང་སྒོར་བཞི་ཐུན་དུ་བཤད་ཀྱང་གནད་མ་གོ་བར་ཟད་དོ། གདམས་པ་འདིའི་ལུགས་ལ་རླུང་སྣ་ནས་མི་གཏོང་བར་ཁ་ནས་མཆུ་སོ་མ་རེག་ཙམ་གྱི་བར་ནས་ཤིན་ཏུ་དལ་བུས་འབྱུང་འཇུག་བྱེད་པ་སྟེ། རླུང་དལ་བ་བསྟེན་པས་རིག་པ་བཙོན་དུ་གཟུང་བ་ཞེས་བྱ་སྟེ། སྒོ་བའི་རླུང་འགྲོ་འོང་གི་རྣམ་པ་ཅན་རང་བཞིན་གྱིས་དག་པས་རིག་གདངས་སྙིང་གར་ཐིམ་ནས་སེམས་རྟོག་རང་ཞི་ལ་སོང་སྟེ་རིག་སྟོང་རྗེན་པ་མངོན་དུ་འཆར་བའོ། སྤྲུལ་པའི་རླུང་བཞིས་ནི་བསྐྱོད་ཅིང་འདེགས་སོ། ཞེས་པ་ནི། །ཁྱད་པར་གྱི་རྩ་ཆེན་བཞི་སྟེ། རླུང་གིས་ཐམས་ཅད་བསྐྱོད་ཅིང་སྣང་སྲིད་ཀུན་འདེགས་པ་ལྟར། ཁྱད་པར་གྱི་རྩ་བཞིས་འོད་གསལ་གྱི་སྣང་བ་ཐམས་ཅད་བསྐྱོད་ཅིང་བོན་ཉིད་མངོན་སུམ་ནས་ཉམས་སྣང་གོང་ནས་གོང་འཕེལ་འདེགས་པར་བྱེད་དོ། ཐིག་ལེ་དྲུག་པ་ལས། སྤྱིར་ནི་བཞི་བསྟུས

༄། ཕུང་པོ་འདི། རྩ་བའི་དྭ་བ་ཡིན་གྱུར་ཀྱང་། དོན་བྱེད་ནུས་པའི་རྩ་བཞིར་ཡོད། ཅེས་པ། ཀ་ཏི་གསེར་གྱི་རྩ་ཆེན། དར་དཀར་སྣལ་མ། ཕྲ་ལ་འཁྱིལ། །སེལ་
ཟུག་ཅན་དང་བཞི་ཡིན་ནོ། དེ་ལས་གསེར་གྱི་རྩ་ཆེན་ནི་དབུ་མའི་དབུས་ནས་སྙིང་དུ་འབྲེལ་པར་གནས་ལ། སྙིང་པོ་འོད་གསལ་གྱི་གདངས་སྙིང་དབུས་ན་གཡུང་དྲུང་ཡོངས་སུ་རྫོགས་པའི་ལྷ་
ཚོགས་དང་། དྲུང་ཁང་གི་ཁྲོ་བོ་རྣམས་དང་། དེའི་གདངས་རྩ་རྣམས་ཀྱི་ཐིག་ལེ་རྣམས་འཆར་བའི་རྟེན་བྱེད། དར་དཀར་སྣལ་མ་ལྟ་བུའི་ནང་རྩ་འགྲེང་བུའི་ནང་རྩ་འགྲེང་བུ་གཅིག་ལ་
གཉིས་སུ་གྱེས་པའི་སྣ་གཅིག་མིག་གཡས་སུ་བྲུག་ནས་ཕྱིར་ཡུལ་ལ་འཇུག་པའི་རྟེན་བྱེད། གཅིག་ཚངས་བུག་ལ་བྲུག་ནས་ངོ་བོ་སྟོང་གདངས་རིག་པ་རྟོག་མེད་ཆེན་པོ་འཆར་ལ། ཚད་ཐེབས་ཀྱི་དུས་ན་ཐིག་ལེ་
ལྔའམ་དགུ་བརྩེགས་སུ་འཆར་བའི་རྟེན་བྱེད། ཕྲ་ལ་འཁྱིལ་ནི་འཁོར་ལོ་བཞིའི་དབུས་ནས་མིག་གཡོན་པར་བྲུག་ནས་རང་བཞིན་འོད་གདངས་རང་ལ་དངོས་སུ་འཆར་བའི་རྟེན་བྱེད། སེལ་ཟུག་ཅན
ནི་སྙིང་ནས་མིག་ཏུ་འབྲེལ་ནས་རང་ལ་སྣང་ཞིང་ནང་དུ་ནུབ་པའི་རྟེན་བྱེད་དོ། ཐུགས་རྗེའི་རིག་གདངས་སྒྲོ་རྩ་ན་སེམས་སུ་འཆར་བའོ། ཕྱུལ་པའི་མེ་བཞིས་ནི་རྟོད་སྐྱམས་སོ། ཞེས་པ་ནི།

སྒྲོན་མ་བཞི་སྟེ། རྒྱང་ཞགས་ཆུའི་སྒྲོན་མ། ཐིག་ལེ་སྟོང་པའི་སྒྲོན་མ། །དབྱིངས་རྣམ་དག་གི་སྒྲོན་མ། ཤེས་རབ་རང་བྱུང་གི་སྒྲོན་མ་དང་བཞིས་ནི་རིག་པའི་གདངས་སྐུ་དང་ཞིང་
ཁམས་སུ་སྣང་བ་གང་ཡང་དངོས་སུ་གསལ་ལ། ཐམས་ཅད་ལ་ཡེ་ཤེས་ཀྱི་ནུས་ཆ་སྐྱོམས་པས་སྐུ་གསུམ་ལམ་དུ་ཁྲིད་པར་བྱེད་དེ། དཔེར་ན་སྲིད་པའི་མེ་ཆེན་པོས་སྣང་སྲིད་ཐམས་ཅད་ལ་སྟོད་
སྐྱོམས་པས་རྩེ་བཙུད་དང་སོ་འབྲས་ཐམས་ཅད་སྨིན་པར་བྱེད་པ་ལྟ་བུའི་ནང་བཞུགས་ཀྱི་མན་ངག་དམ་པ་ཡིན་ཏེ། རིག་པ་རྩལ་དབང་གི་རྒྱུད་ལས། སྒྲོན་མ་རྣམ་བཞི་ནང་གི་བསྟན་པ་ཡིན།
ཞེས་སོ། དེའང་རྣམ་པར་ཅུང་ཟད་ཕྱེ་ནས་བཤད་ན། བཞུགས་སྟངས་དང་གཟིགས་སྟངས་གཉིས་ལ་མིག་རྒྱང་ཞགས་ཆུའི་སྒྲོན་མ། ཕྱིའི་ནམ་མཁའ་དག་པའི་ཀློང་དུ་གཏད་པས་འོད་
གདངས་སྔོ་རབ་ཤིན་ཏུ་དག་པ་ཞིག་ཐོག་མར་སྣང་ལ། དེ་ལས་མཆེད་པའི་ཚུལ་དུ་འོད་ལྔའི་གདངས་ཁ་དོག་ལྔ་པ་ཟ་འོག་ཁ་ཕྱེ་བ་ལྟ་བུར་གསལ་བ་ནི་སྙིང་ནང་གི་འོད་གསལ་ཕྱི་རུ་གསལ་བ་སྟེ།
གསེར་གྱི་ཞུན་མ་ལས། ཕྱི་དབྱིངས་ནམ་མཁའ་སྟོང་པ་ལ། ཚོ་ཀྱའི་འོད་གསལ་མངོན་སུམ་མཐོང་། དཀར་དང་སེར་དང་མཐིང་ག་དང་། དམར་དང་ལྗང་དང་དྲུག་ཁའི་

༄། མདོག ཅེས་སོ། དེའང་ཕྱི་དབྱིངས་ནམ་མཁའ་སྤྲས་ཁ་ཅིག་གིས་ཕྱིའི་ནམ་མཁའ་སྤྲིན་མེད་རྒྱང་པ་དེ་ལ་ཕྱི་དབྱིངས་ཞེས་ངོས་འཛིན་པ་ནི་མི་རིགས་ཏེ། ནམ་མཁའ་སྐྱེས་བུ་དང་
འབྲེལ་པ་མ་གྲུབ་ལ། སྒྲོན་མ་སྐྱེས་བུ་ཡོད་མེད་ཀྱི་རྗེས་སུ་བྱེད་པའི་ཕྱིར། ནམ་མཁའ་གོ་འབྱེད་འཆར་གཞིའི་ཆ་ཙམ་ལས་དབྱིངས་དངོས་མ་ཡིན་ལ། ནང་གི་ནམ་མཁའ་གདངས་སྟོ་བ
དེ་ཕྱིར་ཤར་བ་ལ་ཕྱི་དབྱིངས་ནམ་མཁའ་ཞེས་བརྗོད་པ་ཏེ། གསེར་གྱི་ཕྲེང་བ་ལས། ཕྱི་དབྱིངས་ནམ་མཁའ་དག་པའི་དཀྱིལ། ནང་དབྱིངས་སྒྲོན་མ་དག་ཏུའོ། ཞེས་སོ། འདིའང་
ཕྱི་དབྱིངས་དང་ནང་དབྱིངས་ཞེས་སོ་སོར་བརྗོད་ཀྱང་འཇའ་འོད་ཀྱི་གུར་ཁྱིམ་དུ་མི་གསལ་བ་གསལ་བར་གོ་འཕོས་པ་ཙམ་ལ་བཤད་ཀྱི། ཕྱི་ནང་གཉིས་བཅས་སུ་སྣང་བ་ལྟ་བུར་བཤད་པ་མ་ཡིན་ནོ།
དབྱིངས་ཀྱི་སྒྲོན་མ་དེའི་ནང་དུ་ཐིག་ལེ་སྟོང་པའི་སྒྲོན་མ་ཞེས་པ། ཀོ་མོའི་རྒྱལ་རྫ་བོར་བའི་རྣམ་པས་མཚོན་པའི་ཐིག་སྒྲུམ་འོད་ལྔའི་སུ་ཕྲུད་ཅན་སྣང་བ་ནི་ལས་ཀྱི་རླུང་དག་པའི་ཆ་ལས་བྱུང་ཞིང་། །
དེར་རྒྱང་ཞགས་གཟིགས་སྟངས་ཀྱིས་གཏད་པས་ནང་གི་རིག་པ་གསལ་དངས་བྱེད་ལ་ཡུལ་མེད་རྗེན་པ་ཞིག་ཉམས་སུ་སྐྱོང་བ་དེ་ནི་ཤེས་རབ་རང་བྱུང་གི་སྒྲོན་མའི་ངོ་བོ་ཡིན་ལ། དེ་ལས་ཡུལ་ཤེས་ཀྱི་

58

ཤེས་རབ་རྩེ་ལ་སྦྱར་བ་དང་། ཚིག་དོན་སྐྱོང་རྩོལ་དུ་འཆར་བ་ནི་དེའི་ཚུལ་ཡིན་ལ། དེ་ལས་ལྷག་མཐོང་གི་རིག་པ་གཡུང་དྲུང་ལུ་གུ་རྒྱུད་མུ་ཏིག་བསྟར་ལ་བརྒྱུས་པའམ། གསེར་སྐུད་
ཐིང་བ་ལྟར་སྣང་བ་ལ་ཤེས་རབ་ཀྱི་གདངས་ཞེས་བྱ་སྟེ། ངོ་བོ་གཅིག་ལ་ལྡོག་པའི་ཆ་ནས་དབྱེ་བའོ། གསེར་གྱི་ས་གཞི་ལ་ནི་གནས་བཅས་སོ། ཞེས་པ་ནི། དབྱིངས་ཉིད་རིག་པའི་
གནས་བསྟན་པ་སྟེ། དབྱིངས་ནི་མཐིང་ག་ལས་ཁ་དོག་ལྔར་མཆེད་པའི་འོད་གདངས་ཡིན་ལ། རིག་པ་དངོས་ནི་སྙིང་ནང་ན་ཡོད་ཀྱང་གདངས་ཕྱིར་གསལ་བས་རིག་པ་ཞེས་བཏགས་ཏེ་ལུ་གུ་རྒྱུད་
དུ་སྣང་བ་ལ། ནང་བཞུགས་དང་ཕྱིར་གསལ་གྱི་ཆ་ནས་ངོ་བོའི་རིག་པ་དང་ལྷག་མཐོང་གི་རིག་པ་ཞེས་བརྗོད་པ་ཡིན་ནོ། གསེར་གྱི་ས་གཞིའི་སྐབས་དབྱིངས་དེ་ན་སྣང་བ་ཐམས་ཅད་ནང་གི་རིག
པའི་གདངས་ཕྱིར་ཤར་བས་བཟང་ངན་སྤང་བླང་མེད་པར་བསྟན་པའོ། ཀ་བ་ཆེན་པོ་བཞིས་ནི་བསོད་ནམས་ཀྱི་རྒྱན་བསྒྲིང་ངོ་། ཞེས་པ་ནི། སྣང་བ་བཞིའོ། དེའང་སྣང་བ་བཞི་
ནི། སྤྲོས་བྲལ་རིག་པའི་རྩལ་དབང་ལས། བོན་ཉིད་མངོན་སུམ་ཉམས་སྣང་གོང་འཕེལ་དང་། རིག་པ་ཚད་ཕེབས་བོན་ཉིད་ཟད་པ་བཞི། ཞེས་གསོམས་སྤོབས་ཀྱི་ཕྲུད་པ་ལས་འོག་མ་བ་ལྟར་

59

༄། དག་ཅ་དག་འབྲས་ཀྱི་ཚུལ་དུ་སྣང་བའི་ས་མཚམས་བཞིའི་བཤད་པ་བྱུང་ནའང་། ལམ་སྦྱར་བུལ་ཀྱི་ཁྱད་ནམ་མཁའ་དང་ས་གཞིའི་འགྲོ་ས་ཅན་ལྟ་བུའི་ཁྱད་ཆེའོ། དེ་ལས་དང་པོ
བོན་ཉིད་མངོན་སུམ་གྱི་སྣང་བ་བཤད་པ་ནི། གོང་དུ་བཤད་པའི་གནད་རྣམ་པ་བཞིས་གཟུན་པས། སྙིང་གའི་བདེ་གཤེགས་སྙིང་པོའི་གདངས་དབྱིངས་འཇའ་ཚོན་རིས་དང་པོ་མཐོང་བ་ནས
བཟུང་། །ཐིག་ལེ་སྟོང་པའི་སྒྲོན་མ་འོད་རྒྱུམ། ཐིག་ཕྲན་གསུམ་འབྲེལ་སོགས་འགྲོ་འོང་གི་ཆ་བཅས་གསལ་འགྲིབ་ཅན་དུ་འཆར་ལ། དེ་དག་གི་གོ་མཚམས་སུ་ཉི་མ་དང་ཟེར་བཞིན་ཊོ་བའི་
རིག་པ་སྟོང་གསལ་བརྗོད་དུ་མེད་པའི་གདངས་ལྷག་མཐོང་གི། རིག་པ་གཡུང་དྲུང་ལུ་གུ་རྒྱུད་དུ་སྣང་བ་དེ་ཉིད་ཅུད་དང་མེ་ལོང་གི་གཟུགས་བརྙན་བཞིན་ནང་གི་རིག་པ་དངོས་དང་
བདག་ཉིད་གཅིག་པར་ཤེས་དགོས་ལ། དེ་ལྟར་མ་ཤེས་ནས་རིག་པ་རྩལ་གདངས་ཕར་སྣང་གི་རྟོག་འཛིན་བྱེད་དེ་བས་བར་ཆད་ན་ལུག་རྒྱུད་དངོས་པོར་འཛིན་པར་གོལ་བའོ། དེའི་ཕྱིར་རིག་པ་
དེ་རྩའི་གནད་ལ་བརྟེན་ནས་གྲོལ་བའི་རྟགས་སུ་ལུ་གུ་རྒྱུད་ཕྲ་ཞིང་འཚུབ་པའི་བྲེང་ཡོད་ལ། ཐིག་ལེ་ལ་བརྟེན་ནས་གྲོལ་བའི་རྟགས་སུ་འཚུབ་མཚམས་ན་ཐིག་ལེ་ཕྲ་མོ་བྲུང་འབྲེལ་ཡོད་ཅིང་། རྒྱུང་

60

གི་གནད་ལ་བརྟེན་ནས་གྲོལ་བའི་རྟགས་སུ་འགྲོ་འོང་ཅན་དུ་ཡོད་པའི་ཡན་དུ་མི་འཇུག་པར་དབྱིངས་དང་ཐིག་ལེའི་ར་བར་འཇུད་པ་ལ་མཁས་དགོས་སོ། དེའང་ཐོག་འབེབས་ལས། ཐབས་ཤེས་
ཟུང་འབྲེལ་གནད་ཀྱི་རྩལ་སྦྱང་ལ། ཞེས་ཡུལ་གནད་ཉིན་མོར་ཤེས་རབ་བོན་སྐུའི་རྟེན་ཉི་རི་དང་མན་ཤེལ། མཚན་མོར་ཐབས་ལོངས་སྐུའི་རྟེན་ཟླ་རི་དང་རྒྱ་ཤེལ། ནང་རུབ་ཟུང་འབྲེལ་
སྤྲུལ་སྐུའི་རྟེན་ནེ་རི་སོགས་ལ་དང་པོའི་ཚེ་རྟེན་ལ་མ་རེག་ཙམ་དུ་བལྟ་ཞིང་གོམས་སུ་གཞུག་པས་འོད་སྣང་དེ་དག་ཇེ་གསལ་ཇེ་བརྟན་དུ་འགྲོ་ལ། སྒོ་གསུམ་དལ་མེད་རྒྱུང་སེམས་རང་ཞི་ལས་ནང་དུ་
ཉམས་རྟོགས་ཁྱད་པར་ཅན་དང་། ཚིག་དོན་ལ་སྦྱར་ལས་ལྷག་པའི་ཤེས་རབ་སྐྱེ་བས་ཡེ་ཤེས་ཀྱི་གསུམ་ཆ་ལ་དབང་ཐོབ་པའོ། འདིའི་དུས་སུ་བར་ཆད་ནའང་རང་བཞིན་སྤྲུལ་པར་དབུགས་
འབྱིན་པའོ། རྟག་སྒྲོན་མ་ལས་དབྱིངས་སྤྲིན་འཚམ་ནས་བྲལ་དུས་སུ་འཕོས་ན་རང་བཞིན་སྤྲུལ་པར་བསྒྲོད་པར་གསུངས་པ་ཡང་ཉམས་གོང་འཕེལ་གྱི་འགོ་ཟིན་པར་བཞེད་ཀྱང་དེ་མངོན་སུམ་པའི་
མཐར་ཐུག་ཡིན་པས་ཕོ་བོས་དོན་གཅིག་ཏུ་རྟོགས་སོ། དེའང་ཕྱིའི་དབྱིངས་སྣང་གི་རྟགས་དང་པོ་ཙམ་མཐོང་བས་མ་ཡིན་པར་ནང་དུ་རིག་པ་གོམས་པའི་དབྱིངས་རིག་ཟུང་དུ་འབྲེལ་བའི་གནད་

ཁ

༄། ཀྱིས་ཡིན་ཏེ། རྟགས་སྦྱོར་བུ་ལས། དབྱིངས་དང་རིག་པ་འདྲེས་པ་ཡིས། །རང་བཞིན་སྤྲུལ་པའི་ཞིང་དུ་སྐྱེ། ཞེས་པས་སོ། གཉིས་པ་ཉམས་སྣང་གོང་འཕེལ་ནི། གོང་བཞིན་
ཉམས་སུ་བླངས་པས་དབྱིངས་རིག་རེས་གསལ་རེས་མི་གསལ་བ་ལས། སྣང་བ་ཆེར་མཆེད་དུས་དབྱིངས་རིག་སྨིན་འཚམས་ནས་བྲལ་བར་འགྱུར་ཏེ། ཡེ་ཤེས་ལྔའི་འོད་ལྔ་ཀྱིན་འཁྱིང་
དང་། རྩིབས་ཤར་དང་། གུ་ཆད་དང་། རེ་ཌྷེའི་རྣམ་པ་དང་། ཡུལ་གྲུ་ཙམ་དུ་སྣང་བ་ནི་ཁ་དོག་གི་སྣང་བ་དང་། ཐིག་ཚགས་ཀྱི་རྣམ་པ། སྣ་བ་སྣ་ཕྱེད། མི་རྟོག་
གི་ཚོམ་བུ། །རིགས་རྟགས། མཁར་ཐབས་སུ་སྣང་བ་ནི་དབྱིངས་ཀྱི་སྣང་བ་སྟེ་མཁའ་ལས་འོད་སྨིན་པ་ཞེས་བྱའོ། དེ་ནས་མཆོད་རྟེན་དང་། ཐུགས་ཀྱུ་དང་། །རྩེ་གསུམ་དང་།
རེ་གཅིག
མདའ་དང་། མདུང་རྩེ་ལྷ་བུ་སྣང་བ་ནི་དབྱིངས་ལས་ཡེ་ཤེས་སྨིན་པ་ཞེས་བྱ་སྟེ། དབྱིངས་ཀྱི་རྒྱན་རྫོགས་པའི་ཚད་དོ། ཐིག་ལེའི་སྒྲོན་མ་ཡང་སྲན་མ་ཙམ་ནས་བསེ་ཤུབ་ཙམ་དུ་རིམ་གྱིས་
འཕེལ་ཞིང་དེ་ལ་འོད་ལྔའི་སུ་ཕྲུད་རྒྱས་པོར་སྣང་བ་ནི་རིག་པ་སྨིན་པ་སྟེ་སྙིང་པོར་བཅུད་དུ་དྲིལ་བ་ཞེས་བྱའོ། རིག་པའི་ཁུ་བྱུག་ལས། གཟའ་དང་རྒྱ་སྐར་ནི་ཀེད་ནས་འཆར་རོ། ཞེས་པའི་བཛྲ་ཚིག་ཀྱང་

འདི་དག་གིས་བསྒྲོལ་བ་ཡིན་ནོ། རིག་པ་ཞུ་གུ་རྒྱུད་ཀྱང་འདབས་ཆགས་འཕུར་སྐྱོན་པ་དང་། རི་དགས་རྩིབས་ལ་རྒྱུག་པ་དང་། ཤ་ར་ཁ་དལ་གྱིས་འགྲོ་བ་དང་། བུང་བ་མེ་ཏོག་ལ་ལྡིང་བ་ཙམ་དུ་དལ་བུར་
འགྲོ་བའོ། མདོར་བསྡུ་ན་ཇི་ཙམ་གོམས་པ་བརྟས་པ་བཞིན་འོད་སྣང་རྒྱ་ཆེ་དང་རིག་པ་རྗེ་བརྟན་དུ་འགྲོ་ཞིང་མཐར་གང་དུ་བལྟས་པའི་སྟོང་ཁམས་འོད་གསལ་གྱི་སྣང་བས་ཁྱབ་ཅིང་གཡོ་འགུལ་མེད་པར་
ཁ་རེ་གཉིས
གནས་པ་ཡིན་ལ། འོད་སྣང་དེ་དག་རེ་ཞེ་ཙམ་ལ་མཆེད་དུས་ལྷ་སྣང་ཀྱི་གནད་ནི་ཞང་ཞུང་གི་སྙན་རྒྱུད་ལས། ཟླ་གམ་མཐོང་དང་དཀར་ཤས་ཆེ། ཀྱིན་ལ་བལྟ་བ་གནད་ཡིན་ལ། ཀྱིན་འཁྱིང་མཐོང་དང་
དམར་ཤས་ཆེ། དེ་ལ་ཕྱུར་ལ་བལྟ་བ་གནད། །གྲུ་བཞི་མཐོང་དང་སེར་ཤས་ཆེ། གཡས་སུ་བལྟ་བ་གནད་ཡིན་ནོ། ཟླུམ་པོ་མཐོང་དང་ལྗང་ཤས་ཆེ། དེ་ལ་གཡོན་ལ་བལྟ་བ་གནད། གྲུ་གསུམ་མཐོང་དང་
མཐིང་ཤས་ཆེ། ཐུར་དང་དབུས་ལ་བལྟ་བ་ཡིན། ལྔ་ལྡན་མཁར་ཐབས་མཉམ་པར་བལྟ། ཞེས་པ་ལྟར་རོ། དེའང་ཡེ་ཤེས་མཁར་ཐབས་ལ་སོགས་པའི་དུས་ན་འདུག་སྟངས་མི་འགྱུར་བའོ། ཐིག་ལེ་མ་འཕེལ་
ན་མིག་དབུས་སུ་དྲིལ་ནས་འོད་རྩ་གཅུད་པའོ། འོད་བྲ་ཡས་ན་སྨིན་ཐག་ཏུ་གཏད་པའོ། རྟོག་པ་འཐོར་ན་རླུང་འཆིང་ཞིང་འཁྱེན་པའོ། དབྱིངས་ཀྱི་གནད་དབུས་སུ་བསྡུ་ཞིང་མིག་ཟུར་ནས་ཕྱིད་དེ་བལྟ་བའོ།

ཁ

༄། རིག་པའི་གནད་ཞུ་གུ་རྒྱུད་མཁའ་ལ་དབྱུང་བའོ། སྐུ་མཐོང་དུས་དེ་རྫོགས་པར་བྱེད་པའི་གནད་གདངས་དེ་ལ་མི་འགྱུར་བར་བལྟ་བའོ། འདི་དག་གནད་ཡིན་ནོ། ཉམས་
འཕེལ་ཁར་བར་ཆད་པའི་གྲོལ་ཚད་ནི། དབྱིངས་རིག་སྨིན་མཚམས་བྲལ་ནས་ཡེ་ཤེས་བཞི་སྦྱོར་གྱི་སྣང་བས་གྲོལ། གུ་ཆད་ཀྱི་རྣམ་པར་ཤར་ན་ཆོས་བུའི་སྣང་བས་གྲོལ། དབྱིངས་སྣང་རྒྱས་
འཁྲིགས་སུ་པད་འདབ་བཞི་བཞིས་བརྒྱན་པའི་ཆོས་བུར་ཤར་ན་འོད་གསལ་ཤར་བའི་སྐད་ཅིག་མར་གྲོལ། མདོར་ན་ཁ་དོག་དང་དབྱིབས་ཀྱི་སྣང་བ་རྫོགས་པ་ན་བར་ཆད་ཀྱང་ལྷུན་གྲུབ་ཀྱི་སྣང་བས་
གྲོལ་བས་སྲིད་པའི་བར་དོ་རང་སོག་པ་ནི་སྒྲོན་མ་མའི་དགོངས་པ་ཡིན་ནོ། ཐིག་ལེ་བསེ་ཤུབ་ཙམ་དུ་སྣང་དུས་ན་ཐིག་ལེ་ཚད་དུ་ཕྱིན་པ་ཡིན་ཏེ། དེ་ལས་ཆེར་འགྲོ་བའི་ངེས་པ་མེད་ལ།
རེ་གསུམ
ཐིག་ལེ་དེ་དག་རེ་རེ་བཞིན་འོད་ལྔའི་སུ་ཕྲུད་ཅན་ནང་དུ་ལྷ་སྐུ་ཀྲུང་པ་རེ་རེ་སྣང་བ་ན་ཉམས་སྣང་མཐར་ཕྱུག་པས་འཕེལ་ཟད་པ་ཡིན་ནོ། གསུམ་པ་རིག་པ་ཚད་ཕེབས་ཀྱི་སྣང་བ་ནི། རིག་པའི་གཤིས་ལ་
སྐུ་གསུང་ཡེ་རྫོགས་སུ་གནས་པ་དེ་ཉིད་ལམ་གནད་ཟབ་མོས་བཅིང་པས་ཚད་ལ་ཕེབས་པའི་དུས་ན་རིག་པའི་ཡོན་ཏན་ལོངས་སྤྱོད་རྫོགས་པའི་སྐུའི་དཀྱིལ་འཁོར་ལམ་གྱི་དོན་དུ་གཉེར་བྱའི་མཐར་ཕྱུག······

64

ཀྱི་འབྲས་བུའི་མཚན་དཔེ་ཡོན་ཏན་ཐམས་ཅད་མ་ལུས་པ་མེད་པ་འདིར་ལམ་གྱི་སྣང་བ་ལ་རྩལ་རྫོགས་པ་ནི་རང་བཞིན་རྫོགས་པ་ཆེན་པོའི་ལམ་ཁྱད་དུ་འཕགས་པའི་གནད་ཅིག་ཡིན་ནོ། དེའི་ཕྱིར་ན་
རིག་པའི་ཡོན་ཏན་འཕེལ་བའི་ཆ་སྐབས་སུ་གྱུར་པ་ལས་ཡེ་ཤེས་ལྔའི་འོད་ཉིད་ལ་བྱིན་ཚུད་པས་ཐིག་ལེ་ལྔ་ཚོམ་ཤར་བའི་དུས་ན་སྤྲུལ་སྐུའི་སྣང་བ་མཐར་ཕྱིན་པ་ལས་བྱུང་བའི་སྐུ་ཕྱེད་པ་ནས་སྐུ་རྒྱང....
པའི་བར་དང་། ལོངས་སྐུའི་ཡེ་ཤེས་ཚད་དུ་ཕྱིན་པ་ལས་བྱུང་བའི་ཀུན་སྣང་ལ་སོགས་པའི་རིགས་ལྔའི་བདེ་གཤེགས་རྣམས། སྐུ་རྒྱང་ནས། །རྒྱན་རྫོགས་དང་། ཡུམ་
དང་བཅས་པའི་བར་དུ་འཆར་ལ། བོན་སྐུའི་སྣང་བ་རྣམ་པར་དག་པ་ལས་བྱུང་བའི་གཙོ་དང་འཁོར་གྱི་ཚོམ་བུ་ཐ་དད་པའི་དཀྱིལ་འཁོར་སུ་ཁྱུད་ར་བ་དང་བཅས་པར་གསལ་བ་ཏེ། ཐོག་
འབེབས་ལས། སྨིན་པའི་རྟགས་ཚད་རྒྱན་རྫོགས་སྐུ་རུ་གསལ། ཞེས་སོ། དེ་ཡང་རིག་པ་ཁྲུ་གུག་ལས། གསལ་བའི་སྒྲོན་མ་ལྔ་ནི་དབུའི་གཙུག་ནས་སྐྱེས་སོ། ཞེས་པས་རིག་པ་
ཚད་ལ་ཕེབས་པའི་དུས་ན་ཡེ་ཤེས་ལྔ་མངོན་དུ་གྱུར་པ་བསྟན་ཏེ། དེ་ཙམ་ན་ཕྱི་སྣང་བ་ཚད་ལ་ཕེབས་ཏེ་ཆོས་བཅས་ཀྱི་སྣང་བ་རང་དེངས་པས་སྟོང་པ་ཉིད་ཀྱི་ཡེ་ཤེས་མངོན་དུ་གྱུར། མཐོང་ཚད

65

༄། ལ་འོད་གསལ་ཆེན་པོའི་སྣང་བ་འབྱམས་ཀླས་པས་མེ་ལོང་ལྟ་བུའི་ཡེ་ཤེས་མངོན་དུ་གྱུར། གང་ཤར་རང་སྣང་མཉམ་གདལ་རིས་མེད་ལ་བདག་གཞན་དུ་ཕྱེས་པ་མེད་པས་མཉམ་པ་ཉིད་
ཀྱི་ཡེ་ཤེས་མངོན་དུ་གྱུར། ལུས་ཚད་ལ་ཕེབས་ཏེ་སྣང་བ་མ་ལུས་པ་རྒྱལ་བ་རིགས་ལྔའི་ཞིང་དུ་གསལ་བའི་སྐུ་རྣམས་ཀྱི་ཐུགས་ཀ་ནས་འོད་ཟེར་ལྔ་སྤྲོལ་བྱུང་བ་རང་གི་སྙིང་དབུས་སུ་ཐུག་ནས་འབྲེལ་
བར་སྣང་། མཛོད་སྤུ་ནས་འོད་ཟེར་འཇོམ་གང་གསལ་བ་ལས་ཡེ་ཤེས་ཀྱི་རླུང་གིས་ཐིག་ལེ་འཁར་གཞོང་ཙམ་པ་དགུའམ་ལྔ་བརྩེགས་མ་འདྲེགས་པ། དུང་ཁང་དུ་ཁྲོ་བོའི་དཀྱིལ་འཁོར་གསལ་
བ་དེའི་གདངས་སྙིང་ཕྱོགས་ན་འབར་བ་བརྒྱད་ཅུ་དང་། .སྙིང་ནང་ཞི་བའི་དཀྱིལ་འཁོར་ལས་ཐད་སོ་ཐམས་ཅད་གཡུང་དྲུང་ཡོངས་སུ་རྫོགས་པའི་ལྷ་ཚོགས་རྣམས་འཆར། འོད་རྩ་ཕྲ་མོ་རྣམས་
སུ་ཡེ་ཤེས་ཀྱི་གདངས་གསལ་བས་བ་སྤུའི་སྒོ་དང་རྡུལ་ཕྲ་རབ་རེ་རེའི་གོ་ན་སངས་རྒྱས་ཀྱི་ཞིང་ཁམས་དཔག་ཏུ་མེད་པ་རང་གསལ་ལ་མ་འདྲེས་པར་མཐོང་བས་སོ་སོར་རྟོག་པའི་ཡེ་ཤེས་མངོན་དུ་གྱུར།
སེམས་ཚད་ལ་ཕེབས་ཏེ་ཀུན་ཏུ་རྟོག་པའི་སེམས་དང་ཡིད་དང་རྣམ་པར་ཤེས་པ་རྣམས་ཐུབ་ནས་རང་རིག་པ་མངོན་དུ་གྱུར། ཤེས་པ་གང་དུའང་ཚུད་པས་ཐེམ་པོ་འགྲུལ་བ་དང་གཞན་གྱི་སེམས་ཤེས་

66

པ་ལ་སོགས་མངོན་ཤེས་དྲུག་དང་། ཕ་རོལ་གྱི་ཡུལ་དང་རྒྱལ་བའི་ཞིང་ཁམས་ཚད་མེད་པ་མཐོང་བ། ཤེས་རབ་དང་ཏིང་ངེ་འཛིན་གྱི་སྒོ་དཔག་ཏུ་མེད་པ་ལ་དབང་འབྱོར་བས་བྱ་བ་ནན་ཏན་
ཀྱི་ཡེ་ཤེས་མངོན་དུ་གྱུར། མདོར་ན་ལུས་ཀྱི་རྡོས་པ་དག་པས་རྩ་རླུང་རང་དག དེ་དག་པའི་སྒྲོ་བུར་གྱིས་བསྡུས་པའི་ཚོགས་པ་ཞིག་སྟེ་ལུས་སེམས་ཀྱི་འབྲེལ་མངོན་གྱུར་རགས་པ་ཡོག
ཕྲ་བ་རིག་པའི་ཆ་ལ་བག་ལ་ཉལ་བ་ཙམ་གྱི་སེམས་དེ་ཉིད་སྐད་ཅིག་རེ་ཤར་བ་ལ་འཁོར་བའི་སྣང་ཆ་མཐོང་བས་འཁོར་འདས་གཉིས་ཀའི་ཆ་འཛིན་པ་ཞེས་བྱ་སྟེ། སྐར་མདའ་རྒྱུག་པ་ལྟར་དབྱིངས་
སུ་ཡལ་བས་ལས་དང་བག་ཆགས་ཀྱི་རྒྱུན་ཆད་པའོ། འདིའི་དུས་ན་སྐུ་གསུམ་ལམ་སྣང་དུ་རྫོགས་པ་ཞེས་བྱ་སྟེ། རིག་པ་ཁྲུ་གུག་ལས། གསང་བའི་ཡིག་འབྲུ་གསུམ་ནི་ཐུགས་ལ་བཀོད།
ཅེས་དེ་བཞིན་གཤེགས་པའི་ཁམས་ལ་སྐུ་དང་ཡེ་ཤེས་ཀྱི་ཡོན་ཏན་ཡོད་པ་དེ་ཉིད། འདིར་དབང་པོའི་སྒོར་མངོན་སུམ་པ་ཉིད་སྣང་བར་བྱེད་པ་ནི་རང་བཞིན་རྫོགས་པ་ཆེན་པོ་འདི་མིན་པ་ལམ་གཞན་
གྱིས་ནི་མ་ཡིན་པས་གསང་ལ། ཡིག་འབྲུ་གསུམ་གྱིས་མཚོན་པ་ཡེ་གཞི་མན་ཆད་ཀྱི་འབྲས་བུའི་མཐར་ཐུག་སྐུ་གསུམ་པོ་དེ་ཉིད་འདིར་ལམ་གྱི་སྣང་བ་ལ་འཆར་བ་ལ་ཐུགས་ལ་བཀོད་ཅེས་བྱའོ།

ཐ་

སོ་བཞི་

༄། །འདི་ཁ་ཅིག་སྟོང་གཟུགས་འཕྲུལ་སྣང་དུ་འདོད་པ་དང་། ཁ་ཅིག་དོན་དམ་དུ་འདོད་པ་གཉིས་ཀ་མ་ཡིན་ཏེ། ཁམས་དེ་བཞིན་གཤེགས་པའི་རང་གདངས་ཡིན་པས་མ་འཁྲུལ་ལ། །
རིག་གདངས་ཕྱིར་ཤར་བའི་གཟུགས་བརྙན་ཡིན་པས་དོན་དམ་དངོས་སུ་མི་འཐད་དེ། སྙིང་པོའི་རང་གདངས་ཡིན་པས་ཕྱི་སྣང་ཟད་དགོས་པའི་ཕྱིར་རོ། །བཞི་པ་བོན་ཉིད་ཟད་པའི་སྣང་བ་ནི།
གནད་ཟབ་མོ་ལ་བརྟེན་ནས་རླུང་གི་གཡོ་བ་ཡེ་ཤེས་སུ་འཕེལ་བའི་ཚད་ཕེབས་ཀྱི་ཟླ་བ་ཉ་བ་ལྟ་བུའི་སྣང་བ་དེ་མར་ཐྲི་ནས་ཐིག་ལེ་ལ་ཐུག་པ་ལ་སོགས་པའི་འོད་གསལ་གྱི་སྣང་བ་ཐམས་ཅད་བོན་ཉིད་གང···
དུ་འང་བརྗོད་དུ་མེད་པའི་དབྱིངས་སུ་ཐིམ་ནས་ཅི་ཡང་མི་སྣང་བ་ལ་ཟད་ཞེས་བྱ་སྟེ། དོན་དམ་པར་གནམ་སྟོང་གི་ཟླ་བ་ཅི་ཡང་མེད་པ་ལྟར་སྣང་ཡང་རང་གི་ངོ་བོ་ལ་འཕེལ་འགྲིབ་གང་ཡང་མེད་པ··
བཞིན་དུ། སྣང་བ་ཡར་འཕེལ་དུས་ན་ཆེར་མ་སོང་། །མར་ཟད་དུས་ན་ཆུང་དུ་མ་སོང་སྟེ། དང་པོའི་འོད་ཆེན་གང་ལ་གང་བ་མེད་ཅིང་ཐྲི་བ་མེད་པ་ཞེས་བྱའོ། ཟད་ཕུགས་ལ་
རིམ་གྱིས་ཟད་པ་ནི་སྣང་བ་བཞི་ཚད་དུ་ཕྱིན་ནས་ཟད་པའོ། ཅིག་ཅར་དུ་ཟད་པ་ནི་བོན་ཉིད་མངོན་སུམ་མཐོང་བ་ལ་གོམས་པར་བྱས་པས་གོང་འཕེལ་དང་ཚད་ཕེབས་ཀྱི་སྣང་བ་མ་སྐྱེས་པ་ཟད་པ་ནི་

བློ་མཆོག་སྟེ་རེ་རེ་ཙམ་སོ། གང་ལྟར་ཡང་ཟད་པའི་དུས་ན་ཕྱི་འོད་ལྔའི་སྣང་བ་སྐུ་དང་བཅས་པ་དང་། ནང་སྐུ་ལུས་དབང་པོ་ཡུལ་གྱི་བོན་དང་། གསང་བ་རྣམ་པར་རྟོག་པའི་སེམས་
ཐམས་ཅད་ཟད་པ་སྟེ། ཕྱི་ཡུལ་དང་ནང་ལུས་ཀྱི་རྟོས་བཅས་ནི་ཚད་ཕེབས་ནས་ཟད་ལ། འདིར་ཀུན་གཞིའི་ཆའི་སེམས་ཀྱིས་བསྡུས་པ་རྣམས་བག་ཆགས་ཕྲ་བ་ས་བོན་དང་བཅས་པ་ཐམས
ཅད་ཟད་པའོ། ཕྱི་སྣང་ཟད་དགོས་པའི་གནད་ནི་རིག་པ་གཡོ་བྱེད་ཀྱི་རླུང་དང་བྲལ་ནས་ངོ་བོའི་ནང་དབྱིངས་སུ་བཙན་ས་ཟིན་དགོས་ལ། དེ་མ་ཟད་ན་ཁམས་གསུམ་ལས་གྲོལ་མི་ནུས་པས།
ཟད་དུས་རིག་གདངས་དང་ལས་རླུང་མཉམ་དུ་ཟད་ནས་ཡེ་ཤེས་ཀྱི་རླུང་དང་ལྷན་ཅིག་ཏུ་ནང་དབྱིངས་སུ་གནས་པ་ཡིན་ནོ། འདིའི་དུས་ན་ཐོབ་པ་གཉིས་འབྱུང་བ་ནི། སྐྱེ་བ་ལ་དབང་ཐོབ
པས་སེམས་ཅན་གྱི་དོན་མཛད་ན་སྣང་བ་རིམ་གྱིས་ཟད་དུས་ལག་སོར་ལྔ་འོད་ཀྱིས་དཀྲིགས་པར་སྣང་བ་ལ་ཤེས་པ་གཏད་པས་འཕྲུལ་སྣང་རང་སོག་ནས་རྟེན་དང་བརྟེན་པའི་སྣོད་བཅུད་ཆུ་ཟླ་ལྟ་བུར་མཐོང
ལ། རང་ལུས་ཀྱང་རང་བཞིན་མེད་པ་མེ་ལོང་གི་གཟུགས་བརྙན་ལྟར་སྣང་བ་ལ་འཕོ་བ་ཆེན་པོའི་སྐུར་བཞེངས་པ་ཞེས་བྱ་སྟེ། འཇའ་ལུས་པ་ཉི་ཤུ་རྩ་བཞིའི་གྲལ་དུ་ཚུད་པ་ཡིན་ནོ། དེ་ལྟ་

ཐ་

སོ་ལྔ་

༄། །བུའི་ལུས་བཟུང་བ་དེ་ནི་གཞན་མིག་མ་དག་པས་རྗེས་བཅས་མཐོང་ལ། རང་ལ་ཟང་ཐལ་དུ་སྣང་བས་སྐད་ཅིག་ལ་ལུས་མི་སྣང་བ་མཛད་ནའང་ཆོག་པའི་ཚུལ་སྣེ་སྦུགས་ཀྱིས་ཇེ་ཏ་པི་ཧྲི་
ཙ་ལ་ཕྱིའུ་རྟེད་ལེགས་མེད་བཏགས་ནས་ལས་བཅོལ་བའི་མོད་ལ་ཡལ་ནས་མི་སྣང་བར་བཤད་པ་དང་། ལུང་བོན་ལྷ་གཉེན་རྗེ་ཆེ་དབང་དང་སྐབས་སུ་མི་དང་མི་བཞིན་དུ་འཕྲད་ནས་ཡང་གར་སོང་མེད
པར་ཡལ་ནས་སོང་བར་བཤད་པའི་ལོ་རྒྱུས་བཞིན་ནོ། དེའི་དུས་ན་བསམ་གྱིས་མི་ཁྱབ་པའི་ཕྲིན་ལས་ཀྱིས་རིགས་དྲུག་གི་སེམས་ཅན་གྲངས་མེད་པའི་དོན་དངོས་དང་རྒྱུད་ནས་མཛད་པའི་ཚུལ་ནི
ཀྱིར་ཆེན་དྲན་པ་ནམ་མཁའི་དགོངས་སྤྱོད་ཟླ་ན་མེད་པ་རྗོགས་པར་བྱའོ། ཁྱད་པར་དུ་མིའི་འགྲོ་བ་སུམ་སྟོང་ལ་རང་གི་རིག་པ་བཙུག་པས། དེ་དག་ཀུན་ཀྱང་འབྱུང་བ་དག་ནས་སངས་རྒྱའོ།
འཇུག་པ་ལ་དབང་ཐོབ་པ་ནི་སྐུའི་རྣམ་པ་དེ་ཉིད་ཀྱི་དུས་དེར་གཞན་དོན་རླབས་ཆེ་མི་འབྱུང་ན་སེམས་ཅན་སུམ་སྟོང་གྲོལ་བར་མཛད་པའི་མོད་ལ་རང་གི་རྐང་ལག་གི་སོར་མོ་འོད་ཀྱིས་དཀྲིགས་པར་སྣང་བ
ལ། སྐབས་འདི་ནས་ནང་དབྱིངས་སུ་འཇུག་པ་དང་། ཕྱིར་སྣང་བ་ཆུར་ཐོག་པའི་ས་མཚམས་ཡིན་པས་ལག་སོར་ལ་མ་གཏད་པ་དབྱིངས་སྣང་ལ་གཏད་པས་ལུས་དང་སྣང་བའི་རང་གདངས་ནང་

ཀུ་ཁྱི་ན

དབྱིངས་སུ་ཐིམ་ནས་རིག་པ་དབྱིངས་ན་འཁྱིལ་བའི་ཚུལ་དུ་སྐུ་དང་ཡེ་ཤེས་འདུ་འབྲལ་མེད་པར་གཞོན་ནུ་བུམ་པའི་སྐུའི་བདག་ཉིད་དུ་བཞུགས་ནས་གཟུགས་སྐུ་གཉིས་ཀྱི་ཕྲིན་ལས་འཁོར་བ་སྟོངས་པར་···
མཛད་པའི་ཚུལ་དབྱིངས་རིག་རིན་པོ་ཆེའི་མཛོད་ལས་རྒྱ་ཆེར་འདོམས་ཟིན་ཏོ། དུས་བཞི་རྒྱལ་མོ་བཞིས་ནི་མཐའ་ཉེན་ནོ། ཞེས་པ་ནི། མཐའ་ཉེན་བཞི་སྟེ། མཐའ་ཉེན་བཞི་ནི། གསེར་
གྱི་ཉུན་མ་ལས། མི་འགུལ་གསུམ་ལ་གཞི་བཅས་ལ། སྡོད་པ་གསུམ་གྱིས་ཚད་བཟུང་ངོ་། ཐོབ་པ་གསུམ་གྱིས་གཟེར་གདབ་པ། གདེང་བཞིས་གྲོལ་ཚད་བསྟན་པའོ། །ཞེས་བཞི་
ལས། དང་པོ་མི་འགུལ་བ་གསུམ་ནི། ལུས་འདུག་སྟངས་ལས་མི་འགུལ་བས་རྩ་རླུང་རང་དལ། མིག་ལྟ་སྟངས་ལས་མི་འགུལ་བས་སྣང་བའི་འཁེལ་ཆེ། སེམས་བརྗོད་མེད་ལས་མི་འགུལ་བས
དབྱིངས་རིག་ཟུང་དུ་ཆུད་པར་བྱེད་དོ། གཉིས་པ་སྡོད་པ་གསུམ་ནི། ལུས་བྱ་བ་ལ་མི་གནས་པར་སྡོད་པས་བྱ་བྱེད་རང་དག རླུང་རང་དལ་ལ་སྡོད་པས་རྣམ་རྟོག་གཡོ་རྒྱུན་ཟད།
སྣང་བ་འགུལ་འཕྲིགས་མེད་པར་སྡོད་པས་ཞིང་ཁམས་ཚད་ལ་ཕེབས་པར་བྱེད་དོ། འདིའི་ཚེ་རྟགས་སྒོ་གསུམ་ལ་འཆར་བ་དང་ཚད་ནི་ལམ་གྱིས་བཟུང་བ་གཉིས་ལས། དང་པོ་ལ་བཞི་ལས་··

70

ཁ

ཞེ་ཁྱ་ཀ

༄། བོན་ཉིད་མངོན་སུམ་གྱི་དུས་ན། ལུས་ཉུས་སྤྲལ་མཁར་གཞོང་དུ་བཙུག་པ་ལྟར་གཡོ་མེད་དུ་གནས་པ་ནི་རྩ་དལ་བའི་རྟེན་འབྲེལ་ལས་བྱུང་ངོ་། རྫོགས་པ་ཆེན་པོ་བྱེད་པ་དང་བྲལ་བའི་
གཟེར་ཡན་ལག་ལ་ཐེབས་པས་བྱེད་པ་རང་སར་དག་པས་བྱེད་པ་མེད་པའི་ཡེ་ཤེས་རང་བྱུང་དུ་ཤར། ངག་ཤུགས་པ་ལྟར་སྨྲ་བ་མེད་པ་ནི་རྩའི་ནང་དུ་རྣམ་ཤེས་ཆུད་པ་ལས་བྱུང་ངོ་། བརྗོད་གཞི་
དང་བྲལ་བའི་གཟེར་ངག་ལ་ཐེབས་པས་བརྗོད་གཞི་ངག་མྱ་ངན་ལས་འདས་ནས་གསུང་འགག་པ་མེད་པའི་ཡེ་ཤེས་ངང་གིས་ཤར། སེམས་མཁའ་འགྲོ་སྐྱི་ལ་ཟིན་པ་ལྟར་བཟུང་སར་ཟིན་པ་ནི་རིག་པ་
འོད་གསལ་དང་འདྲེས་པ་ལས་བྱུང་ངོ་། འཛིན་མེད་རང་གྲོལ་གྱི་གཟེར་སེམས་ཀྱི་སྣང་བ་ལ་ཐེབས་པས་ཡུལ་གྱི་སྤྲོས་པ་རང་དག་ལ་སོང་བའོ། གཉིས་པ་ཉམས་གོང་འཕེལ་གྱི་དུས་ན།
ལུས་སྐྱེས་བུ་ནད་ཀྱིས་གདུངས་པ་ལྟར་ངོ་ཚ་དང་བྲལ་བ་ནི་རླུང་དབུ་མར་ཆུད་པ་ལས་བྱུང་ངོ་། བྱ་བ་གཞི་དང་བྲལ་བའི་གཟེར་སྒོ་ལ་ཐེབས་པས་བྱ་བའི་གཞི་ལུས་མྱ་ངན་ལས་འདས་ནས་སྐུ་སྐྱེ་བ་མེད་
པའི་ཡེ་ཤེས་ངང་གིས་ཤར། ངག་སྨྱོན་པའི་རང་ཚིག་རྡོལ་བ་ལྟར་གང་བྱུང་སྨྲ་བ་ནི་ཡེ་ཤེས་གཅིག་ཏུ་མི་གནས་པ་ལས་བྱུང་ངོ་། ངོས་བཟུང་དང་བྲལ་བའི་གཟེར་བརྗོད་ཚིག་ལ་ཐེབས་པས་ངེས་པ་

71

ཀུ་ཁྱི་ན

མེད་པའི་ཡེ་ཤེས་རང་ལུགས་སུ་ཤར། སེམས་སྐྱེས་བུ་དུག་གིས་མྱོས་པ་ལྟར་འདུ་འཕྲོ་ཆུང་བ་ནི་རིག་པའི་རྩལ་སྐྱེ་བ་མེད་པ་ལས་བྱུང་ངོ་། །མ་སྐྱེས་རང་གྲོལ་གྱི་གཟེར་དྲན་པ་ལ་ཐེབས་པས་དྲན་
རྟོག་རང་ཡལ་འཛིན་མེད་དུ་རང་དག་ལ་སོང་བའོ། གསུམ་པ་རིག་པ་ཚད་ཕེབས་ཀྱི་དུས་ན། ལུས་གླང་ཆེན་འདམ་དུ་ཆུད་པ་རང་སྟོབས་ཀྱིས་འཐོན་པ་བཞིན་བྱ་རྩོལ་རྫོགས་པ་ནི་ཡེ་ཤེས་ཀྱི་
ཤུགས་ཐོན་པ་ལས་བྱུང་ངོ་། ཐོགས་པ་མེད་པའི་གཟེར་ལུས་ཀྱི་བྱ་བྱེད་ལ་ཐེབས་པས་བྱ་བ་གྲུབ་པའི་ཡེ་ཤེས་རང་དབང་དུ་འགྱུར། ངག་གྲུལ་བུམ་གྱི་ཕྲུ་གུ་སྨྲ་ལེན་པ་ལྟར་ཅི་སྨྲས་གཞན་གྱི་ཟ་བར
འཇུག་པ་ནི་ཤེས་རབ་ཡེ་ཤེས་ཀྱི་དབང་དུ་སྙིང་རྗེ་འདུས་པ་ལས་བྱུང་ངོ་། བརྗོད་པ་མི་འགག་པའི་ཡེ་ཤེས་ཀྱི་གཟེར་ངག་གི་བརྗོད་ལས་ལ་ཐེབས་པས་བརྗོད་བྱ་ལས་འདས་པའི་ཡེ་ཤེས་རང་བྱུང་དུ་
ཤར། སེམས་འབྲུམ་ནད་བྱུང་བ་ཁྲིས་སོག་མེད་པར་ལྟར་རང་ཡལ་ཁྲིས་མི་ཐོག་པ་ནི་གོམས་པ་ཀློང་དུ་གྱུར་པ་ལས་བྱུང་ངོ་། སྐད་ཅིག་མ་རྫུར་བྱེད་ཀྱི་གཟེར་དྲན་བྱེད་ཀྱི་ཡིད་ལ་ཐེབས་པས་སྤྲོས་པ་ཉེ་བར་ཞི་
བའི་ཡེ་ཤེས་རང་དབང་དུ་འགྱུར་བའོ། བཞི་པ་བོན་ཉིད་ཟད་པའི་དུས་ན། ལུས་དུར་ཁྲོད་ཀྱི་མི་རོ་བཞིན་ཡ་མི་ང་བ་ནི་སེམས་འོད་གསལ་གྱི་ཀྲ་བར་ཆུད་པ་ལས་བྱུང་ངོ་། འཛིགས་མེད་

72

ཁ

ཚ་བདུན་

༄། གདིངས་ལྡན་གྱི་གཟེར་དམིགས་པ་ལ་ཐེབས་པས་གཉེད་མ་བརྒྱུས་མཐའ་ནས་བསྐོར་ཀྱང་ཞམ་ང་བག་ཚ་མེད་པ་ནི་རྩོལ་བའི་སེམས་རྩོལ་མེད་གཡུང་དྲུང་གི་གྲོང་དུ་ཕྱི་དྲན་ལས་འདས་པའི་རྟགས།
ངག་བྲག་ཅའི་རྣམ་པ་ལྟར་ཕ་རོལ་གྱི་རྗེས་སུ་ཟློ་བ་ནི་རྩ་གནས་ཀྱི་ཡི་གེ་རླུང་གི་ཐིག་ལེར་རྫོད་པ་ལས་བྱུང་སྟེ། བརྗོད་མེད་རང་གྲོལ་གྱི་གཟེར་སེམས་ལ་ཐེབས་པས་བརྗོད་འཛིན་མེད་པའི་ཡེ་ཤེས་རང་
ཕྱུགས་སུ་ཤར། སེམས་ནི་བུན་ལྟར་སྣང་ཅིག་ལ་རང་ཡལ་དུ་སོང་བ་ནི་འཁོར་བ་རང་དེངས་པ་ལས་བྱུང་སྟེ། འཕྲུལ་མེད་ཡེ་ཤེས་ཀྱི་གཟེར་སེམས་ལ་ཐེབས་པས་དྲན་གཞི་སེམས་ཕྱི་དན་ལས
འདས་ནས་ཐུགས་འཕྲུལ་པ་མེད་པའི་ཡེ་ཤེས་ལ་དང་གིས་གནས་པའོ། དེ་དག་ལས་ལུས་ཀྱི་རྟགས་བཞི་ནི་དབང་བཞིའི་གཞི་ལ་ངེས་པ་ཐོབ་པ་ལས་བྱུང་ལ། ངག་གི་བཞི་ནི་དབང་བཞིའི་ལམ་གྱི་
ངེས་པ་ཐོབ་པ་ལས་བྱུང་ལ། ཡིད་ཀྱི་བཞི་ནི་དབང་བཞིའི་འབྲས་བུ་མངོན་དུ་གྱུར་པ་ལས་བྱུང་བའོ། གཉིས་པ་ཚད་མི་ལམ་གྱིས་བཟུང་བ་ནི། བརྩོན་འགྲུས་ཀྱི་རིམ་པས་རབ་མི་ལམ
རྒྱུན་ཆད་ནས་གཉིད་འོད་གསལ་དུ་འཆར་བ་ནི་འདིར་འཚང་རྒྱ་བར་ངེས་པའོ། །འབྲིང་མི་ལམ་མི་ལམ་དུ་ཤེས་ནས་རང་དབང་བསྒྱུར་ནུས་པ་ནི་བར་དོར་འཚང་རྒྱའོ། ཐ་མ་བག་ཆགས་དན་

73

༄ཀ་ཧི

པའི་མི་ལམ་རྒྱུན་ཆད་ནས་བཟང་པོ་ཤ་སྟག་ཏུ་མི་བ་རྣམས་ནི་རང་བཞིན་སྤྲུལ་པར་དབུགས་འབྱིན་པའོ། གསུམ་པ་ཐོབ་པ་གསུམ་ནི། གསེར་གྱི་ཞུན་མ་ལས། སྣང་བ་ཉིད་ལ་དབང་ཐོབ་
པས། ཀྱེན་སྣང་ཐམས་ཅད་གྲོགས་སུ་འཆར། ཕུང་པོ་ཉིད་ལ་དབང་ཐོབ་པས། རྡོས་བཅས་མི་སྣང་འོད་དུ་གསལ། གསང་བ་རླུང་སེམས་དབང་ཐོབ་པས། རྣམ་རྟོག་དབྱིངས
སུ་ནུབ་པའོ། ཞེས་སོ། བཞི་པ་གདེང་བཞི་ནི། སངས་རྒྱས་ཀྱི་ཡོན་ཏན་ཐོས་ཀྱང་ཐོབ་ཏུ་རེ་བ་དང་མ་ཐོབ་ཀྱི་དོགས་པ་གཉིས་ཀ་མེད་པ་སྟེ། རང་རིག་ལས་གཞན་པའི་སངས་རྒྱས
ཡོགས་ན་ཕྲའི་རྩེ་མོ་ཙམ་ཡང་མེད་པར་ཐག་ཆོད་པ་དང་། ངན་སོང་གསུམ་གྱི་སྡུག་བསྔལ་དང་ཚེ་ཚད་ཐོས་ཀྱང་མི་ལྡང་བའི་རེ་བ་དང་ལྡང་གི་དོགས་པ་གཉིས་ཀ་མེད་པ་སྟེ། རང་རིག་གདོད་
ནས་སྐྱེ་བ་མེད་པས་འཁོར་བར་འཁྲུམས་མཁན་མ་གྲུབ་པར་ཐག་ཆོད་པའོ། འཁོར་རྣམ་པ་བཞིས་ནི་བཀའ་སྩོད་བྱེད་དོ། ཞེས་པ་ནི་ཤེས་རབ་བཞི་སྟེ། དེའང་རྣམ་པར་འབྱེད་བྱེད་ཀྱི་
ཤེས་རབ་ཀྱིས་བོན་ཐམས་ཅད་མ་འདྲེས་པར་རྣམ་པར་སོ་སོར་འབྱེད། རྣམ་པར་སྤྱོད་བྱེད་ཀྱི་ཤེས་རབ་ཀྱིས་བོན་ཐམས་ཅད་རང་རིག་ལ་སྤྱད། རྣམ་པར་གྲོལ་བྱེད་ཀྱི་ཤེས་རབ་ཀྱིས་བོན་

74

ཁ

ཚ་བརྒྱད་

༄། ཐམས་ཅད་རང་གྲོལ་དུ་གཏན་ལ་ཕེབས། རྣམ་པར་སྨྱོད་བྱེད་ཀྱི་ཤེས་རབ་ཀྱིས་བོན་ཐམས་ཅད་རང་རིག་ཀ་དག་གང་ཡང་མ་ཡིན་པའི་དབྱིངས་སུ་བསྡུད་པར་བྱེད་དོ། དེ་ལྟར་ཐོད་རྒྱལ་གྱི་
གནད་བཞི་བཅུ་ཚ་གཉིས་དང་ལྡན་པའི་གདམས་ངག་གིས་ཟིན་པའི་རྣལ་འབྱོར་པ་འཕྲུལ་སྣང་གི་འཁོར་བ་སྒྲོ་བུར་བའི་ཆ་ཐམས་ཅད་རང་དག་ལ་སོང་ནས་རང་བཞིན་གྱིས་གཞི་ཀ་དག་གི་རང་ས་ན་རིག
པའི་གཏན་སྲིད་གདོན་མི་ཟ་བར་ཟིན་པར་འགྱུར་བར་ངེས་པའོ། །དོན་གཉིས་པ་དབང་པོ་འབྲིང་བར་དོར་གྲོལ་བའི་གདམས་པ་ལ་རང་བཞིན། འཆི་ཀ། བོན་ཉིད་ཀྱི་བར་དོ་དང་
གསུམ་ལས། དང་པོ་ནི། ཐོག་མའི་གཞིར་ལྷུན་གྲུབ་ཀྱི་སྣོས་བཀོད་པའི་སེམས་ཅན་གྱི་ཀུན་གཞིར་ཉོན་མོངས་སྡུ་མས་བཞག་པའི་བག་ཆགས་དཔེར་ན་མེ་ལོང་ལ་གཡའ་ཁམས་ལྡན་གྲུབ་ཏུ་ཡོད
པས་གཡའ་དྲིས་མོས་པ་ལྟ་བུ་ལ། ཕྱི་མའི་ལས་ཉོན་བསྐྱེད་པའི་ས་བོན་དུ་གྱུར་པས་ལས་ཟ་དད་པ་བསགས་པའི་དབང་གིས་གནས་རིགས་བདེ་སྡུག་བར་པར་འཕེན་པའི་མཐུ་ཡོད་པས་ནུས་པ་ཞེས་རྩ
བ་འབྲུ་པ་པའི་སེམས། ཕྲད་པར་མི་རྣམས་ནི་ཕུང་ལྷས་བཅིངས་པས་སྐུ་ལྔའི་སྣང་བ་བསྒྲིབས། །ཁམས་དང་སྐྱེ་མཆེད་ཀྱིས་བཅིངས་པས་འོད་གསལ་དང་། ལས་ཉོན་གྱིས་བཅིངས

75

76

པས་ཡེ་ཤེས་དང་བོན་ཉིད་ཀྱི་སྣང་བ་བསྒྲིབས་ནས་འཁྲུལ་སྣང་རང་ཁ་མ་ལ་སྤྱོད་པས་སྲིད་པ་ཕྱི་མས་ཕྱི་མའི་སྡུག་བསྔལ་འདྲེན་པས་མཐའ་མེད་པར་མནར་བའི་རང་བཞིན་ལ་སྙིག་སེམས་ཀྱིས་ཐར་པ་འདོད་པས་ལམ་འདི་ལ་དང་པོ་ཐོས་པས་བློ་སྦྱོང་། བར་དུ་བསམ་པས་གཏན་ལ་ཕབ། ཐ་མར་སྒོམ་པས་མངོན་དུ་བྱེད་ལ་རྟེན་འདིའི་སྟེང་ནས་འཁོར་བར་ཕྱིར་མི་ལྡོག་པའི་ཉམས་ལེན་ལ་བློའི་གདེང་ཚུད་པར་བྱ་དགོས་པ་ནི་གསེར་གྱི་ཞུན་མ་ལས། རང་བཞིན་གནས་པའི་བར་དོ་རུ། ཐོས་བསམ་སྒོམ་ལ་ནན་ཏན་བྱེད། ཅེས་སོ། གཉིས་པ་འཆི་ཁའི་བར་དོ་ནི། རབ་བུ་ཆུང་ལྟ་བུར་འཆི་བའི་གང་ཟག་ནི་འཆི་མི་འཆིའི་རྩིས་གདབས་ཟད་པས་གདམས་པ་འདི་མི་དགོས་ལ། འབྲིང་ཁྱི་ཀན་ལྟར་འཆི་བའི་གང་ཟག་འབྲིང་གི་རབ་ཡུལ་རྐྱེན་གྱིས་མི་གནོད་པས་རྒྱ་ལམ་དང་གྲོང་ཁྱེར་གྱི་སྟོང་མཐོར་འཆི་བ་དང་། འབྲིང་གི་འབྲིང་དེ་དག་ལས་འདས་པར་རི་ཕུག་གམ་ལུང་སྟོང་དམ་སུས་ཀྱང་མི་མཐོང་སར་འཆི་བ་དང་། ཐ་མ་རྒྱལ་པོ་ལྟར་འཆི་བ་ནི། ན་བའི་དུས་སུ་ཡང་སྨན་དང་རིམ་གྲོ་སོགས་བྱེད། འཆི་དུས་ཡང་ཉེ་གྲོགས་ཀྱིས་བསྐོར་ནས་སྨྲེ་ངག་ཁ་ཆེམས་འཇོག་ནས་འཆི། ཤི་ནས་ཀྱང་དགེ་བ་དང་བདུན་ཚིགས་དང་རོ་སྲེག་ལ་སོགས་པ་བྱེད་དོ།

77

༄༅། དེ་ལྟར་ཤི་བ་ནི་རྫོགས་པ་ཆེན་པོའི་ཉམས་ལེན་ལ་གདིང་མ་ཚུད་པའི་རྟགས་ཡིན་ཏེ། དོན་གྱི་རྣལ་འབྱོར་མ་ཡིན་ནོ། དེ་ནི་ལམ་ལ་མ་ཞུགས་པའི་སྐྱེ་བོ་དག་གི་འཆི་ལུགས་སོ། དེས་ན་ལམ་ལ་སྦྱོངས་པའི་རྣལ་འབྱོར་པ་སྐུ་དང་ཡེ་ཤེས་ལ་འཇུག་པ་འོད་གསལ་སྤུབས་འཇུག་པ་རྣམས་ནི། སེང་གེའི་ཉལ་ལུགས་ལ་གནས་པའི་ཤེས་པ་མིག་ལམ་ནས་དབྱིངས་རིག་དབྱེར་མེད་ཀྱི་ངོན་ལ་སྤྲོ་བསྡུ་མེད་པའི་ངང་ནས་འཚོ་བའི་འདུ་བྱེད་བཏང་བའི་སྐད་ཅིག་ལ་གྲོལ་བར་འགྱུར་ཏེ་ཐ་མ་ལས། འབྱུང་བསྡུད་འཆི་ཁའི་བར་དོ་ལ། མ་ཡེངས་དྲན་པས་གསལ་བར་གཅེས། འོད་གསལ་གདམས་པའི་གནས་ལུགས་གཟུང་། ད་ལྟའི་ཉམས་ལེན་སྐྱེལ་མ་འདྲ། བར་དོའི་སྣང་བ་སྲུན་མ་འདྲ། སྐད་ཅིག་གཅིག་ལ་གྲོལ་བར་ངེས། ཞེས་སོ། ད་ལྟའང་ནམ་མཁའ་དྭངས་པ་ལ་མིག་དང་སེམས་གཏད་ནས་དབྱིངས་རིག་བསྲེས་ཏེ། བདག་ངེས་པར་ཤི་ནས་རིག་པ་དབྱིངས་ན་གནས་པའི་དུས་ཡིན་པས་སྤྲོས་མེད་པའི་ཀློང་དུ་མྱ་ངན་ལས་འདའ་བར་བྱའོ་སྙམ་དུ་དབུགས་ཕྱིར་འཕངས་པའི་ཕྱི་ལ་ཤེས་པ་གཏད་མེད་དུ་འཇོག་པ་ནི་གནད་དམ་པའོ། དེའི་ཚེ་ཚིག་གི་སྤྲོས་པ་ལ་ལྟོས་དགོས་པ་རྣམས་ལ་ནི། བླ་མའམ་གཡུང་དྲུང་གི་སྤུན་སྲིང་དམ་ཚིག་ལ་སེལ

78

མེད་པ་གཅིག་གིས་དབྱིངས་དང་རིག་པ་ངོ་སྤྲད་དོ། ཡུལ་དང་གནས་ལ་འཇུག་པ་ནི་ཡེ་ཤེས་ཟང་ཐལ་གྱི་མན་ངག་ལྟར་རླུང་ཐ་མ་ཕྱིར་འགྲོ་དུས་ཏིཀ་ཀི་ཤུ་ཙ་གཅིག་བརྗེགས་མར་བརྗོད་པས་སྙིང་ག་ནས་རིག་པ་ཨའི་རྣམ་པ་དེ་ཚོན་རེ་བཞིན་ཚང་བུག་ནས་ཡར་རྒྱང་གིས་སོང་བ་བསམ་པས་གྲོལ་ལོ། གཞན་ཡང་དུས་དེར་ལམ་མངོན་སངས་རྒྱས་པའི་རྒྱུད་ཀྱི་འབྲིང་རྫོགས་སྐྱུར་འཕོ་བའི་གདམས་པ་ཀྱང་ཉམས་འོག་ཏུ་ཚུད་པར་བྱའོ། གནད་དེ་ལྟ་བུ་དང་ལྡན་པ་རྣམས་ནི་ཐིམ་རིམ་གྱི་ངེས་པ་ལ་མ་ལྟོས་པར་དབུགས་འཕོ་ལུགས་དག་གིས་མྱ་ངན་ལས་འདའ་བ་ཡང་ཡོད་དོ། མན་ངག་ཐབ་ཀྱང་གདེང་དང་མི་ལྡན་པའམ་ཐ་མལ་པའི་རིགས་ལ་རྩ་རླུང་གི་འདུ་བའི་བྱེད་པས་ཕྱི་འབྱུང་བཞི། ནང་ནམ་མཁའ་ལྔ། གསང་བ་སྒྲོག་ལྔ། ཡང་རྫོགས་རླུང་ལྷག་མ་ཉི་ཤུ་དང་བཅས་པའི་ཐིམ་ལུགས་ནི་དབྱིངས་རིག་རིན་པོ་ཆེའི་མཛོད་ལས་ཞིབ་པར་བསྟན་ཀྱང་། འདི་དབང་རྟུལ་གྱིས་རྟོགས་སླ་བའི་ཕྱིར་འབྱུང་བའི་ཐིམ་ཚུལ་ནི། ཐ་མ་ལས། ས་ནི་ས་ལ་ཐིམ་པའི་ཚེ། ལུས་པོ་ལྕི་ཞིང་ཟས་མི་ལེན། ལངས་ཏེ་འགྲོ་བའི་སྟོབས་ཀྱང་ཟད། ཆུ་ནི་ཆུ་ལ་ཐིམ་པའི་ཚེ། ཁ་ཆུ་སྣ་ཆུ་འཛག་པ་བྱེད། མེ་ནི་མེ་ལ་ཐིམ་པའི་ཚེ། ལུས་དྲོད་འཆོལ་ཞིང

ཐ

༄། ཞིང་མཐའ་ནས་བསྡུད། ཆུང་ངེ་ཆུང་ལ་ཐིམ་པའི་ཚེ། ངར་ངར་སོག་སོག་ཡན་ལག་གཡོ། དེ་དུས་མིག་འབྲས་གྱེན་དུ་ཕྱོག པ་རོལ་འགྲོ་བའི་ལྟ་ལྟས་ཡིན། བླ་མའི་གདམས་
ངག་དྲན་པ་གཅེས། ཞེས་སོ། དེ་ནས་རྩ་ཐུན་གྱི་ཁྲག་ཐམས་ཅད་སྙིག་ཙར་འདུས་པའི་བྱེད་ལས། ཁྲག་ཐིག་རིམ་པ་གསུམ་རྒྱབ་པས་དབུགས་ཀྱང་ཕྱུང་གི་རྣམ་པས་རིམ་པ་གསུམ་གྱི་ཐ་
མར་ཕྱི་དབུགས་ཁྲིགས་ཀྱི་ཆད། དེ་ནས་སྣང་མཆེད་ཐོབ་གསུམ་གྱི་སྐད་ཅིག་མ་གསུམ་གྱི་ཉེར་ཐོབ་དྲན་པས་ཟིན་དཀའ་བས་བརྒྱལ་བ་ལྟར་འགྲོ་ལ། དེ་ལས་སངས་ཏེ་སྐད་ཅིག་མའི་ཡེ་བཞུགས་
ཀྱི་འོད་གསལ་སྤྲིན་མེད་པའི་ནམ་མཁའ་ལྟ་བུ་རྩལ་སྣང་དྲན་རྟོག་གང་ཡང་མེད་པ་ཞིག་འཆར་བ་ངོ་ཤེས་པར་བྱས་པས་ཀ་དག་གི་དབྱིངས་སུ་རིག་པས་གཏན་སྲིད་ཟིན་ནས་འཚང་རྒྱ་བ་ནི་གསེར་གྱི་ཕུར་མ་
ལས། སེམས་དང་ཡེ་ཤེས་རྒྱབ་གྱིས་ཆེ། སྐད་ཅིག་དེ་ལ་རྫོགས་སངས་རྒྱས། གཡུང་དྲུང་འགྱུར་མེད་ཨེ་མ་ཧོ། ཞེས་སོ། གསུམ་པ་བོན་ཉིད་བར་དོ་ནི། གོང་གི་ཀ་དག
ནམ་མཁའ་ལྟ་བུ་ཤར་བ་དེར་མ་གྲོལ་ན་ནམ་མཁའ་འོད་གསལ་ལ་ཐིམ་པ་ཞེས་རིག་པ་མིག་ནས་འཐོན་པས་ཉེར་ཐོབ་ཡེ་ཤེས་སྐད་ཅིག་བཞི་པའི་རྗེས་སུ། གཞི་སྣང་འོད་གསལ་ཞེས་ནམ་མཁའི་

79

མཐོངས་སུ་འོད་གསལ་ཡེ་ཤེས་ལྔའི་རང་མདངས་ཁྲ་མོ་རེ་འཆར་བ་དེ་ཉིད་རང་སྣང་དུ་ངོས་བཟུང་བས་གྲོལ་ཏེ། ཡང་རྩེ་ལས། རྒྱུན་ལམ་རིག་པ་མིག་ནས་འཐོན། ནམ་མཁའི་མཐོངས་
སུ་འོད་དུ་འཆར། གདམས་པ་ཅན་རྣམས་གྲོལ་བའི་དུས། ཞེས་སོ། དེ་ལས་མ་གྲོལ་ན་འོད་གསལ་ཟུང་འཇུག་ལ་ཐིམ་པ་ཞེས་སྟར་གྱི་སྣང་བ་དེ་ལས་སྒྲ་འོད་ཟེར་དང་གོམས་འདྲིས་ཅན་ལ་
སྐུའི་སྣང་བ་འཆར་བའི་ཚུལ་ནི་གཟི་བུ་ལས། འོད་ནི་ཞིང་ཁམས་མཐའ་དབུས་མེད། ནམ་མཁར་འཇའ་ཚོན་ཤར་བ་འདྲ། སྒྲ་ནི་དངོས་མེད་སྒྲོང་ན་སྒྲིར། རང་བྱུང་རྒྱུན་མེད་འབྲུག་
སྒྲའི་ཚུལ། ཟེར་ནི་ཚོ་འཕྲུལ་ངེས་མེད་སྟོན། ཟ་འོག་སྣམ་བུ་ཁ་ཕྱེས་འདྲ། གོམས་ཤིང་འདྲིས་པའི་གང་ཟག་ལ། སྐུ་དང་ཞིང་ཁམས་རྫོགས་པར་འཆར། ཞེས་སོ། དེ་དུས་
རང་གི་སྙིང་ག་ནས་འོད་ཀྱི་ཟེར་ཐག་ཤིགས་སྐུ་དེ་དག་གི་ཐུགས་ཀར་འབྲེལ་པར་སྣང་སྟེ། གསེར་གྱི་ཞུན་མ་ལས། ཨོཾ་རྒྱའི་འོད་དུ་གསལ་བ་དེ། འོད་ཀྱི་སྙིང་པོ་ཆེན་གང་བཅས། འོད
ཀྱིས་སྐུ་དང་འབྲེལ་པར་སྣང་། དེ་ལ་མ་ཡེངས་ཆེ་རེར་བཞག ཅེས་སོ། འོད་དེ་ལ་རང་གི་ཤེས་པ་ཐིམ་ན་རིག་པ་འོད་ལ་འཇུག་པ་ཞེས་བྱ་སྟེ། མི་རྟོག་པའི་བསམ་གཏན་ལ་རང་

80

ཐ

༄། བཞིན་དུ་གནས་ལ། སྣང་ལ་དེ་དག་ཟེར་ཐག་ལས་རང་གི་སྙིང་གར་ཚུར་ཐིམ་པ་སྒོམ་བྱེད་ན་འོད་རིག་པ་ལ་ཐིམ་པ་ཞེས་བྱ་སྟེ་རང་ངོ་ཀ་དག་གི་རང་ས་ངོ་ཤེས་པར་བྱས་པས་དེ་ཉིད་དུ་གྲོལ་ལོ།
དེར་མ་གྲོལ་ན་ཟུང་འཇུག་ཡེ་ཤེས་ལ་ཐིམ་པ་ཞེས་བྱ་སྟེ་རང་གི་སྙིང་ག་ནས། འོད་ཀྱི་ཐག་པ་ཤིན་ཏུ་ཕྲ་བ་གཅིག་སྟེང་གི་ནམ་མཁའ་ལ་ཐུག་པ་དེ་ལ་བལྟས་པས་སྣང་བ་དེ་རྒྱ་ཆེ་བར་འཆར་ཏེ། ཐུ་མ་ལས།
ལུས་ནི་འོད་དུ་སྣང་བ་ལ། ཡེ་ཤེས་སྣམ་བུ་ལྟ་ཤར་དུས། རང་ངོ་ཤེས་པ་གནད་དུ་བཟུང་། ཞེས་འོད་མཐིང་ཀ་དང་དཀར་པོ་དང་སེར་པོ་དང་དམར་པོ་བཞིའི་སྣམ་བུ་འཕུར་ལ་མ་རེག་པ། སོ་སོའི་སྟེང་དུ
རང་རང་གི་ཁ་དོག་དང་མཐུན་པའི་ཐིག་ལེ་མེ་ལོང་ཙམ་རེ་ལ་ཐིག་ལྡན་ལྔ་ལྔས་བརྒྱན་པར་འཆར་ལ། དེ་དག་གི་སྟེང་ན་འོད་སྨུག་ཆ་བྱའི་གདུགས་ལྟ་བུ་ཅིག་འཆར་ཏེ། དབྱིངས་སུ་གྲོལ་མ
ཐིན་པས་ཡེ་ཤེས་བཞི་སྦྱོར་གྱི་སྣང་བ་ཞེས་སྒྲ་བཏགས་ནས། དོན་དུ་ཡང་གི་གོ་དོན་བཞིན་སློང་ན་སྣམ་བུ་ལྟ་འཆར་བའང་མ་བཀག་པའི་དེ་དག་ལ་ཡེ་ཤེས་ལྔའི་སྣང་བ་མཉམ་པར་རྫོགས་པའོ། །
དེ་དག་རང་སྣང་དུ་མ་ཤེས་ན་དེ་ནས་ཡེ་ཤེས་ལྷུན་གྲུབ་ལ་ཐིམ་པ་ཞེས་བྱ་སྟེ། ཕར་གྱི་སྣང་བ་དེ་དག་དང་རིག་པ་སྟེང་གི་འོད་རྒྱུས་ལ་འདུས་པ་སྒོམ་བྱེད་པའི་ཚུལ་ལས་སྟེང་ན་ཀ་དག་གི་སྣང་བ་ནས

81

82

མཁའ་གཡའ་དག་པ་ལྟ་བུ། དེའི་འོག་ན་དཔང་ཆེན་ཁྲོ་བོའི་དཀྱིལ་འཁོར། དེའི་འོག་ན་གཡུང་དྲུང་ཡོངས་སུ་རྫོགས་པའི་ལྷ་ཚོགས། ཕྱོགས་མཚམས་ན་རང་བཞིན་སྤྲུལ་པའི་ཞིང་ཁམས།
འོག་ན་རིགས་དྲུག་གི་སྣང་བ་འདུལ་བྱེད་སྟོན་པ་དང་བཅས་པ་རང་སྣང་བ་གཞི་ལས་མ་གཡོས་པའི་གཞི་སྣང་ཞེས་བྱ་སྟེ་འཆར་ལུགས་བརྒྱད་སྣང་བའི་ཚུལ། ཐུགས་རྗེ་ལྟར་ཤར་བས་སྙིང་རྗེའི་ཤུགས་
འཁོར་བ་ལ་འཇུག་པའི་འཁོར་འདས་རྒྱ་མ་ཆད། འོད་ལྟར་ཤར་བའི་སྣང་ཆ་ནང་ན་གསལ། སྐུ་ལྟར་ཤར་བས་སྣང་བ་གང་དུའང་མི་འབྱེད། ཡེ་ཤེས་ལྟར་ཤར་བའི་སྣང་བ་ཟང་ཐལ།
གཉིས་མེད་ལྟར་ཤར་བས་ཤེས་པ་རྩེ་གཅིག་ཏུ་གནས། མཐའ་གྲོལ་ལྟར་ཤར་བས་ངོ་བོ་ཉིད་དུ་སངས། མ་དག་པ་ལྟར་ཤར་བས་སྲིད་པའི་བྱུང་ཁུངས་མ་འགགས། དག་པ་ལྟར་ཤར་བས
ཡེ་ཤེས་མ་བུ་འབྲེལ་པའོ། སྣང་བ་དེ་དག་རང་སྣང་དུ་ཤེས་པའི་བོན་སྐུར་གྲོལ་ཏེ་གསེར་གྱི་ཡང་ཞུན་ལས། ལྷུན་གྲུབ་སྐུ་གསུམ་སྣང་བ་ལ། ཅི་ཤར་ཀློ་ལས་སྒྱུ་མར་ཤེས། སྒྱུ་མ
རང་བཞིན་མེད་པ་ལ། ཆགས་ཞེན་མི་བྱ་ཡན་པ་བསྐྱུར། སྟོང་གསལ་འགག་མེད་ངང་དུ་ཞོག བོན་གྱི་སྐུ་རུ་གྲོལ་བར་ངེས། ཞེས་སོ། སྣང་བ་དེ་དག་ནང་དུ་སྡུད་པའི་ཚེ་ཐིམ

83

༄། ལུགས་བརྒྱད་དུས་གཅིག་ལ་འབྱུང་བའི་ཚུལ་ནི་ཐུ་མ་ལས། ཐུགས་རྗེ་ཐུགས་རྗེ་ཉིད་ལ་ཐིམ། ཉི་མ་ནུབ་པའི་ཟེར་བཞིན་དུ། གདུལ་བྱ་འདུལ་བྱེད་རྣམ་པར་དག འོད་ནི་འོད་ལ་རང་ཐིམ་པས།
ནམ་མཁའི་གཞའ་ལྟར་གསལ་རིག་མེད། སྐུ་ནི་སྐུ་ལ་རང་ཐིམ་པས། གཞོན་ནུ་བུམ་པའི་སྐུ་བཞིན་དུ། མཁྱེན་པ་ནང་གསལ་ཉིད་དུ་གནས། ཡེ་ཤེས་ཡེ་ཤེས་ལ་ཐིམ་པས། མ་པང་
བུ་ནི་འཇུག་པ་བཞིན། རིག་པ་གཞི་ཐོག་ཉིད་དུ་གྲོལ། གཉིས་མེད་གཉིས་མེད་ལ་ཐིམ་པས། ཆུ་ལ་ཆུ་ཐིམ་ཅི་བཞིན་དུ། བོན་ཅན་བོན་ཉིད་གཅིག་ཏུ་འདྲེས། མཐའ་གྲོལ་
མཐའ་གྲོལ་ལ་ཐིམ་པས། ནམ་མཁའ་ནམ་མཁའ་ཐིམ་པ་བཞིན། གཡུང་དྲུང་བོན་གྱི་ངང་དུ་གནས། མ་དག་དག་པ་ཉིད་ལ་ཐིམ། སྲུ་ཡི་ཆེན་ཐག་བཏུལ་བ་བཞིན། འོད་
གསལ་དང་ལས་གཡོ་བ་མེད། དག་པ་ཡེ་ཤེས་སྒོ་ཐིམ་པས། སེང་གེས་གངས་རི་ཟིན་པ་བཞིན། གཡུང་དྲུང་བོན་གྱི་ངང་དུ་གནས། ཞེས་སོ། དེ་ལྟར་ཐིམ་ལུགས་བརྒྱད་ཀྱི་རིག
པ་རང་ཡུལ་དུ་ཐོག་སྟེ། ཀ་དག་ལྷུན་གྲུབ་དབྱེར་མེད་ལ་གནས་པས་ངོ་ཤེས་པ་རྣམས་ཕྱིར་མི་ལྡོག་པར་བོན་གྱི་སྐུའི་གཏན་སྲིད་ཟིན་པ་སྟེ། འཁོར་འདས་དབྱིངས་སུ་ནུབ་སྟེ་གཞི་གྲོལ་ལ་སོང་བ

84

ལྷུན་གྲུབ་ཐིམ་ཚུལ་གྱི་དུས་དེར་ངོ་ཤེས་དགོས་སོ། སྣང་བ་བཞི་པོ་དེ་དག་གང་ལའང་སྤྱིར་བཏང་གི་གདམས་པ་ཁྱད་པར་ཅན་འདི་ཡོད་དེ། བར་དོར་སྒྲ་འོད་ཟེར་གསུམ་གྱི་སྣང་བ་སྲུན་མ་དང་
འདུ་བར་འཆར་བའི་ཚེ། དེ་ལ་སྐྱེལ་མ་དང་འདྲ་བའི་གདམས་པ་གསུམ་དྲན་པར་བྱ་སྟེ། དེའི་ཚེ་བུ་མ་དང་འཕྲད་པ་ལྟར་གང་ཤར་ལ་ཞེ་ཚོམ་མི་ཟ་བར་རང་སྣང་དུ་ཡིད་ཆེས་བྱེད། མི་འགྱུར་བ་གསེར་
གྱི་ཕུར་མའི་དཔེས་ཡིད་ཆེས་ཐོག་ལས་གཞན་དུ་མི་ཡེངས་པར་བཙན་ས་བཟུང་དཔག་ཆེན་གྱི་མདའ་ཚུར་ལ་མི་ལྡོག་པའི་དཔེས་བཙན་ས་བཟུང་བའི་གཤིས་ལ་མི་གཡོ་བར་བཞག་པས་གནད་གསུམ་གཅིག་ཏུ
རྫོགས་ཏེ། སངས་རྒྱས་པ་ནི་ཡང་རྩེ་ལས། དད་པའི་སྣོད་ལྡན་མཁའ་འགྲོ་མ། དུས་འདིར་ངོ་སྤྲོད་ཐོབ་པ་རྣམས། བར་དོ་དེ་རུ་འཛོམས་མི་དགོས། རྐྱེན་གསུམ་འཆར་བའི་སྲུན་མ་གསུམ། སྐྱེལ་མ་གསུམ
གྱིས་སྐྱེལ་བར་བྱེད། གནད་གསུམ་གཅིག་ཏུ་རྫོགས་ཏེ་གྲོལ། ཞེས་སོ། དེ་དག་གི་གྲོལ་རྐྱེན་རྗེས་དྲན་དྲུག་ནི། བར་མ་དོའི་སྣང་བ་མཐོང་བས་རྐྱེན་བྱས་ནས་ཡི་དམ་ལྷ་དྲན་ནས་ཞལ་མཐོང་། དེས་བླ་མ
དྲན་པའི་མོད་ལ་མདུན་དུ་བྱོན་ནས་མན་ངག་སྟོན། གདམས་པ་དྲན་པས་གང་ཤར་རང་སྣང་དུ་ཤེས། དེ་ནས་ལྟ་བ་དྲན་པས་དབྱིངས་ཀ་དག་དྲན་ནས་དེའི་སྙིང་དུ་བསམ་གཏན་ལ་གནས་དགོས་པ

ཞ ཞེ་གསུམ

༄། དྲན་ནས་གྲོལ་ཏེ། །གསེར་གྱི་ཞུན་མ་ལས། བླ་མ་དྲན་དང་གདམས་པ་དྲན། ཡི་དམ་ལྷ་དྲན་ལྷ་བ་དྲན། དེ་ལས་གདོད་མའི་དབྱིངས་དྲན་པས། དེ་སྟེང་བསམ་
གཏན་གནས་པ་དྲན། ཞེས་སོ། དེ་དང་དུས་མཉམ་པའི་ཚུལ་དུ་མངོན་ཤེས་དྲུག་འཆར་ཏེ། དབང་པོ་དག་པས་དབང་དྲུག་གི་མཐོང་བ་དག ཤེས་རབ་དག་པས་བློ་དང་ཡིད་དཔྱོད་
དང་བྲལ། ཡེ་ཤེས་དག་པས་སེམས་ཅན་གྱི་དུས་གསུམ་གྱི་སྐྱེ་གནས་དང་འཆི་འཕོ་ཤེས། ཉིང་འཛིན་དག་པས་སེམས་ལས་སུ་རུང་། ཟག་པ་ཟད་པས་རང་དོན་མཐར་ཕྱིན་ནས་རིགས་
དྲུག་གི་སྐྱེ་གནས་མཐོང་ནས་གཞན་དོན་དུ་སྤྲུལ་པ་འགྱེད་ནུས། མཁྱེན་པ་དག་པས་སངས་རྒྱས་ཀྱི་གཟིགས་པ་ཕྱིན་ཅི་མ་ལོག་པར་མཐོང་བ་ནི་སྔ་མ་ལས། དབང་པོ་ཤེས་རབ་མཐོང་བ་དག །
ཡེ་ཤེས་དག་དང་ཉིང་འཛིན་དག ཟག་པ་ཟད་དང་མཁྱེན་པ་རྫོགས། ཞེས་སོ། གྲོལ་ཚད་ཀྱང་རབ་སྐད་ཅིག་མ་གསུམ་ན་གྲོལ། འབྲིང་ལྔ་ན་གྲོལ། ཐ་མ་ཉི་ཤུ་རྩ་གཅིག་ན
གྲོལ་བ་ཐོབ་པའོ། དོན་གསུམ་པ་རང་བཞིན་སྤྲུལ་པའི་ཞིང་དུ་དབུགས་འབྱིན་པ་ནི། གོང་དུ་ལྷུན་གྲུབ་ཀྱི་སྣང་བ་ཤར་དུས་དེ་མ་གྲོལ་བའི་དབང་པོ་ཉེར་གཅིག་པའི་ཐ་མ་དེ་ཉིད་སྲིད་པའི་བར་

ཀྱང་ཡིག

དོ་མི་ལམ་འདྲ་བ་འཆར་བའི་ཚེ། འདིའི་སྒོ་མཐོང་བ་ནྲམས་དྲན་པ་སད་ནས་ཐོན་དུ་བོན་ཉིད་བར་དོ་ངོས་མ་ཟིན་ནས་སྲིད་པའི་བར་དོར་ཁ་འཁྱིལ་པ་དེ་ཤེས་ཏེ། ད་ནི་རང་བཞིན་སྤྲུལ་པའི་
ཞིང་དུ་འགྲོ་བར་བྱའོ་སྙམ་པ་ཙམ་གྱིས་ཞིང་ཁམས་དེ་ར་རྫུས་ཏེ་སྐྱེ་བའི་ཚུལ་གསེར་གྱི་ཕྲེང་བ་མ་ལས། སྲིད་པའི་བར་དོར་ངོ་ཤེས་ནས། རིགས་དྲུག་སྐྱེ་བའི་བག་ཆགས་ཟད། སྤྲུལ་པའི་སྐུ་ཙ་
དབུགས་འབྱིན་ཅིང་། སྨོན་ལམ་དག་པས་མཚམས་སྦྱོར་ཏེ། ཕྱི་མར་ལྷག་མེད་ཨེ་མ་ཧོ། ཞེས་སོ། དེ་ལ་ད་ལྟ་རིག་པ་ཚངས་ཕུག་ནས་འོད་ཀྱི་གོང་ཕུར་དམིགས་པ་སྐར་མདའ་རྒྱུག་པ
ལྟར་འཕེན་པ་དང་། དེའི་དུས་ན་ཞིང་དེ་དྲན་ནས་ཤར་ལ་སོགས་པར་རིག་པ་ཨའི་རྣམ་པར་ཞིང་གི་གཙོ་བོའི་ཐུགས་ཀར་ཡང་ཡང་འཕངས་པ་ལ་ནན་ཏན་བྱའོ། ཞིང་ནི་ཤར་མངོན་པར
དགའ་བ་ན་སྟོན་པ་གསལ་བ་རང་བྱུང་། བྱང་ལས་རབ་རྫོགས་པ་ན་སྟོན་པ་དགེ་ལྷ་གར་ཕྱུག ནུབ་པདྨ་བརྩེགས་པ་ན་སྟོན་པ་བྱེ་བྲག་དངོས་མེད། ལྷོ་དཔལ་དང་ལྡན་པ་ན་སྟོན་པ་དགའ་
བ་དོན་འགྲུབ། དབུས་ལྷུན་གྱིས་གྲུབ་པ་ན་སྟོན་པ་འོད་དཀར་གནས་འཛིན་གཡུང་དྲུང་འཆང་ཆེན་པོ་དང་ལྔ་ལ། རང་རང་གི་འཁོར་རྫུས་ནས་སྐྱེས་པའི་བྱང་ཆུབ་སེམས་དཔའ་ཁྲིཙ་དང་བྱ་

ཞ ཞེ་བཞི

༄། མོ་ནྲམས་ཞིང་ཁམས་རང་རང་གི་ཁ་དོག་ཅན། རང་རང་གི་གཙོ་བོས་རང་རང་གི་འཁོར་ལ་བོན་འཆད་པ། ས་གཞི་ནྲམས་ཀྱང་རིན་པོ་ཆེ་ལས་གྲུབ་པ། དེ་དག་ཏུ་སྤྲུལ་པའི་
བྱ་དང་རི་དྭགས་ཀ་སྒྲང་ལ་སོགས་པ་ཁ་དོག་ཀྱང་ཞིང་ཁམས་རང་མདོག་དང་མཐུན་པ། རིན་ཆེན་སྣ་ཚོགས་ཀྱི་ལྗོན་ཤིང་དང་། ཡན་ལག་བརྒྱད་ལྡན་གྱི་ཆུ་བོ། ཟས་སྐོམ་དང་ལོངས་སྤྱོད་
བསམ་གྱིས་མི་ཁྱབ་པར་འདུག་པ། ཞིང་ཁམས་དེ་ནྲམས་ཀྱི་སྟེང་ཕྱོགས་ན་བོན་ཉིད་ཁྲོ་གཏུམ་འབར་བ་ཞེས་བྱ་བ་སྤྲུལ་པའི་ཁྲོ་བོའི་ཞིང་ཁམས་ཡོད་དོ། དེ་དག་ཏུ་སྐྱེས་པ་ནྲམས་ལོ་ལྔ་བརྒྱ་ན
བར་དོ་མེད་པར་སངས་རྒྱས་ཐོབ་པ་ཤ་སྟག་གོ། དེ་དག་ལམ་མས་བགྲོད་ཀྱི་རིགས་ལྔའི་ཞིང་ཁམས་དང་ཁྲོ་བོའི་དཀྱིལ་འཁོར་འདྲ་ཅང་དུ་ཡོད་ཀྱང་དངོས་ནི་མ་ཡིན་ནོ། ཞིང་ཁམས་དེ་དག་རང་
གི་སྙིང་ག་ན་སྟོང་པ་ཉིད་ཀྱི་ཡེ་ཤེས་ལ་སོགས་པའི་ཡེ་ཤེས་ལྔ་རང་གསལ་བའི་རང་གདངས་དང་། དུང་ཁང་ན་ཁྲོ་བོའི་དཀྱིལ་འཁོར་དུ་ཡེ་ནས་བཞུགས་པའི་སྣང་བ་ལས་རང་བཞིན་གྱིས་སྣང་བའི་ཕྱིར
རང་བཞིན་སྤྲུལ་པའི་ཞིང་ཁམས་ཞེས་བྱའོ། འདིའི་སྒོ་མ་མཐོང་བའི་འགྲོ་བ་ཐལ་ཐ་ལས་བོན་ལ་སྦྱངས་པས་སྐྱ་མ་དང་མི་ལམ་འབྱོངས་པས་གྲོལ་བར་སྲིད་པར་བཤད་ལ། བོན་ལ་གོམས་པ་མེད་

པ་རྣམས་ལས་ཀྱང་ཞིང་དག་པ་ལ་སྨོན་ལམ་འདེབས་པ་དང་། སྐྱབས་འགྲོ་བྱེད་པ་དང་། དད་པ་ཅན་རྣམས་ཀྱིས་མངལ་སྒོ་ངན་པ་ལས་ལོག་སྟེ་བཟང་པོ་དང་འཕྲད་ནས་རྟེན་དག་པ་ཐོབ་སྟེ་ཐོན་དང་
འཕྲད་ནས་ཐར་པ་ཐོབ་པར་འགྱུར་རོ། དེ་ལས་གཞན་པ་ཀུན་སྲིད་པའི་བར་དོར་ཁ་འཁྱོལ་ཏེ་སྔོན་མའི་ལས་ཀྱི་ཤུགས་ཀྱིས་འཕངས་ཏེ། བདེ་སྡུག་བར་མའི་སྐྱེ་གནས་སུ་བརྒྱུད་ནས་མཐའ་
མེད་པའི་འཁོར་བའི་སྡུག་བསྔལ་གྱི་རྒྱ་མཚོ་ལ་ཡང་ཡང་འཁོར་བ་ལས་ལོངས་མེད་པས་དགེ་སྡིག་ཤུང་སླང་ལ་ཞིབ་ཏུ་ནས་འབད་པ་གལ་ཆེའོ། །རྣམ་ཀུན་མི་གཡོ་ནམ་མཁའི་རང་བཞིན་མཁྱེན་པ་ནང་
གསལ་ཡེ་ཤེས་སྐུ། རྗོད་བྱེད་མདོ་རྒྱུད་ཤིན་ཏུ་རྒྱ་ཆེའི་དོན་འབྲས་དྲི་མ་མེད་པ་གང་། ཚིག་གི་སྤྲོས་པ་ཅུང་ཟད་ལེགས་འདོམས་བློ་གྲོས་མི་ཟད་དམ་པའི་གཞི། འདིར་བསྟེན་མཁས་གང་
སྲིད་པ་འདི་ན་འཕགས་སོ་གྲགས་པའི་ཛ་སླས་ཅུར། གང་འདི་བདག་བློའི་པད་མཚོ་ལས་སྐྱེས་ཕན་བདེའི་བདུད་རྩི་སྦྲ་མཁས་ཅན། ཀུན་གྱིས་མ་ཡིན་མཁྱེན་སྤྱན་ཡངས་པའི་གཟིགས་ན་དངོས་
པོའི་དེ་ཉིད་མཐོང་། དེ་ཕྱིར་དབྱིངས་རིག་ཟབ་དོན་སྙིང་པོ་སྐོར་ཡང་ཅུང་ཟད་འདི་བཀོད་པས། ལེགས་གང་ཤེས་ན་དེ་ཉིད་འདི་ཡི་གདུལ་བྱ་དམ་པའི་རྗེས་འགྲོ་གཤེན། སྲིད་པའི་སྣང་

༄། ཚུལ་ཉོན་མོངས་དཔུང་ཆེའི་བུད་ཤིང་ཐལ་བར་བསྲེགས་པའི་མེ། སྡུག་བསྔལ་རྒྱ་གཏེར་གཏིང་ནས་སྐེམས་བྱེད་ཡེ་ཤེས་ཉི་མ་འབུམ་གྱི་འོད། མཆོག་གསང་ལམ་འདི་ཀུན་བཟང་མི་
གཉིས་ཡེ་ཤེས་བླ་མའི་རང་གཟུགས་ཅན། རྟོགས་པའི་ནང་བྱན་མིན་ཀྱང་སྔོན་ལས་སད་པས་ཁོང་ནས་འདི་བཞིན་བྱུང་། དེ་ལྟར་ནའང་རྗེ་བོའི་གནས་ལུགས་ཟབ་ཅིང་ཆ་ཕྲ་བརྟག་དཀའི་གནས།
འདི་ན་མཁས་པ་བསྟེན་མིན་ཆུང་ནས་མ་སྦྱངས་ཅུང་ཟད་བཀོད་བྱས་ཀྱང་། འགལ་འཁྲུལ་ནོར་བའི་རང་བཞིན་མཆིས་སྲིད་ཚུར་མཐོང་བྱིས་པའི་བློ་ཅན་ཕྱིར། ཉེས་གང་དེ་ཀུན་རྒྱལ་དང་དེའི་
སྲས་བློ་མཆོག་མངའ་བའི་མདུན་སར་མཐོལ། གང་དག་དེ་ལས་བྱུང་བའི་རྣམ་དཀར་ལེགས་ཚོགས་འོད་སྟོང་འཕྲོ་བ་གང་། །གཤེན་བསྟན་ཟབ་ཡངས་མཁའ་ལ་རྟག་འཆར་ཡེ་ཤེས་འོད་སྣང་
འབར་བའི་གཟིམས། སྲིད་པའི་མ་རིག་མུན་སྤྲུག་རབ་གཅིལ་ངོ་བོ་ཀ་དག་སྟོང་ཆེན་ཞིང་། །རང་བཞིན་ལྷུན་གྲུབ་གཞོན་ནུ་བུམ་སྐུའི་གཏན་སྲིད་ཀུན་གྱིས་ཟིན་གྱུར་ཅིག འདི་ན་རྒྱ་བའི་
བྱིས་པའི་གྲོགས་དང་འགྲོགས་རྣམས་ཆགས་སྡང་སྐྱི་ལ་འཐོགས། སྲིད་པའི་ཕུན་ཚོགས་རྨི་ལམ་ནོར་བཞིན་སྙིང་པོ་མེད་པར་འབྲལ་བར་ངེས། འདི་སྣང་ཆེ་གྲགས་འདོད་གདུངས་ཞགས་པས་རང་

རྒྱུད་དམ་དུ་བཅིངས་པ་གང་། འདི་ནས་ཕར་ངོས་སྣང་བ་མ་ངེས་བདེ་སྡུག་བར་མའི་ལས་དབང་གཙོ། འདི་ཀུན་རང་བསྲིག་མི་དབྱུང་རང་གིས་བསྒྲུབ་པའི་ངང་ཚུལ་འདི་ཤེས་ནས། ཡ་ཀི་
ཞི་བའི་ནགས་སུ་གནས་གང་ཨུ་དུམ་ཝ་རའི་མེ་ཏོག་བཞིན། དམ་པའི་རྣམ་ཐར་འཛིན་པ་གང་དེས་གདམས་པ་འདི་ལ་གཏན་གྲོགས་འོས། དེ་སྐད་རྗེས་འཇུག་སྐལ་ལྡན་དེ་ལ་ཕོ་བོས་གདམས
སོ་སྙིང་ལ་བཅང་། གང་ན་འདུ་འཛིའི་བྱ་བས་སྟོངས་པའི་རི་བོང་སྐྱོན་པའི་ཁྲི་གར་བཅས། མ་བཟོས་བཀོད་ལེགས་བྲག་གི་ཁང་བཟང་ཐད་ནས་ཕུ་རྒྱུའི་ལྷུང་ལྷུང་སྒྲོག སྒྲུ་སྟུག་བྱ་
ཚོགས་སྙན་པའི་དབྱངས་ཀྱིས་ཀུན་ནས་བདག་ལ་བསྟོད་པ་བཞིན། ལྷ་ཡུལ་འཕོས་འདྲའི་གནས་སུ་འགྲོ་དེའི་རྗེས་ནས་ལྷ་བཅས་མི་རྟག་འཛོར། གྲོགས་དག་ཕུང་ཀྲོལ་བསྐྱེད་པའི་གཞི་ཆེ་སྲིད་
འདིའི་འཚོར་པས་ཅི་བྱར་ཡོད། ཤིན་ཏུ་དུལ་བའི་ངང་པ་དུ་མའི་བརྟེན་པའི་ནགས་ཚལ་སྨན་ལྗོངས་སུ། སྲིད་པའི་མི་བདེ་གང་མེད་དེ་ནི་ཞི་བའི་ས་ཆེན་བརྟེན་པའི་གནས། འདུ་འཛིའི་
བྱ་བ་རིང་དུ་བསྲིང་ནས་རྫོགས་ཆེན་བསྒོམ་པའི་སྙིང་ཇོ་བཙུག འདི་ནི་དེར་གནས་སྐྱེས་བུའི་རྟག་ཏུ་ཉམས་དང་བསྟུན་ཅིང་སྤྲས་སུ་སྨན། འགྲོ་དོན་ཆས་པའི་རྣལ་འབྱོར་བདག་ནི་དར་ཙམ

ཁ། ཞེ་དྲུག

༄། འདི་ན་བྱུང་ཙམ་ཡིན། མཚན་སྙན་གྲགས་པའི་ས་གསུམ་ལྷེར་བའི་གདམས་པའི་གནས་ཀུན་བསྟན་ནས་ཡོད། ཁོ་བོའི་འདི་འཕྲད་ལས་ཅན་གང་དེ་གཙུག་མ་འོད་གསལ་དང་གཉས་ཤོག
ཅེས་པ་འདི་ནི་རྗེ་བཙུན་བྱང་པ་ཁྲོ་ཚང་གི་མཆོག་སྤྲུལ་གྲུབ་བརྙེས་ཀྱི་སྐྱེས་བུ་དམ་པ་གསུང་རྫུང་མཐོང་གྲོལ་རྩལ་དང་། ལྷག་པར་བྱ་བཏང་སྤྲུལ་སྐུ་ཚེ་དབང་འགྱུར་མེད་ནས་ཁྲི་གཞིའི་ཤོག་བུ་བཅས
ཕུལ་ནས་བསྐུལ་བའི་ངོར། ཐེག་པ་མཆོག་གི་རྣལ་འབྱོར་པ་རིག་པ་རང་ཤར་གྱིས་རྩ་གསུམ་མཁའ་འགྲོའི་འདུ་གནས་གཡུང་དྲུང་ལྷུན་པོའི་རིའི་དགའ་ཚལ། དབྱར་དུས་ན་འཇའ་ཚོན་གྱི་གུར་
ཁང་དང་། རྒྱུམ་འཁྲིགས་དང་། སྤྲིན་རྒྱུག་དང་། ཅིབས་ཤར་དང་། ཟླ་གམ་དབྱིབས་དཀྱིལ་ཅིང་། དགུན་མེ་ཏོག་གི་ཆར་མཛད་པ་དུས་དུས་སུ་འབབས་པ། སྟོད་
བཅུད་ཀྱི་ཐོས་ལེན་ཅིང་བསིལ་བཅུད་རྐང་པས་འཐུང་བའི་ལྗོན་ཤིང་དྲུང་གི་སྡོང་པོ་ལ། ཟངས་ཀྱི་ཤུན་པ་དང་། གཡུའི་ལོ་མ་དང་། ཡལ་ག་དང་། འདབ་མ་རྒྱས་པ། གསེར་གྱི་འབྲས་བུ་
སྨིན་པ་བདུད་རྩིའི་ན་བུན་འཁྱིགས་པ། ག་བུའི་དྲི་བསུང་ཀུན་ཏུ་འཐུལ་བའི་ཕང་ཕུང་གི་ཁོང་གསེང་ན་ཕྱུ་བསངས་ནམ་མཁའི་བུ་མོས་ཏ་ལྷང་ཞིག་གིས་འཇུམ་ཟེར་དང་བཅས་པའི་སྙིང་ལ་དགའ་བ་ཅི་ཡང་

ཀློང་ཐིག

སྨིན་པ། འཁྲི་ཤིང་གི་རྩེ་རྣམས་སུ་བྱ་ཕྱུག་གི་བྱ་རིགས་དུ་མས་སྙན་པའི་དབྱངས་རྟག་ཏུ་འབྱིན་པ། དོན་གྱི་རྣལ་འབྱོར་པ་བཅུ་ཕྲག་དུ་མས་རོལ་པའི་གནས་སུ་བྲིས་པའི་ཤུ་གི་པ་ནི་རང་གི་སྙིང་
བུ་ཤེས་རབ་མཆོག་ལྡན་མིང་གིས་བྱས་པས་རྫོགས་པ་ཆེན་པོའི་བསྟན་པ་དར་ཞིང་རྒྱས་པའི་རྒྱུར་གྱུར་ཅིག ༄། ཨོཾ་སྭ་སྟི། ཀ་དག་གདོད་མའི་གཞི་ལས་མ་གཡོས་པའི། དང་པོའི
སངས་རྒྱས་མཁྱེན་རབ་ཡེ་ཤེས་སྐུ། རང་སྣང་གཏིང་གསལ་གཞོན་ནུའི་བཙུན་མོ་བཅས། དུས་གསུམ་རྒྱལ་བའི་སྤྱི་མེས་གང་དེར་འདུད། དགོངས་བརྡ་སྙན་ཁུང་བརྒྱུད་པའི་ཡང་གསང་ཐོན།
སྙེ་གསུམ་རྫོགས་ཆེན་འོ་མཚོའི་བཅུད་ཕྱུང་བཞིན། རྒྱ་ཆེའི་ལམ་བཟང་ཅུང་ཟད་ཚིག་གི་ལམ། མ་ལུས་སྨོན་མཁས་རིག་པ་རང་ཤར་རྒྱལ། གཡུང་དྲུང་བོན་མཆོག་རྒྱ་ཆེའི་ས་གཞི་ལས། ཟླ་མེད་
འབྲས་བུའི་ཐེག་པ་གསེར་ཞུན་བཞིན། སྐལ་ལྡན་བློ་རབ་སྙིང་གི་ནོར་མཆོག་ཏུ། ཀུན་ལ་སྣང་མཛད་གང་ལའང་འཇིགས་མེད་དབང༌། དེ་ཕྱིར་བློ་གྲོས་ཡངས་པའི་ལྷ་ལམ་ལ། ཐོས་
བསམ་སྤྲིན་བཀོད་ཕན་བདེའི་རྣམ་བཀྲ་ཅན། རྫོགས་པའི་འབྲུག་སྒྲ་ཉིད་འཛིན་རྣམ་འགྲོས་ལས། ལེགས་བཤད་ཀྱུ་ཆར་འབེབ་མཛད་བླ་མ་དེའོ། རིམ་བརྒྱུད་ཐེག་པའི་གཉེར་དཔོན་རྣམས་

ཁ་ཀློང་ཐིག་ཞེ་བདུན་འཕེལ་སོ།

༄། ཀྱིས་ཀྱང་། མཐོང་མིན་དུས་གསུམ་བློ་ལས་འདས་པའི་དོན། །རྩོལ་མེད་རང་གྲོལ་དགོངས་པ་རྗེན་གཅེར་དུ། སྟོན་འདི་དྲི་མེད་སྙིང་པོའི་དགོངས་པའི་བཅུད། དེ་ཕྱིར་བློ་
ཆེན་སྟོང་གི་འཇུག་པའི་སྒོ། ཕྱར་དུ་སྒྲུབ་པར་ཚུལ་ཁྲིམས་གཡུང་དྲུང་གིས། དངོས་རྗེས་ཡོན་སྦྱར་བོན་སྦྱིན་ཟད་མེད་དུ། ཕྱིས་འབྱུང་སྐལ་ལྡན་རྣམས་ལ་དགའ་སྟོན་བྱས། དེ་ལས་
བྱུང་བའི་རྣམ་དཀར་དགེ་ཚོགས་དེས། སྲིད་གསུམ་མུན་ནག་འཁྲུལ་བའི་འགྲོ་མང་ཁམས། མ་རིག་མུན་ཚོགས་རབ་བཅོམ་ཞི་བའི་དབྱིངས། ཐར་པ་དམ་པའི་གྲོང་དུ་དབུགས་
འབྱིན་ཤོག ཅེས་པའི་ཕྱར་བྱང་ཤུང་དུ་འདེབས་དམ་པའི་དངོས་སློབ་ཤེས་རབ་མཆོག་ལྡན་གྱིས་བྱས་ཤིང་བྲི་བོའི་ཡི་གེ་མཁན་ཚུལ་ཁྲིམས་བསྟན་འཛིན་དབང་པོས་བགྱིས་པ་དགེའོ། |

If you would like to find out more about the teachings of Lopon Tenzin Namdak or the activities at the Tritan Norbutse Bönpo Monastery in Nepal, Menri Monastery in Dolanji, India, or the Ligmincha Institute in the United States, please write to:

Nyima Wangyal, Abbot
Tritan Norbutse Bönpo Monastery
PO Box 4640
Kathmandu, Nepal